WITHDRAWN

DATE DUE

THE DUTY AND OFFICE
OF
A LAND STEWARD

This is a volume in the
Arno Press collection

HISTORY OF MANAGEMENT THOUGHT

Advisory Editors
Kenneth E. Carpenter
Alfred D. Chandler

Consulting Editor
Stuart Bruchey

See last pages of this volume
for a complete list of titles

THE DUTY AND OFFICE
OF
A LAND STEWARD

Edward Laurence

ARNO PRESS
A New York Times Company
New York • 1979

Editorial Supervision: BRIAN QUINN
Reprint Edition 1979 by Arno Press Inc.

Reprinted from a copy in the Harvard University
Library

HISTORY OF MANAGEMENT THOUGHT
    AND PRACTICE
ISBN for complete set: 0-405-12306-X
See last pages of this volume for titles.

Manufactured in the United States of America

———

Library of Congress Cataloging in Publication Data

Laurence, Edward, d. 1740?
    The duty and office of a land steward.

    (History of management thought)
    Published in 1727 under title: The duty of a steward
to his lord.
    Reprint of the 2d ed., 1731, printed for J. and J.
Knapton and others, London.
    1. Farm management--Great Britain--Early works to
1800. 2. Agriculture--Great Britain--Early works to
1800. I. Title. II. Title: Land steward.
III. Series.
S562.G7L38 1979   630'.0941   79-7549
ISBN 0-405-12333-7

THE
DUTY and OFFICE
OF A
LAND STEWARD:

Reprefented under

Several Plain and Diftinct ARTICLES;
wherein may be feen the INDIRECT
PRACTICES of feveral STEWARDS, tending
to LESSEN, and the feveral Methods likely
to IMPROVE their Lords Eftates.

To which is added an

APPENDIX,

SHEWING

The WAY to PLENTY;

Propofed to the FARMERS:

Wherein are laid down General Rules and Directions for the
Management and Improvement of a FARM.

The Second Edition,
With ALTERATIONS and ADDITIONS.

By *EDWARD LAURENCE,*
LAND SURVEYOR.

LONDON:

Printed for J. and J. KNAPTON, at the *Crown,* in *St. Paul's Church-yard;* J. PEMBERTON, at the *Buck,* againft St. *Dunftan's* Church, in *Fleet-ftreet;* J. OSBORN and T. LONGMAN, at the *Ship,* in *Pater-nofter-Row;* and J. SHUCKBURGH, at the *Sun,* near the *Inner-Temple-Gate* in *Fleet-ftreet.* M. DCC. XXXI.

To Her GRACE the

Dutchess of *Buckingham-shire* and *Normanby.*

MADAM,

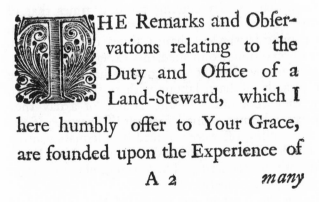 HE Remarks and Obser-
vations relating to the
Duty and Office of a
Land-Steward, which I
here humbly offer to Your Grace,
are founded upon the Experience of

A 2 *many*

many Years, and on fuch Reafon-
ings as have had the Honour of *Your
Grace*'s Approbation : Upon both
thefe Accounts, I am perfuaded, they
will be readily entertain'd by Perfons of the higheft Rank, who are
chiefly concern'd in them ; and by
thofe more efpecially who have already fuffer'd thro' the *Knavery* and
Unfaithfulnefs of their Stewards. And
as it was for the fake of fuch that I
undertook this Work, it is a peculiar
Satisfaction to me, that I have the
Honour of fending it into the World
under the *Patronage* and *Protection*
of a Perfon eminently diftinguifh'd
for a *Superior* Judgment and *Good*
Senfe ; for an uncommon *Sagacity*
in finding out *TRUTH*, and an
unweary'd Application in the lay-

ing open and punifhing *FALS-
HOOD.*

WERE I able to attempt the moſt
imperfect Sketch of Your Grace's
Character, I ſhould mention that
ſingular Candour and Condeſcen-
ſion, that Eaſineſs of Acceſs to Infe-
riors, which I have ſo often experienc'd, and which ſo naturally at-
tracts Love and Admiration: I ſhou'd
mention the Tryals Your Grace has
had of almoſt *every* Fortune, and
under *every* Relative Duty, in Life;
what *Prudence* in all of them; what
Firmneſs and *Courage* under the
greateſt Difficulties; what *Humani-
ty* and *Generoſity* have in their turns
preſided in your Life, and produc'd
the

the juſteſt Conduct under ſo various Circumſtances.

B u t I cannot omit what has fallen more fully under my Obſervation, and ought in juſtice to be taken notice of, That with an unuſual Aſſiduity and Application to Buſineſs Your Grace has ſurmounted the greateſt, and ſeemingly inſuperable Difficulties, in the *preſerving* and *retrieving* an Eſtate ready to be *ſwallow'd up in Ruin*; not ſo much by the Neglect, as the *Villany* of a Set of unjuſt Stewards, who had made all manner of ill Uſes of the late Duke's *Abſence* from them.

A Deſign truly worthy of a Parent's Care ; which *few* Ladies with ſuch an unwearied Force and Reſolution

lution cou'd have purfued and executed ; *Few* wou'd have had an
Inclination to undertake ; efpecially
at a time when Your Grace was Mi-
ftrefs of Your own Actions, and in
a Seafon of Life which might naturally have led you to pafs away the
Hours in that profperous Indolence
and Eafe you were left poffeffed of.

THAT Your Grace may long
Live, and have the Pleafure of feeing the wife and noble Ufe the *Duke
of Buckingham*, your Son, will make
of all the Advantages you have pro-
cur'd him ; That he may daily add
to thofe great Improvements, which
he already promifes, and which cannot fail of *flowing* from the Prudent
Care you have taken, and continue

to

to take, of *his Education*; as it is
the greateſt Satisfaction Your Grace
propoſes in Life, ſo is it the moſt *ſin-
cere* Wiſh of,

MADAM,

Your Grace's

Moſt Dutiful, and

Moſt Obedient Servant,

EDWARD LAURENCE,

THE
PREFACE.

THE *Misfortunes and Loſſes that have befallen ſeveral of the* Nobility *and* Gentry *throughout the Kingdom, on account of ei-ther the* Ignorance *or* Knavery *of* bad Stewards, *will of themſelves be a* ſufficient Apology *for this Undertaking ; even tho' the* Subject *itſelf is* wholly new, *and the Attempt of finding out a Remedy for a ſpreading an unhappy Diſeaſe be difficult and dangerous.*

'Tis now above Twenty Years ſince I firſt began to apply myſelf to Survey No-blemens *and* Gentlemens *Eſtates ; and at*

the

the same time to make the most Exact Observations about the different Methods of Husbandry *and* Improvement, *where-ever I went. This naturally led me into an Acquaintance with* Stewards *and* Farmers ; *and when I had made myself a tolerable Master of what was both their* Duty *and their* Interest *to pursue, I soon found room to Complain (within myself) of great, of very great, Misfortunes which* Lords *and* Gentlemen *too frequently lay under, from the Ignorance and Slothfulness of some, and the* Knavery *and* Wickedness *of others.*

The Consideration of these things, I own, made so deep an Impression upon my Mind, that I quickly brought myself to these two following Resolutions: First, Not to engage myself in the Office *and Business of a* Steward, *let the Proposals and Offers be ever so* advantageous: *And, secondly, To publish to the World, some time or other, my Thoughts about the* Duty *of a Steward, chiefly with a View of correcting* Miscarriages, *and removing the Scandal which too often so* justly *attends the Office.*

The

The first of these Resolutions I have hitherto preserv'd, under *pretty strong* and *repeated Temptations from several Quarters to* break *it : And the second I am now performing, at a time when the whole* 𝕻𝖔𝖎𝖈𝖊 *of the Kingdom hath founded with Indignation against a* 𝕱𝖔𝖗𝖌𝖊𝖗𝖞 *and consummate piece of* 𝕭𝖎𝖑𝖑𝖆𝖓𝖞 *in a* 𝕾𝖙𝖊𝖜𝖆𝖗𝖉, *grown* immensely rich *by a series of other* Unrighteous Designs *contriv'd against a* 𝕸𝖎𝖓𝖔𝖗 *and* Infant.

And altho' I am not so vain as to think this short Essay will have any such abiding Effect upon the Morals of Persons concern'd, *as quite to wear out the Disgrace usually attending the Office, or tempt me to* break *my* first *Resolution ; yet at least this Pleasure and Satisfaction I shall have in this Performance, that I shall* honestly *lay before the World what I have gather'd from* labour'd *Diligence and Observation, and what I take to be* right *in the* Office *and* Duty *of a* Steward, *with respect both to what he* ought, *and what he* ought not *to do. And if in performing this I use a Familiarity proper to make me understood, I hope it will not*

a 2   *be*

be imputed to me as a Fault, by thoſe of a politer *Taſte, whilſt at the ſame time it may manifeſtly appear, that I aim to promote thoſe two* valuable *and* much-wanted *Things* (the ſame in every *Place, and reſpected in every Age*) Truth *and* Honeſty.

In *directing the* Duty *and* Office *of a* 𝕾𝖙𝖊𝖜𝖆𝖗𝖉, *I found myſelf alſo under a Neceſſity of ſaying* ſomething *to the* 𝕱𝖆𝖗𝖒𝖊𝖗, *whoſe Duty in many Caſes is pretty ſtrongly connected with that of the* Steward, *and without whoſe Diligence and Skill the* Steward *himſelf labours under* great Difficulties *and* unjuſt Reproofs. *I have therefore added an* APPENDIX, *wherein are laid down* (gather'd from long Obſervation and diſtant *Parts*) *ſuch* ſhort Rules *and* Directions *for the Management and Improvement of a* Farm, *as I purpoſe* (GOD *willing*) *ſome time or other* much *to enlarge upon.*

THE

THE
CONTENTS.

Introduction.

THE Method which Noblemen *and* Gentlemen *should take when their Estates have been under a long Course of bad Government by former Stewards, so as they may* retrieve *the* Loss.
Pag. 2

The ill Consequence of making small Farms *great ones all at once.* ———— ———— —— 4

The proper Methods to be taken, when Tenants do not sufficiently understand the best and latest Arts *of Husbandry.* —— ———— 6

The Evils and Inconveniencies which Gentlemen lie under in employing Country-Attorneys (*not skill'd in Husbandry*) *for their Stewards.* — 7

The Indirect Practices *which some Stewards have made use of, to* lessen *the Value of their Lord's Estates, in order to Enrich themselves.* —— 8

To prevent in some measure the 'foregoing Evil, Gentlemen should be persuaded to allow their Stewards an handsome Salary. —— —— 13

If Tenants are rack'd too high in their Rent, they will have no Encouragement to Improve their Farms ; but, on the contrary, will be tempted to 𝕚𝕞𝕡𝕠𝕧𝕖𝕣𝕚𝕤𝕙 *them, especially as their Leases expire.* —— —— —— 14

Old-rented Estates ought to be rais'd ; as for many other Reasons, so also on account of the constant sinking of the Value of Money. —— 15

The Method too often taken to advance Estates by way of 𝔓𝔬𝔲𝔫𝔡𝔞𝔤𝔢, *is neither* just *nor regular, because it often falls light on some Tenants, and heavy on others.* —— —— 17

The most probable and successful Method of treating with Tenants about the Value of their Farms, is by making exact Calculations. —— 18

The best Method to be taken when Tenants combine together, and will not suffer any Advance of Rent. —— —— 22

The Method taken by a Person of Quality for the Government and Choice of his Stewards. 24

An Address to the Legislative Power, for an Interposition to prevent the Abuses and Mischiefs occasion'd by common Water-mills. —— 30

Articles

Articles relating to the Duty of a Steward.

Article I. *A Steward should not undertake more Business than he can well perform, and a Wrong is done for want of regular Surveys; it being the least part of the Business of a Steward to collect the Rents.* —— —— —— 33

Art. II. *A Steward ought to be well vers'd in* Country-Business, *and in all the* new *Arts of* Improvement, *before he undertake that Office.* 34

Art. III. *The Steward's Business is to assign what Parcels of Lands are proper for* Pasture *and* Meadow, *and what others for* Tillage: *That the* Tillage *laid down for Grass be re-enrich'd with proper Manure.* —— —— 35

Art. IV. *The Steward should, at least once a Month, ride over the whole Estate, taking Memorandums of the Tenant's Methods of Improvements, and of his Stock of* Cattle, &c. —— 37

Art. V. *No fresh* Pasture *or* Meadow-Ground *of the better sort to be plow'd up, without agreeing to further Covenants.* —— —— 38

Art. VI. *Ditches to be scowred up, and Trenches open'd, by Direction of the Steward. A Method given for draining Ground.* —— —— 40

a 4   Art.

Art. VII. *Cow-dung not to be burnt for Fuel; Farms are impoverish'd by it.* —— —— 45

Art. VIII. *The Steward's Care is to prevent paring and burning the Soil, which sinks the Rents soon after. Rape, Hemp, Flax, and Woad not to be suffer'd without further Covenants and Considerations.* —— —— 46

Art. IX. *The Manure bred on every Farm should (by the watchful Eye of the Steward) all be laid on the Lord's Lands, and not (as is too common) on the Freehold-Lands adjacent.* —— 49

Art. X. *The Steward to watch the Mole-catcher, that he perform his Duty.* —— —— 50

Art. XI. *That the Lordship be not overstock'd with Rabbits, except on large Moors and Commons at a considerable distance from Inclosures.* 51

Art. XII. *The Steward should not suffer any part of a Farm to be let to Under-Tenants, especially Freeholders: The Inconveniencies which attend that Practice shewn.* —— —— 52

Art. XIII. *His Business to lay small Farms into great ones: To be done discreetly as the Heads of poor Families happen to fall.* —— — 54

Art. XIV. *To watch for all Purchases of Freehold Estates within his Lord's Manor: Not for himself, but his Lord's Advantage.* —— 56

Art. XV. *Some Methods propos'd to prevent a Steward's being impos'd upon in purchasing Estates.* —— —— — 61

Art. XVI. *Farm-Houses to be kept up in good Repair by the Tenants: Some Methods propos'd to prevent*

prevent a conſtant Rent-charge upon Eſtates by unknown and endleſs Deductions. —— 63

Art. XVII. The Steward ſhould not ſuffer the Tenants to over-ſtock their Farms by over-joyſting near the time of their leaving the Farm : The ill Conſequence of that Clown-Craft Practice ſhewn. 66

Art. XVIII. His Buſineſs not to ſuffer Mounds and Hedges to decay : The manner of plaſhing Hedges given, with Directions to weed the Quicks. 70

Art. XIX. Enquiry to be made by the Steward after Coal, Tin, and Lead-Mines within his Lord's Eſtate ; and to diſcover, if poſſible, all Bribes to ſtifle Enquiries. ——— 77

Art. XX. Before Incloſing, Draining, &c. are enter'd upon, an Eſtimate of the Charge ſhould be ſent to his Lord, that he may firſt ſee the Coſt. 78

Art. XXI. The Obſervation of the Steward to be a Cheque upon the Farmer, that he keep a ſufficient Stock of Cattle : And his way to know the Value of the Farm, is for ſeveral Years to obſerve the Crops. ——— ——— 81

Art. XXII. The Steward ſhould not ſuffer Poachers to deſtroy the Game, but ſhould proſecute 'em, to prevent that Idleneſs which commonly ends in Poverty, or ſomething worſe. ——— 89

Art. XXIII. He ſhould alſo make himſelf Maſter of all the ancient Cuſtoms within his Lord's Manors. ——— —— 91

Art. XXIV. Where his Lord is the Impropriator, the Steward ſhould let the great Tythes, with all the

*the Advantages attending them, to fuch Tenants
only as have the worft Land.* —— 95

Art. XXV. *The Steward is to watch the* Park-
keeper, *that he perform his Duty in all the
Parts mention'd.* White-thorn Pollards *and
true* Chefnuts *are recommended to be planted in
Parks, as great Supports to the* Deer *in the
Winter. A Method of driving a Park laid
down, and keeping a Book for that purpofe recommended.* —— —— 97

Art. XXVI. *Managing* Woods *to the beft advantage, and keeping an Account, by way of Table,
of every fingle Tree recommended.* —— 103

Art. XXVII. *Improving wet and boggy Lands recommended to the Care of Stewards, and the beft
Method of doing it given: As alfo the Ufe of the
Spirit-Level, in order to float Meadows and let
off the Water.* —— —— 115

Art. XXVIII. *Method of improving large uninclos'd Lands by moveable Hurdles, or Pofts and
Rails, laid down. What Cattle are proper to
ftock fuch Lands, and the Advantages attending
fhewn.* —— —— 117

Art. XXIX. *A Steward's Care is to order the Tenants Houfes to be cover'd with* Slate *or* Tile,
*not only to prevent Accidents by Fire, but like-
wife to preferve the* Straw *for Manure.* 120

Art. XXX. *His Care alfo 'tis to prevent all Waftes
made by Tenants; particularly not to fuffer the
erecting of* Brick-kilns *without further Covenants.* —— —— 121

Art.

CONTENTS. xix

Art. XXXI. *Breeders of Horses should not rent the best Land: The Inconveniencies thereof shewn.*
122

Art. XXXII. *The Steward's Care is, to order all the Bye-roads leading thrô' the Estate to be made good. The Method of doing it.* — 123

Art. XXXIII. *He should not parcel out Lands to small Freeholders, where there happen to be large Commons without Stints. The Inconveniencies attending that Practice shewn.* 124

Art. XXXIV. *He should be well satisfied of a Tenant's Ability and Substance before he lets a Farm; otherwise many Inconveniencies follow.*
127

Art. XXXV. *'Tis the Steward's Business to ease the Tenants, and rid them of Vagrants and Strangers. Arrears of Rent occasion'd thereby. Some Methods hinted at by way of prevention.* 128

Art. XXXVI. *His Care in having the Estate exactly survey'd and mapt, set forth. Errors committed by Surveyors who use the plain Table. A Description of Mr. JONATHAN SISSON's new-invented Theodolite, for Surveys in the most exact manner.* — — 132

A Survey of the Manor of K. in the County of H. with the Particulars of the several Farms improved by the said Survey, and an Abstract drawn from it. — — 148

An

An Abstract of general Covenants *left with the Steward of the Court, to be inserted in all the Tenants Leases ; of general use to most Estates.*
159

A familiar Method of making up Accompts for the use of Stewards *when they deliver them up to their* Lord.　181

A particular Account of the Prices *of the several sorts of* Artificers Works *relating to ordinary Buildings, and the Repairs of* Farm-Houses, Mills, &c. *Also the Prices of the several sorts of Works relating to* Husbandry : *Of great use to All, and a Thing hitherto much wanted.* 208

A new and concise Table of Timber-measure *ready cast up, design'd for general Use.*　219

APPEN.

APPENDIX.

Art. I. *A*N approved *Method of destroying* Wild Oats. —— pag. 243

—— II. *Four Fields in Tillage better than three: The Reasons given. Also the Advantage shewn of sowing Beans and Pease* under-furrow, *and the Method of doing it.* — 245

—— III. *A Method to improve Land over-run with* Shrubs, Underwood, Moss, *and full of Bogs.* — — 247

—— IV. Sea-coal Ashes *recommended as a great Improvement of* Pasture *and* Meadow *Ground.* 248

—— V. *A Method of improving poor Land without any* 𝕾𝖚𝖕𝖊𝖗𝖎𝖓𝖉𝖚𝖈𝖙𝖎𝖔𝖓 *of Dungs or other Manures.* — — 249

—— VI. Clover, Trefoil, *&c. are shewn to be vast Improvers of poor Land design'd for Grass; with a view of turning it again for Tillage.* 251

—— VII. *The Mistakes of the* North *shewn, in sowing both their Winter and Summer Corn too late.* —— —— —— 252

Art.

Art. VIII. *Great Improvements to be made by* Lime *and* rolling *the Land.* — 255

—IX. *Cautions against laying down Land in high Ridges; the Inconveniencies thereof shewn.* 256

—X. *Improvements to be made by mixing Dung and Ditch-earth together, as practis'd in* Essex. 257

—XI. *A new Method of making* Oxen *fat in a cheap and expeditious way, when* Hay *is dear.* 258

—XII. *The great Advantage of keeping the Fallows clean and free from Weeds, with the Method of doing it.* — — 259

—XIII. *Seed-Corn to be steep'd longer than is commonly practis'd: The Method of preparing it.* 260

—XIV. *A new and approv'd Method of ordering Calves and Lambs, so as to make them exceeding white and fat.* — — 261

—XV. *A new Way of sowing upon poor Land, by way of Improvement.* — 265

—XVI. *A List of artificial Grass-seeds: The Quantity of Seed to be sown on an Acre; the Soil they like; the Time of sowing them, and the Price of the Seed in* London. — 268

—XVII. Turnips *great Improvers of Land: The Method of houghing them.* — 272

Art.

CONTENTS. xxiii

Art. XVIII. *An Abstract of the several* Dungs, *shewing their Nature and Properties.* 279

— XIX. *An Abstract of the several sorts of* Soils, *with proper* Dungs *and Manures suitable to their several Natures.* — 291

— XX. *How some general Annoyances to a Farm may be remov'd without any great Charge.* 295

Adver-

Advertisement.

N**Oblemens** and **Gentlemens Estates** **surveyed**, in order to their Improvement; and Books of Maps, with the Particulars drawn from the said Surveys; shewing (under the proper Columns) the several sorts of Lands, whether *Arable*, *Pasture*, *Meadow*, or *Woodland*, in the possession of each Tenant:

By *EDWARD LAURENCE*,

And his AGENTS.

Who may be heard of at Mr. *Knapton's*, a Bookseller, at the *Crown* in *St. Paul's Church-yard*; or at *Richard's* Coffee-House near *Temple-Bar*, or at the Rev. Mr. *Laurence's* at *Bishops-Weremouth* in the Bishoprick of *Durham*.

N. B. The said Mr. EDWARD LAURENCE having had *long* Experience in *Country Business*, and the Nature of *Farms*; and having given full Satisfaction to a considerable part of the *Nobility* and *Gentry* by his own *Surveys*, which have enabled him first to *value*, and then to *let* or *sell* their Estates to the *best* Advantage; and likewise by drawing up *proper* Covenants to oblige their Tenants to keep up their Farms in a *due* Course of Husbandry: Gives Notice, That he is ready to serve the Nobility and Gentry farther, in **Valuing** and **Letting** their Estates, not only from his *own Surveys*, but from those already done; and likewise gives Intelligence of *Estates* that are to be *Bought* and *Sold*.

THE
DUTY and OFFICE
OF A
LAND STEWARD.

The Introduction.

THE following ARTICLES being sent into the World in a plain, familiar Dress, and with a Freedom becoming an Artless HONESTY and *Simplicity*, I was willing, by way of *Introduction*, to advertise both *Nobleman* and *Steward* of some Particulars, which I conceive, may be

B   of

of Ufe to *both*, and which I fhall make ufe
of with the fame Ingenuous Freedom.

THAT the Art of *Husbandry* is of late
Years greatly improv'd, is an undoubted
Truth, confirm'd by every Day's Experience;
and accordingly many Eftates have already
admitted their *utmoft* Improvement; but
much the greater number ftill remains of
fuch as are fo far from being brought to
that Perfection, that they have felt *few*, or
none, of the Effects of Modern Arts and
Experiments.

WHEN therefore a Lord of a Manor, either by his own Obfervation and Skill finds,
or by the Advice and Experience of Others
is made to underftand, that fuch Eftates, or
fuch Parts of his Eftate, have been under a
long Courfe of *bad* Government by *former
Stewards*, or have otherwife fuffer'd by
long Indolence and Neglect, altho' 'tis his
great Wifdom to lofe no Time in entring
upon a Reformation; yet he fhould not
immediately think that *All* is to be fet right
on a fudden; but Time and Patience muft
be

be allow'd, and then fomething may be done to Satisfaction: Nay, fomething more muft alfo be allow'd to recover and rectify great Diforders; for if the Land hath been *pared* and *burnt*, or *over-plough'd* and *mow'd*, or otherwife impoverifh'd by felling the Hay and Straw off the Premifes; or if the Fences have gone to ruin, by the Careleffnefs of a Steward and Tenant; or if 'tis over-run with *Thorns*, *Whins*, and other Trumpery: In all, or any of thefe cafes, a Sum of Money *muſt* be allow'd and expended to make good Deficiencies; and this, before the Landlord can, or ought fo much as to think of, any Advance of Rent: And therefore to anfwer his End moft effectually, and to do Things to the beft Purpofe, a Refolution fhould be taken to keep fuch Farms in hand, till they are a little reduc'd into Order; and after that, to let 'em to the beft Advantage. If fome fuch Method is not taken, I am pretty well affur'd, 'twill be very difficult to find Tenants that will anfwer either Rent or Expectation, except a *very long* Leafe be granted, to make the Farms in fome meafure their own.

TENANTS in the *North*, who rent but
fmall Farms, have, generally fpeaking, but
little Subftance wherewith to make any ex-
penfive Improvements. This indeed is a
Misfortune, but 'tis fuch a one as requires
Time to mend and alter. To alter Farms,
and to turn feveral little ones into great
ones, is a Work of Difficulty and Time;
for it would raife too great an *Odium* to
turn poor Families into the wide World,
by uniting Farms all at once, in order to
make an Advance of Rents: 'Tis much
more reafonable and popular to be content
to ftay till fuch Farms *fall* into Hand by
Death, before the Tenant is either rais'd or
turn'd out. I remember an Inftance, in my
Surveys, of a Gentleman who was for making fmall Farms into great ones, all at once,
the Confequence whereof foon after appear'd to be this; That the *Church* and
Poor's Affeffments fell fo heavy upon the
remaining Tenants, that the Lord of the
Manor was foon brought to difcover his
Miftake by re-admitting the poor Tenants,
and difpofing the Farms partly in the fame

ftate

ſtate they were in before, and to content himſelf to allow *Time* to compleat his Deſire of *improving his Eſtate* in *that Way* of making the Farms larger.

THE true Remedy therefore for this Misfortune is not the *violent* one of *forcing* them beyond their Power, but the *gentle* and *rational* one of *perſuading*, and *inſtructing* them in all the thriving *Arts* of making the beſt of their Farms, that they may be able, not only to *pay*, but to *advance* their Rents. I have known ſeveral Inſtances of Tenants that held their Lands at an Eaſy *Old* Rent, and yet, for want of being inſtructed in the New Methods of *Lime, Turneps, Graſs-Seeds,* &c. were ſtill poor, and hardly able to pay that *Old* Rent, much leſs could they bear any Advance: But yet, as ſoon as they became better inſtructed by the Steward to practiſe all the beſt and lateſt Methods of Husbandry, they preſently could bear an Advance of Rent; and not only *ſuffer'd* it, but grew *richer* upon it, and *thriv'd* better than they did before at the *Old* Rent.

BUT

BUT forafmuch as it will appear, by what follows, that the Steward, if he acts as an *Honeſt* Steward ought to act, will have always his Hands and his Head full of Buſineſs of many kinds, ſo that he may be well excus'd the Trouble of being a conſtant Inſtructor to the Tenants ; and foraſmuch as it is highly convenient to have a living Inſtructor amongſt many ignorant Farmers, to teach them, if poſſible, both by Example and Precept, the readieſt Way to *improve* their Farms, and to *enrich* themſelves, I would advise all Noblemen, and others, who cannot be at hand themſelves to ſet forward Improvements, to get one or two Tenants out of the *South,* and moſt improv'd Countries, to ſhew others the Way by their Example.   And if it ſhall be thought difficult to get Tenants to remove into a ſtrange Country, a proper Perſon ſhould be *hired,* who underſtands the New Methods of preparing the Ground, and ſent over, as well to manage a Farm in hand for his Lord, as to direct and inſtruct others, till they ſee with their own Eyes

how

how much better *the Land gives her Encreafe*, order'd and manag'd with Wifdom and Skill.

I cannot forbear here to take notice, that Noblemen andGentlemen lie under greatEvils and Inconveniencies, when they fuffer themfelvesto be perfuaded to employ *Country Attorneys* for their Stewards; becaufe it feldom happens that they are well qualified for that Truft.   And indeed, if the Office of a Steward be any whit rightly defcrib'd in the following Articles, and his DUTY fairly explain'd, it may at one View be eafily difcern'd, that this Caution is well founded.   A Steward's Bufinefs is not fuch as may be done as it were *by the by* : 'Tis his *whole* Employment, and a full one too; and therefore he muft *hoc agere*.   The Attorney, if he has any Character, has Bufinefs enough of his own, of the Law, and therefore fhould not undertake the Office of a Steward, which in moft Parts of it, he doth not underftand; neither will his Employment let him : But I would always have the Steward confult the Attorney in mat-

ters

ters relating to the Law, and to attend him at his *Court-keeping*.

I have known Inftances where a Country Attorney has been Steward to feven or eight Noblemen, and others, and yet has done nothing elfe but attend the Court-keeping and collecting of Rents; by which means the Tenants have taken the Advantage of doing what they would with their Farms, quickly leffening the Value of the Eftates by *Over-ploughing*, &c. I have alfo obferv'd on my Surveys, that thefe fort of indolent Stewards are commonly againft the having their Lord's Eftates furvey'd and mapt, for fear of opening a *New Scene*: And yet their very warmnefs againft *Surveys* and *Improvements* (calling the one *unneceffary*, and the other *unpopular*) has been the Occafion of putting all *Oeconomifts* upon them.

FROM thefe, compar'd with the following Reafons in the Articles, it will appear, what a great Truft a Steward has repos'd in him; and how much it is in his power to
Improve,

Improve, or make *worfe*, his Lord's Eftate. For which reafon it behoves every Landlord to ufe his utmoft Caution and Wifdom in the Choice of a Man of HONESTY and UNDERSTANDING for a Steward : However, I fee no reafon why he fhould not be under Covenants, and give Security to perform them as well as the Tenants.

WHETHER the Hints I have here given, and fhall hereafter have Occafion to give, with refpect to *indirect Practices* in many Stewards, be not well founded, I muft leave to Others to judge, who have had a *feeling* and thorow Senfe of that Matter: But I cannot forbear to take Notice of a particular pleafant Incident in my Travels, which (becaufe I was myfelf no Sufferer, nor had any hand in the Suffering of Others) hath often made me fmile.

" As I was, fome time fince, employ'd
" in *Surveying* and *Valuing* a Lord's Eftate
" in the *North*, Curiofity led the Noble-
" man himfelf to go along with me one
" Day, to look about him, to fee how his
" Eftate

" Eftate lay, and to view the Extent and
" Beauty of it. But before we enter'd up-
" on Bufinefs, the *Steward* led us the way
" into his Compting-houfe, or (as he rather
" chofe to call it) his *Oratory*, or Place
" of Devotion ; where he prefently fhew'd
" us (as lying at his Right-Hand) *South's*
" and *Waterland's* Sermons againft the
" growing Heresies of this Age ; Which
" Sermons (faith he, with the *godly* Parts
" of his Eyes lift up, and a devout Coun-
" tenance) I read to my Family every *Sun-*
" *day* Night, left they alfo be tempted to
" *deny the Lord that bought them.* And
" thus, by ordering the matter fo, as to
" appear to his Lord at other times with a
" *Friday-Face* for every Day in the Week,
" he anticipated all Sufpicion of *Knavery*
" or Wrong; infomuch that fometimes, with
" a fingular Pleafure he would exprefs to
" me, *how happy he was in a Steward,*
" *that had fo good and orthodox a Senfe*
" *of Religion!* But, alas! before the Lord
" left the Country, he was told, to his
" forrow, that *The Zeal of his Houfe had*
" *even eaten him up:* For, upon a ftrict
                                        " Enquiry

" Enquiry into his Affairs, the Lord was
" quickly made to underſtand, that his
" godly Steward had bought no leſs than
" Six hundred Pounds a Year, under his
" very Noſe, which he purchas'd by being
" Steward only Fifteen Years; and, by all
" Accounts, he was not worth Ten Pounds
" when he enter'd.   And the method by
" which he acquir'd theſe Riches is no
" leſs remarkable; for it was by receiving
" of the Tenants what he was pleas'd to
" call *Income-money*; telling them, It was
" an antient *Perquiſite* of a Steward : That
" is to ſay, every Year, when he enter'd
" the Tenant's Name anew into his Book,
" he receiv'd a BRIBE, for letting them
" hold their Farms at a *low Old Rent*, in-
" ſtead of an *Improv'd one*.   This was on-
" ly One Part of his *unjuſt Gain*; for he
" likewiſe,   on pecuniary Conſiderations,
" ſuffer'd the Tenants to ſtock ſome of the
" beſt Land with Rabbits, conniv'd at their
" ploughing the beſt Paſtures and Mea-
" dows, and conſented to the *paring*, and
" *burning*, and *ſowing Rape* upon the beſt
" Land, the *vile* and *beggaring* Effects
                              " whereof

" whereof I have fully fhewn in the fol-
" lowing ARTICLES. ,

MOREOVER, it may not be amifs to take
Notice here, that whenever a Steward en-
gageth himfelf in the Bufinefs of Farming
on his own Account, it commonly proves
a Lofs and a Difappointment to his Lord;
becaufe that Bufinefs, if it is minded, (and
he feldom will forget or neglect his own)
takes up fo great a part of his Time, that
fome neceffary Article of Duty muft be
neglected; and it will be impoffible for
him to be upon the watch, as he ought, to
fee that the Tenants perform their Covenants. It is alfo no lefs a Difadvantage to
a Lord, when his Steward (and fuch a Cafe
I have known) turns *Merchant*, by trading
in *Corn, Malt, Butter, Cheefe*, &c. the
Product of the Eftate; for, to my certain
Knowledge, this Practice hath apparently
prov'd a great leffening of the Tenant's Profit, whilft by the *Authority* of the faid
Steward the Tenant is frequently oblig'd,
not only to pay his Rent in fuch Commo-
dities before 'tis due, but alfo at the Steward's

own

own price, and at under-rates. They held indeed their Farms at an *eafy Old Rent*, but if the Steward, by thefe *knavifh*, indirect Practices, raifes an Eftate, it is plain *the Lord pays for it*. And yet, when thefe *vile* Practices were put a ftop to, and the Tenants were advanc'd above a third Part, I have been affur'd, by the Tenants own Confeffion, that they got more Money off their Farms, after their Rents were rais'd, than they did before.

It is therefore, on all Accounts, much the *Wifdom* and *Intereft* of all Noblemen, and others, to allow their Stewards a *handfome Salary*, that they may be able, without new-invented *Perquifites*, to live with Reputation and Credit; by which they will preferve an Authority over the Tenants to keep Bufinefs in order. And if this is not done, the falfe *Oeconomy* of it will foon be paid dear for, in all the artful ways of *fqueezing* and *pinching* both Landlord and Tenant; as may appear by what hath been faid above.

As

As Prudence and Difcretion fhould govern every thing, fo, in following the Example of Others, great regard is to be had to them. In my Surveys I have met with Inftances of private Gentlemen of fmall Eftates living upon the fpot, who, led perhaps by Neceffity or Avarice, did *rack* their Tenants higher than the Land, by the moft laborious Induftry, could make any profitable Return; as hath appear'd by their conftant change of Tenants almoft every two or three years: But if Stewards acting for Perfons of Quality at a diftance, fhould be fo *rigid,* fhall I fay, or *imprudent,* as to practife this Method, they would foon make their Lord, as well as themfelves, very uneafy by the *uncertainty* of the Rentals, by conftant *Arrears,* and by having the Lands often thrown into hand: But the greateft difadvantage of all is, the running a *hazard* of having the Eftate *beggar'd* and *impoverifh'd.* For, if Tenants are not at fome *Certainty,* they will be greatly difcourag'd from being good Husbands; at leaft, from laying out Money whereby to

im-

improve their Farms. So that when a Steward is once fatisfied and convinc'd he hath let a Farm to an *honeft* Advantage, his beft way then is, to let a Leafe for 15 or 21 years, at the fame time taking care to infert *proper Covenants,* fuch as in *this Treatife* he will be fufficiently inftruct-ed in.

BUT I would not have it be fo under-ftood, as if I thought the fame Leafe and Rent were to be a ftanding Rule for *ever.* On the contrary it is certain, that the *Va-lue* of Money every day and year *fluctuates,* and, in the general, hath been continually decreafing; and therefore the Rent of an Eftate in reafon ought to be adjufted to that Rule, and to be rais'd accordingly in pro-portion. Thefe (and the like) Arguments I have ufed with Tenants occafionally, as I found they would hear Reafon. I told them it was unreafonable to expect to rent a Farm *now,* when a fat Goofe is fold for *Two Shillings,* at the fame Rate as *formerly,* when the fame Goofe was fold for a *Groat.* This familiar way of talking to them, I often

often found, made an Impreſſion on them
with Succeſs, when other more reſolute and
rougher Methods fail'd. In treating with
Tenants they ſhould be talk'd with in their
own Language, and by Arguments which
they throughly underſtand, and have a feeling Senſe of. So that if a Steward would
gain his Point, he muſt not hope to do it
in the *bluſtering* manner and method of
ſome Agents, whom I have known ſent
down from *London,* in order to make an
Advance of Rents, who yet know little or
nothing of *Country Buſineſs.* One of theſe
Agents, I remember, came down fully bent
with a Reſolution to advance his Lord's Tenants *Six ſhillings* in the Pound, one with
another; and told them in a haughty, ſhort
manner, that they muſt *turn out* if they did
not comply. Thoſe who rented *ſmall* Farms,
and were themſelves *poor,* were forced to
ſubmit, knowing not what to do, nor where
to go; but the more diſcerning and ſubſtantial Farmers, finding the Agent to talk
more knowingly about *Aſſemblies* and *Ladies,* and underſtood *Dreſſing* better than
Farming, ſoon deſpiſed him, as ignorant of
their

their Affairs, and would not submit; and so
he was forced to return to *London* just as wise
as he came down, without having done any
business to the purpose: for, indeed, he might
have used the same *ridiculous* method of
raising the Rents by *Poundage,* and have
stay'd at home.

WHEREAS had this Estate been prudently
manag'd by a Steward well vers'd in *Country
Business,* and the best methods of Husbandry;
had he had by him an accurate * Survey of
the number of Acres of the several Parcels
of Lands, whether *arable, pasture,* or *meadow,* in the possession of each Tenant; and
had he throughly understood which Farms
would admit of *most,* and which of the *least*
Improvements, he might easily have settled
each Tenant's Farm in a due *proportion* of
Rent to their Satisfaction, without going in
the summary and *unjust* way of *Poundage.*
I call it *unjust,* because it falls heavy
upon *some,* and perhaps light on *others.*
And indeed it is not seldom that I have

* See the Survey at the end of the Articles.

C   known

known a Steward (to ſhew a pretended diligence) has rais'd ſome of the *ſmall* Farms, that did not bring *Griſt to his Mill*, and let the more *ſubſtantial* ones, who were able, go free and unrais'd, for Reaſons not to be named.

IF then Perſons of Quality will ſuffer themſelves to be led into this method of advancing their Eſtates by *Poundage*, it may eaſily be imagin'd what Sorrows and Curſes they will draw upon themſelves, and what ſad undeſirable Work will be made amongſt the ſmall Farms, when it ſhall be once underſtood, that they have been rais'd already.

IF it will not be thought too much antici-pating what is to follow in the *Articles*, I would here obſerve, that a Steward who is maſter of Country-Affairs, and hath made himſelf acquainted with *every* Parcel of Land in each Tenant's Poſſeſſion, when he comes to treat with a Tenant, in order to ſettle a Rent equal to the Value of the Farm, ſhould take his *Pen* in hand, and make

make a *Calculation* with the Tenant, how many *Head* of Cattle his Pasture will keep, according to its Goodness; as also how many *Quarters* of the several sorts of Grain his arable Land will produce one year with another, which may be judg'd of *nearly* by seeing the Crops in the several years: And again, how many *Loads* of Hay may be expected from the Meadows. From these and such other DATA's, he may finish a Calculation of what may be sold off the Farm, which ought to be (as I shall have further occasion hereafter to observe) at least *two Rents*, if it is intended a Farmer should thrive; and *thrive he must*, or else the Landlord will suffer *first* or *last*. By these Methods and fair *Calculations* a Farmer is treated in a familiar, easy way, and you beat, or rather *convict*, him with his own Weapons. But he will not be *bully*'d or *hector'd* into an advanc'd Rent, by those who know no reason for what they do and say: Whereas, by using him with Respect and Civility, and appealing to his own Judgment and Experience, you bring him to Reason and Conviction; you make a Conqueſt by talking in his own way, and ſo *honourably* gain your Point.

I muſt confeſs, I have ſometimes met with ſuch as would not be perſuaded or beat out of their own way of thinking, and therefore would hear *no* Reaſons : In ſuch caſe a Steward, before he begins to make an Advance upon an *old-rented Eſtate*, ſhould have an *over-rack'd* Tenant or two in his Eye ready to put in, if any of the principal Tenants refuſe, after a fair *Calculation* of the Value of their Farms hath been made to them.   This Method I always found to have a good Effect, and was a means of breaking the Neck of a *Confederacy* or *Combination*, which ſometimes will be obſerv'd among the Tenants, when they agree together to make *no Advance*. The firſt Example of a Tenant that will not liſten to Reaſon or Civil Treatment, ſhould be us'd in ſome ſuch manner as followeth : Get it under his own Hand, that he *voluntarily* leaves his Farm on the Terms offer'd, *viz.* Thus :

Sept.

Sept. 20. 1722.

I *Do hereby declare, that I have voluntarily left the Farm which I lately rented of his Grace the Duke of* K----; *and, that I freely confent that the fame fhould be rented by any other Perfon that offers, intending to leave the fame at* L. *Day next.*

Witnefs my Hand,

A. B.

I almoft always found, that when fuch a Certificate as this was offer'd to be fign'd, the Tenant (ftubborn as he was before) *boggled* at it, as thinking that *now* in earneft he muft leave his Farm, if he fets his Hand: Infomuch that he commonly chofe to *confider* of it, and to have Time to ask his Wife leave, and to have her Confent: The Confequence of which was, that he feldom fail'd to come again in a few days, and

C 3   with-

without more ado, to ſtrike up a *Bargain*. But if it ſo happen'd that the Tenant was unperſuadable, and *would* ſign the aforeſaid Certificate, yet this Method was of ſingular Uſe in procuring a *new* Tenant. They commonly make a ſort of Conſcience of taking a Farm over another's head, as they call it; tho', it may be, an abſolute Refuſal has been given; and ſo, for want of ſome ſuch Teſtimony under Hand, that *Shyneſs* would ſtill remain; but, upon producing it, all Difficulties vaniſh'd, and *new* Tenants readily enter'd into Articles.

THIS Method had alſo another good Effect; for it put a ſtop to all further Combinations, and, as it were, *Rebellions* againſt their Lord, uſually carried on in a *ſtupid*, tho' a ſort of *ſacred* manner: For it is uſual with them to aſſemble together round a *great Stone*, upon which they are to SPIT, believing this Practice (join'd with a Promiſe of what they will do, and ſtand to) to be as ſacred and binding as if they had taken a publick *Oath*. In this Contrivance I will

not

not fuppofe that they can prevail upon the
Vicar of the Place to *preach* againft Improvements ; but if they can prevail upon
the *Clark* of the Parifh (as fometimes they
have done) to fet an appofite *Pfalm*, and
make the Congregation *fneer*, they applaud
themfelves for their *Wit*, and conclude their
Bufinefs done.

I am forry to fay thefe fort of mean
Contrivances have fometimes been not a little encourag'd underhand, by the Envy of
fome of the Gentlemen of leffer Eftates, who
tho' they themfelves *ftretch* their Tenants
Rents to the utmoft, yet hate that a Perfon of Quality, living in the *South*, fhould
by his Steward fet up for *Oeconomy* and
Management, fometimes not fparing even
Terms of Reproach, and popular Scandal,
in order to caufe a *mutiny* among the Tenants : Which Misfortune cannot otherwife
be better and more effectually remedied,
than by proper and occafional Refidence,
whereby Great Men (as I fhall have occafion
in the Articles to obferve) endear themfelves to their Country, and thereby pre-

vent

vent the *Odium* which ufually attends the making any Advancement in Rents; whilft it appears that they do not carry away all their Money and Treafure, but are willing to fpend fome of it amongft them, by encouraging *Trade*, and by *Acts* of *Charity*.

I am unwilling to detain the Reader too long from the Subftance of my Defign, or to tire him with too many Particulars in an Introduction; but yet there are two Heads ftill remaining, which, when explain'd, I fhould think, cannot fail to be acceptable to the Publick. And I fhall lay down what I have to fay by way of Addrefs, (1.) to all *Noblemen*, and others, for the *choice* and *management* of their Stewards: And (2.) to the *Legiflative Powers*, that they would interpofe, to prevent the Abufes and Mifchiefs, occafion'd by common WATER-MILLS.

THE firft Head leads me to mention a fingular good Method, taken by a Perfon of Quality, for the Government and Choice of his Stewards, as an Example to others.
This

This good *Oeconomist*, whenever he comes down into the Country, (*and come they must, if they will have their Estates to thrive*) in looking into his Affairs, and the Difposition of his Eftate, ever took care to have *all* his Agents and Stewards along with him, that they might *all* be acquainted with one another's Bufinefs, by knowing the feveral Tenants Methods of managing their Farms, and alfo the true Value of them, that in cafe of Mortality or Removes, there might be no difficulty of a Steward's being a Stranger to any part of the whole Eftate. And to carry this rational Management a little further, I fhould think it very proper, after a Steward hath liv'd five or fix years upon one Eftate, that he be mov'd to live five or fix years upon another ; and fo to continue moving the whole Sett of them round as the Nobleman or Gentleman fees occafion: The reafon of which is very plain and difcernible, *viz.* that hereby they will of confequence prove a *Checque* upon one another.

MORE

MOREOVER, that Perfons of Quality may never be at a lofs (in cafes of Mortality and Removes) to have a proper Steward to fupply a *Vacancy*, it is very advifeable and neceffary, to have always one, or more of the Farmer's Sons in their eye, who are deem'd to be of a fuitable Genius, and whofe Education hath been fuch, that they may be fuppos'd not only to be expert in *Country-affairs*, but to bear the Character of fupporting and purfuing TRUTH and HONESTY. When once the Lord is pretty well affur'd of this, 'twould very much contribute to the End in view, if a Prefent of Ten or Fifteen Guineas apiece was made to the Parents, to have them well inftructed in *Accompts*, &c. and to let fall fomething that may *encourage* their Hopes of being provided for in a better manner than can reafonably be expected from moft Trades and Profeffions, which are obferv'd of late Years to be fo generally overftock'd, that more than half of the Profeffors throughout the Kingdom are driven to Neceffities and Straits. When fome fuch Methods as thefe

are

are taken, whereby the brighter part of the Country Youth are made to hope for *Preferment* in their Lord's Service, or to be recommended to others upon occasion, it may easily be concluded, that no small Advantage must accrue towards the *Improvement* of Estates in general, from a *Nursery* and (as it were) *Seminary* of young Men instructed, as they ought to be, in all the Honest *Arts of good Husbandry and good Accompts.*

Possibly the Freedom I have taken, and the Plainness I have us'd, may be thought by some to need an Apology, because some of the *Articles* at first View may, by *Stewards*, be interpreted as *Ill-nature* in me, as if I had had a *Prejudice* to, or *set my self* against them in general; but, alas! I have neither *Interest* nor *Inclination* to serve in being ill-natur'd or satyrical: I would discourage and detect *Knavery*, and I would do all I can to convince *Stewards* that *Honesty* and *Truth* are the best Policy. Stewards indeed are, of all others, under the greatest Temptation to be Knaves, because becaufe they have it fo much in their power to be fuch, with impunity, and without difcovery: They are born like other Men, and have not more Corruptions in their Nature; and, were I to give Inftances, I could name many who are *above* all the little *Arts* of *robbing* their Lord to *enrich* themfelves: And if there are others not true to their Truft, their Faults fhould be writ in their *Foreheads*; and I am not afham'd to fay, *I have done*, and *will do* all I can to make them known, and to prevent indirect Practices for the future.

MOREOVER, if it be ftill objected and ask'd, (as I forefee fome may ask) *Who would be a Lord's Steward, if they muft have fo many Eyes, and fo many Checques upon them?* let fuch confider, that *Lofers* and the *Cheated* have not only a right to complain, but alfo to contrive the beft Methods to fecure and defend themfelves from future *Injuries*. Neither can I think that an *honeft* and *wife* Steward will have any Reafon to diflike thefe Methods; and as for thofe that are otherwife, the World is generally juft and
equitable

equitable enough not to regard their Complaints.

To conclude this Head ; I cannot however avoid faying, that it is the Interest, and should be the Resolution, of every Nobleman, when he is persuaded he hath a *faithful* Steward, to study to make him as easy as possible by all fitting *Encouragements,* and not to *listen* to, or entertain every *officious Story* that will be told, except there be very good grounds; much less to discharge him on the account of *Suspicion* only. To do that (*and yet that is too often done*) were the sure way never to be serv'd with *Truth* and *Honesty :* For it may be a Temptation to some Stewards, when they find their Office is precarious, to make the best they can of it in a *little* time, by ways not altogether *justifiable* ; *Encouragement* goes a great way towards putting *evil* Thoughts out of their Minds. I remember an Instance of the *Generosity* of a certain Lord, that when his Steward had balanc'd a faithful Account, and had observ'd that the Estate was *improv'd,*

prov'd, would make him a handfome Prefent, befides the Allowance of his fettled
Salary.

Much the fame may be faid with refpect
to Tenants; if they are bound down to
hard Meafures and Articles, regarding only the Intereft of the Lord, they will have
no Encouragement to *improve* their Farms,
but on the contrary will be tempted to
contrive ways to *evade* the Force of their
Leafes to fupply Deficiencies, efpecially as
they are near *expiring*, attended with fuch
Expoftulations as thefe: *What Encouragement have we to improve, if we muft
pay for it when our Leafes are out, upon
that* very *account ?*

The fecond Head leads me to an Addrefs to the Legislative Powers, that
they would interpofe (for the Good of the
Publick, and their own fakes) to prevent
the Abufes and Mifchiefs occafion'd by
Water-Mills. For it is well known,
that moft of the loweft Meadows and beft
Lands in *England* are more or lefs affected

and

and hurt by Water-Mills, which sometimes wholly prevent the draining and drawing off such stagnating Waters, as tend to spoil the very *best Land*; and at other times prevent the great Advantages which the Meadows near Rivers might receive by being *flooded* with *Freshes* and *White-water*. In short, they cause the overflowings of large and brave Estates, to their *utter Ruin*; and they prevent the Improvements which might be made upon others; to say nothing here of the dead Weight which they ever prove upon the good Designs of making Rivers *navigable*.

All which Abuses, I am well assur'd from a Person of undeniable Judgment and Skill in such Affairs, may be perfectly remedied, and the necessary Business of grinding Corn, *&c.* as effectually perform'd, as ever was in the common Methods.

The Commissioners of *Sewers* have little Encouragement to take pains, and perform their Duty, whilst they constantly find their Designs prove abortive, on account

count of the prefent Scituation of *Water-Mills*; the fettling of which Inconveniencies, I refer to the Confideration of Perfons in Power, and others, whofe Eftates are hurt thereby.

Article

Article I.

I Begin with a Maxim which is highly to be regarded, *viz.* That a Steward undertake not more Bufinefs than he can truly and regularly and *honeftly* perform. And this Caution is to be underftood, not only of fuch *variety* of Bufinefs and Affairs of different Kinds, as tend to diftract the Head, but even of a *multiplicity* of proper Bufinefs relating to a Steward ; efpecially if that Bufinefs happen to lie in many and diftant Parts : For (as it will appear in the following *Articles*) it is the leaft part of the Bufinefs of a Steward to collect the Rents ; and he may as effectually wrong his Lord for want of proper and *regular Surveys,* as for a Neglect in gathering his Rents.

Arti-

Article II.

NO one fhould undertake the Bufinefs of a Steward till he is fully acquainted with Country Affairs, fo as to be able, upon *all* occafions, to direct and advife fuch Tenants as do not underftand the *beft* and *lateft* Improvements in Husbandry. And this Knowledge is the more neceffary, becaufe fometimes a Farm ill manag'd by a former Tenant, happens to fall into the Lord's hand ; and then a regular and experienc'd Skill in the Steward will be very feafonable, as well as of great Service to his Lord, by fhewing an *Example* of good Husbandry to the reft of the Tenants.

Arti-

Article III.

A Steward fhould at the *firft* entring into his Service, make himfelf Mafter
of the Quantity and Quality of *every* Parcel
of Land occupied by the feveral Tenants ;
and this will enable him to confider and
advife what Parcels are proper to be kept
for *Pafture* and *Meadow*, and what other
Parcels for *Tillage :* An Example whereof
is drawn out from an accurate Survey at
the end of this Treatife *. But it fhould
be added here, that great Care ought to
be taken, that *none* of the Tenants be allow'd to have much above a third Part of
the Farm in Tillage in any one Year, (except 'tis fuch poor Land as is fubject to be
over-run with Trumpery for want of ploughing) obliging them alfo to lay the fame
down, after a reafonable Term of years,

* See the Survey.

with

with proper * Grafs-Seeds ; *viz.* after about four Crops taken, and two Summer Fallows given. And the fame Care fhould be had, that the Lands, when laid down, be fupply'd, and re-enrich'd with a proper Quantity of Manure; Twenty Loads of Dung fuppofe upon an Acre, or Ninety Bufhels of Lime. A confiderable Strefs fhould be laid upon the due Performance of this Article; becaufe, from *long* Experience and *repeated* Obfervation, it hath *ever* appear'd to me, that the laying down Lands *poor*, without proper Supplies, hath been the *Ruine of many Farms*, and put a Stop to *all* fuch reafonable Advance of Rent as might have been made, by rendering it almoft impoffible (without an *immenfe* Charge) to reftore its former *Riches* and *Strength*.

* See the Appendix.

Arti-

Article IV.

A Steward fhould endeavour to make himfelf Mafter of the *Method* that every Tenant takes, to raife his Lord's Rent, as well as to provide for his Family: And if he finds a Tenant, either th,o' Ignorance or Indolence, not likely to thrive, or does not proceed in a due Courfe of Husbandry, that then he firft *admonifh* and *inftruct* him; and if he proves *ftubborn* and *unper-fuadable*, afterwards to *difcharge* him, and put another in his room, before he run too far *behindhand* in his Rents, which is a fure Fore-runner of an irretrievable Pover-ty, and a too fevere Tryal of a good-natur'd Landlord. To prevent therefore the worft Extremity, and that thefe and the follow-ing *Articles* may be moft effectually per-form'd, *a Steward fhould ride over the whole Eftate at leaft once a Month*, in order to view both the Lands and Stock of

the

the Tenants carefully and diftinctly, taking MEMORANDUMS of the fame from time to time; which will prove no fmall *Cheque* upon the feveral Tenants, and will be of confiderable Advantage to both *Landlord* and *Tenant*.

Article V.

A Steward, on his Survey round his Lord's Eftate, fhould be careful to obferve that the Tenants do not plough up any frefh Pafture or Meadow Ground, without firft giving Notice to the Lord of the Manor, or fuch Agents as he fhall appoint. According to the beft of my Obfervation and Judgment, I could never find but that it is the *Intereft* of every *Landlord* to fuffer the Tenant to grub up *Whins*, *Thorns*, and *Broom*, that have over-run fome of the *worfer* fort of Land, and then to ufe it for Four or Six Years in *Tillage*, without any Expectation of Advance of Rent, provided

the

the fame be laid down with * Grafs-Seeds
(of which more hereafter) and a proper
Quantity of Dung. But if the Land be of
the better fort, and (which is frequently
the Cafe) by age fubject to grow over with
Mofs; in fuch cafe, altho' it is of real Advantage to the Land to turn it up with
the Plough, yet a confiderable † Encreafe
of Rent ought to be made for the *Advantage* of ploughing fuch *frefh* Ground, for
three years only: And the Tenant fhould
be oblig'd to lay down the fame with a-
bout Twenty Loads of Dung, or Ninety
Bufhels of Lime, upon an Acre, according
to the Nature of the Land; which is fully
fhewn in the Appendix.

* See the Appendix.   † See Steward's Accompts.

Arti-

☙❧☙❧☙❧☙❧☙❧☙❧☙❧☙❧☙❧☙❧

Article VI.

A Steward, on his Surveys, ſhould ſtrict-
ly obſerve and order, that the Lord's
Tenants, as well as thoſe of the Freeholders, do conſtantly, from time to time, as
need requires, cleanſe and ſcowr up their
Ditches, in order to carry off the Water into the *Vales*, *Rivers*, or *Sewers*, if any
ſuch there be, within the ſaid Manors. For
which purpoſe it is requiſite that the Steward
be always oblig'd to attend the Court-
Leet and Court-Baron, in order to Present ſuch Tenants as have been guilty of
Neglects in the aforemention'd Particulars,
that they may be *fined* according to Law.
The Force of this Article, in making Stewards
the Agents in this Affair, lieth here: That
it is known by Experience and Obſervation,
if they are not *preſented* by the Steward,
the Tenants will not *preſent* one another;
which occaſions great Delays and Diſap-
pointments, to the manifeſt damage of

Eſtates.

Eftates. It is alfo very proper, that a Steward fhould be qualified to be one of the Commiffioners of *Sewers*, that he may be an Inftrument always at hand to pufh forward the Performance of this Article, and the executing the commendable Huf-bandry of fcowring and cleanfing the feve-ral Ditches and Trenches, which otherwife would foon become of little or no ufe.

N.B. For the better Direction of a Steward, it may not be amifs in this place to mention an excellent part of good Husbandry much practis'd in the *Weft* of *England*, where they plough Trenches about two foot deep with a Plough made on purpofe with a double Coulter: After that they dig the faid Trenches till they are full four foot deep, and confiderably wider at the top than at the bottom, into which they caft all the green Brufh-wood of *Black-thorns, Withies, White-thorns*, &c. which they can mufter up together, laying flat Stones upon them, to keep them tight together; and then the Drain is finifh'd by filling the Trenches up with the Rubbifh plough'd and dug out of them.

This

This Method teaches the Farmer the Advantage of having his over-moist Ground always dry; and, for the future, he will have the Profit of losing no part of the Herbage. Again,

I hope it will not be thought too great a Digression, if for the Steward's Direction and Information, I here transcribe Mr. *Switzer*'s recommended Method of draining Land by artificial Tubes or Trunks of Clay, which, he saith, hath prov'd one of the most useful Inventions that has been found out in any Age, and will do in *pasture*, *arable*, or *wood-lands*, provided you work deep enough. " Be provided then (saith
" he) of three or four narrow Spades about
" eight inches wide, and fifteen inches long,
" with a Handle put into a Socket and
" Ring, with a Tread round it, to set the
" Foot upon to dig; and at every twenty
" foot asunder, if the Ground lie near a
" Level, dig a narrow Trench of about ten
" inches, or a foot wide at most, quite
" through, at twenty foot asunder, and a
" full foot and half within the Clay:
Then

" Then take a wooden Rowl of about five
" inches diameter at one end, of four foot
" long, and four inches diameter at the
" other ; and placing this Rowl at the bot-
" tom of the Trench, take the Clay you
" had before dug out, and with a Ram-
" mer ram it in round the Rowl, which
" will form a perfect Tube : And the
" Rowler being bigger at one end than
" the other, you may, by the help of
" a Chain faften'd to the bigger end, pull
" it out of the Tube; fo that proceeding
" four foot at a time, you go through your
" Trenches from end to end, taking care
" to keep the Extremities of the Tube
" open. He faith, there fhould be a Han-
" dle of about four foot long, mortis'd into
" the great end of the Rowl, by which the
" Workmen fhoggle about the Rowl, fo
" as to loofen it in the Tube, by which
" means the Rowl will be the eafier drawn
" out by the Chain. But before that is
" done, you are to punch a Hole about
" three inches diameter through the ramm'd
" Clay upon the top of your Rowl, through
" which Perforation all the Water is to pafs
that

" that comes from the Ground above, down
" into the underground Drain or Tube be-
" low. But ftill, to keep this perforated
" Hole open, fmall artificial Faggots of
" green Wood fhould be laid upon it, with
" a broad Tile at top, to fecure it from
" any Impreffion that may come from a-
" bove: And thus (faith he) you have a
" clayey Field as hollow and unfit to re-
" tain ftagnated Water as a Sieve. Thefe
" Tubes he has known perform their of-
" fice twelve years, even in plough'd Lands,
" where the diforder of Horfes might be
" fuppos'd to fpoil the whole Scheme. It
" cofts about Twenty Shillings an Acre,
" each Drain at about twenty foot diftance.
[See *Switzer's* Fruit-Garden.]

Arti-

Article VII.

A Steward on his Survey fhould narrowly watch and obferve, that the
Tenants do not gather the *Cow-dung* together on heaps, in order firft to *dry* it, and
then to *burn* it; as is too frequently practis'd, both in *York-fhire* and *Lincoln-fhire*,
where Fuel is fomething fcarce, to the no
fmall damage and prejudice to the Farm.
The ufing *Hogs-dung*, inftead of *Soap*, to
wafh their Linnen, deferves fome notice,
and fhould not be indulg'd to excefs.

Arti-

Article VIII.

A Steward fhould likewife on his Surveys diligently obferve, whether any
of the Tenants do pare and burn the Soil
of any part of their Farms : For tho' this
is a Practice of late years brought up, and
encourag'd by the Farmers, for their own
immediate Advantage, and by *Art* made to
look *plaufible*, efpecially where Avarice or
Indigence are addrefs'd to by prefent Re-
wards; yet, led by *long* Experience, and
certain Knowledge, I am *fure* nothing hath
more tended to the *falling* of Rents and
the *ruine* of Eftates than * *Denfhiring*, as
it

---

* I have often met with Rebukes from feveral Farmers, and others, who are fond of *Denfhiring*, or Burning of *good* as well as *bad* Land : And they have wonder'd that I fhould be againft this *Noble* Improvement
(as they call it) fince there are fuch *vaft* Quantities of poor
Land in *England*, that they have by a long continuance
in Pafture contracted fuch a four Juice, that the
Land would be worth *nothing* without *paring* and burning the Soil: And they have told me, they have (by this
Method)

it is call'd from its firſt practice in *Devon-*
ſhire; where they now own, by way of
Proverb, that tho' it is good for the *Father*,
it is bad for the *Son*. And what brings on
the deſtruction of a Farm the ſooner, is the
ſtill *viler* Practice of the Farmer, who too
often ſows *Rape* after burning; than which
there cannot be a greater Beggarer, eſpecially of good Land; for it ſtrikes a deep Root
into the Soil, and quickly fetches out all
(or moſt) of the terreſtrial Matter fit for Vegetation; inſomuch, that the Land ſo a-
bus'd *ſeldom* or *never* is known to come to
itſelf again. And again; while the Steward
is watching to prevent Abuſes, he ſhould
not neglect to reſtrain the Tenants from
ſowing *Hemp, Flax, Woad, Weldt, Madder*;

Method) receiv'd ſuch Crops as would purchaſe the Inheritance of the Land. Suppoſing this to be true, yet I
would have them conſider, that *all* or moſt of the *Ni-*
trous Particles, by this Method, muſt be *drawn* from
the Land, eſpecially when the Practice is continued,
which is generally done; and ſo conſequently they can
expect to receive but very *little* Advantage from the
Land for the future. Therefore the *ſureſt* way to improve ſuch poor Land, is to turn it up with the Plough,
and to ſow ſuch Seeds upon it as the Nature of the
Land requires, and to plough in the Crop at *Midſummer*.
N. B. This Method is more fully treated of in the Appendix.

and

and from planting *Hops* or *Potatoes*; (except in fmall quantities for their own private ufe.) ALL which Vegetables are very deftructive to Land, becaufe *they breed no Manure* ; they *take from*, but *give nothing back to* the Earth : For which reafon the Practice fhould be difcourag'd, and indeed not fuffer'd, even on the beft Land, without a very *valuable* * *Confideration* made to the Landlord, not exceeding the Term of Three Years at moft. And, after that, the utmoft Care muft be taken that the Land be laid down not in too high Ridges, and with a fufficient quantity of fuch Dung or Lime as can be got for breeding Grafs and † fwarding the Land : *Coal-afhes* and *Horfe-dung* for heavy Land, and *Cow dung*, *Lime*, or *Marle* for light Land.

* See Steward's Accompts.
† As the 'foremention'd Lands are defign'd to be continu'd for Pafture, fo it is advifeable to fow them with the natural *Hay-feed*, allowing Ten or Fifteen Bufhels to an Acre, where it can conveniently be got, near any confiderable City or Market-Town. This hath been practis'd with great Succefs, becaufe thefe natural Graffes do not wear out, as the artificial ones do.

Arti-

Article IX.

I T is also the great Care and Duty of a Steward to see that whatsoever Manure, or materials for Manure, his Lord's Estate produces, such as * *Coal-ashes, Kilp-ashes, Were,* &c. be only used and dispos'd of to his Lord's Tenants, and not to the Freeholders, or their Tenants round about; that these Privileges may appear to be real and valuable Advantages attending their Farms.

* The disposing of the 'foremention'd Manure to the Freeholders round the Country, is practis'd *very* much by such Stewards who make *haste* to be *rich* by this Article, as well as many others mention'd in this Treatise.

E   *Arti-*

Article X.

A Steward fhould have a watchful Eye, that the Mole-catcher perform his Duty in deftroying that noxious Animal, efpecially in the Spring and Breeding-time. Lazy Tenants are apt to think Moles do little or no Harm, and fo they are too of-ten neglected : But fure I am, the Mifchief is great where they are numerous ; for, in a dry Summer following, little Grafs will grow where the Soil is much burrow'd, and made hollow. Twelve-pence a dozen for what the Mole-catcher deftroys, is a better Bargain than to give yearly Wages, becaufe it is a common Practice for fuch Perfons to abufe the Truft repofed in them, when they are paid by the Year. It is alfo the Care of the Steward to fee that each Tenant do le-vel the Meadow and Pafture Ground, as near as poffible in the *Spring*, and to fpread the Mole-heaps and Ant-banks, to prevent

the

the Stroke of the Sythe's being interrupted, and hinder'd from coming too near the Ground; it being an *undeniable Truth*, that one Inch at the bottom is worth four at top.

Article XI.

A Steward fhould take care, that no Part of his Lord's Eftate be ftock'd with Rabbits, except it be on very large *Commons* or *Moors*, at leaft Three Miles diftant from Enclofures or Common-Fields. At two Miles diftance they will often *ftrole* for Food, to the great prejudice of the neighbouring Farmers, as well as to the Woods ufually kept in hand. The mifchief that has been done by Rabbits is very vifible and remarkable, on his Grace the Duke of *Buckingham's* Eftate in *Lincolnfhire*; where the indolent Steward fuffer'd the Tenants to ftock their Farms with Rabbits upon a light blowing Sand, which when

E 2 burrow'd

burrow'd by them, becomes eafily fubject
to the Violence of the Winds; and accordingly above One hundred and fifty Acres
of good Land, of a neighbouring Farm,
have been cover'd with a deep Sand in lefs
than a Year: But, fince that, proper Methods and due Care have been taken to
prevent the like damage, by keeping the
Rabbits on the outfide of the Eftate; which
may eafily be continued with care and
watchfulnefs; being well fatisfied they
may be kept within Bounds by the common Methods of *Ferreting* and *Netting*.

Article XII.

A Steward fhould likewife be careful
and vigilant, that none of the Tenants
do *let* any part of their Farms to *Under-
Tenants*; which I have known frequently
practis'd, with much *Hurt* and *Prejudice*
to the Land. For tho' the chief Tenants
themfelves are apt to cry out before they
are

are hurt, yet I have made it my frequent
Obfervation (as I have been upon my Surveys) that the Farmers are not a little *cruel*
to one another, in *racking* up the Lands
to twice the Value; at which *exceffive*
Price they commonly *fet* it to an *Under-
Tenant*; which Extortion naturally puts the
faid Under-Tenant upon ufing indirect means
to get the *Heart* out of the Land: And yet
that Lofs, in the end, of confequence falls
hard on the Landlord. But all pretences
for doing this, may in great meafure be
prevented by the Steward's *Care*, in laying the Farms as *compact* together as poffible, that the Tenant may not be tempted
to let any ufelefs Part of his Farm to an
Under-Tenant. Neither indeed fhould a
Steward fuffer any of his Lord's Lands to
be let to the *Freehold Tenants* within or
near his Lord's Manor, becaufe 'tis a natural Contrivance, or Piece of *Cunning*, in
them to lay all or moft of their Manure
upon their own Land, to the great *Improvement* of the one, and *Beggary* of the
other: And, by virtue of this abominable
CLOWN-CRAFT Practice, when they think

E 3   proper,

proper, and when their own turn is ferv'd, they'll give it up, as having already got what they intended.

Article XIII.

A Steward, as much as in him lieth, and without Oppreffion, fhould endeavour to lay all the fmall Farms, let to poor indigent People, to the great ones. But this muft be done with Difcretion, as it may be with Reafon and Juftice, as the Heads of Families happen to fall, without continuing the Farms to the poor Remains, who may as well betake themfelves to other Employments; or if unable, had better be provided for otherwife : And this will be a means of keeping a multitude of Poor out of the Parifh, who generally care not to come where they muft live by hard Labour.

NEVER-

NEVERTHELESS, in fome Inftances, and near any populous trading Town, it may be very proper to let Lands in fmall Parcels to an inferiour *working* People, who can make great Advantages by felling Milk; or to a *trading* People, who will give more than it could be let for otherwife, for their convenience ; chufing rather to have Provifions of their own at the beft hand, than to go to Market to buy at a dearer rate. I have known very confiderable Improvements made on Noblemen's Eftates fituated near the Sea, by granting Leafes of the Ground for building Houfes upon the Wafte, at an eafy rate for the firft Term of Ten or Twelve years, by way of encouragement ; and afterwards they have readily fubmitted to a confiderable Advance of Rent for a fecond Term; by which means the Place by degrees foon became very populous, ready for a Charter to be made a trading Market-Town, and at the fame time able to fix advanc'd Rents (even double to their former Value) on all the neighbouring Eftates. This noble Example of good Husbandry

E 4   having

having been compleated by that great Oeco-
nomift Sir *Walter Caverly*, near *Leeds* in
Torkſhire, (whoſe beautiful Seat ſtands upon
the River *Air*) ſhould animate and encourage Others to the like Improvements, who,
by laying out conſiderable Sums of Money
in building *Fulling-Mills* upon the River,
has tempted the Cloth-makers to come and
ſettle there with their Families ; infomuch
that his Eſtate and Lands round about
quickly advanc'd, and doubled the old
Rent.

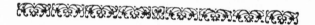

Article XIV.

A Steward ſhould not forget to make
the beft Enquiry into the Diſpoſi-
tion of any of the Freeholders within or
near any of his Lord's Manors, to ſell their
Lands, that he may uſe his beft Endeavours to purchaſe them at as reaſonable a
Price as may be for his Lord's Advantage

3   and

and Convenience. Some Inftances there have been of Stewards, who, after they have made *hafte* to be rich, have made thefe Enquiries for *their own* fakes, and have purchas'd out the Freeholders, thereby making an Eftate for themfelves, even within their own Lord's Manors; infomuch that fometimes I have known it fo order'd that the Lord's Tenants have been call'd to do Suit and Service at his own Court. But, for the fake of *Honour* and *Honefty*, I hope thefe Inftances are rare; and fo I content myfelf to have given this Hint, ftill perfuading the vigilant Steward to be zealous, for his Lord's fake, in purchafing all the Freeholders out as foon as poffible, efpecially in fuch Manors where Improvements are to be made by *inclofing* Commons and Common-Fields; which (as every one, who is acquainted with the late Improvements in Agriculture, muft know) is not a little advantageous to the Nation in general, as well as highly profitable to the Undertaker. If the Freeholders cannot *all* be perfuaded to fell, yet at leaft an Agreement for *Inclofing* fhould be pufh'd forward

ward by the Steward, and a Scheme laid
wherein it may appear, that an exact and
proportional Share will be allotted to every
Proprietor; perfuading them firft, if poffible, to fign a Form of Agreement, and
then to chufe Commiffioners on both fides.

If the Steward be a Man of good Senfe,
he will find a neceffity of making ufe of
it all, in rooting out *Superftition* from a-
mongft them, as what is fo great a hindrance to all *noble* Improvements. The
Subftance of what is proper for the Proprie-
tors to fign before an Inclofure is to be
made, may be conceiv'd in fome fuch Form
as followeth.

" Whereas it is found, by long Expe-
" rience, that Common or Open Fields,
" where-ever they are fuffer'd or continu'd,
" are great Hindrances to a publick Good,
" and the honeft Improvement which every
" one might make of his own, by dili-
" gence and a feafonable charge : And
" whereas the common Objections hitherto
" rais'd againft Inclofures are founded on
                                    " Miftakes,

2

" Miftakes, as if Inclofures contributed ei-
" ther to hurt or ruine the Poor ; whilft
" it is plain that (when an Inclefure is
" once refolv'd on) the Poor will be im-
" ploy'd for many Years, in planting and
" preferving the Hedges, and afterwards
" will be fet to work both in the Tillage
" and Pafture, wherein they may get an
" honeft Livelihood : And whereas all or
" moft of the Inconveniencies and Misfortunes
" which ufually attend the *open Waftes*
" and common Fields have been fatally ex-
" perienc'd at ———, to the great Difcou-
" ragement of Induftry and good Husban-
" dry in the Freeholders, *viz.* That the
" Poor take their Advantage to pilfer, and
" fteal, and trefpafs ; That the Corn is fub-
" ject to be fpoil'd by Cattle, that ftray
" out of the Commons and Highways ad-
" jacent ; That the Tenants or Owners, if
" they would fecure the Fruits of their
" Labours to themfelves, are obliged ei-
" ther to keep exact Time in fowing and
" reaping, or elfe to be fubject to the Da-
" mage and Inconvenience that muft at-
" tend the *lazy* Practices of thofe who fow
                                    " unfea-

" unfeafonably, fuffering their Corn to ftand
" to the beginning of Winter, thereby hin-
" d'ring the whole Parifh from eating the
" Herbage of the common Field, till the
" Frofts have fpoil'd the moft of it: For
" thefe Reafons, and for many more which
" might be affign'd to encourage Induftry,
" and to afcertain a Security to every Man
" of enjoying the quiet Poffeffion of his
" Labour and Care, we whofe Names are
" underwritten, being Freeholders, do agree
" to the Inclofing, and to the immediate
" fetting about the Work of an Inclofure
" in the common Fields of ———, and to
" bring it to perfection with all convenient
" fpeed.

N.B. I have often lamented the Misfortune that attends Noblemen's and Gentlemen's Eftates, where only a *part* of the
Common Fields have been inclos'd, becaufe
the Tenants carry *all* or moft of the Manure bred upon the inclos'd part, to the
Fallows in the Common Fields; which indeed *want* it, becaufe they are conftantly
kept in Tillage: Yet, neverthelefs, this unequal

equal Management impoverifhes the inclos'd
part *not a little*; therefore the moft effectual way to prevent this *growing Evil*,
is to endeavour (as foon as poffible) to inclofe the *whole :* Till this is perform'd, the
Steward fhould fee that the Tenants fpend
the quantity of Manure bred on the inclos'd Part, upon the Land which produced
it, in order to reftore (in fome meafure) the
Riches that *conftant* mowing may have taken from the Meadows.

Article XV.

IT is another confiderable Part of the
Duty of a Steward, whenever an
Offer is made of felling an Eftate adjoyn-
ing upon his Lord's other Manors, to go
to every one of the Tenants, endeavouring to fee all their Acquittances for as
many years paft as poffible, that he may
be able to acquaint his Lord if it is an old-
rented

rented Eftate ; and if any Advance hath been made, he will by that means fee what it is. It hath been a Practice of late years, not much to be commended, to RACK up the Tenants beyond what the Eftate will bear, in order to fell it with advantage; which method is not ftrictly *honeft*. And I have likewife found it too frequently practis'd, before an Eftate is to be fold, provided the Tenants will but agree to give an advanc'd Rent, the Landlord privately confents to pay what the Tenant paid before, *viz.* the *Poor's*, the *Church*, and the *Conftable's* Af-feffments; and it is not feldom that, be-fides thefe, a Sum of Money is given into the bargain : Whereas, if a Steward is *vigilant* and careful, thefe private Contracts tending to over-rate the value of the E-ftate, may in great meafure be difcover'd; and that difcovery will be of fuch real fer-vice to his Lord, that it will prevent his being impos'd upon in a Purchafe.

Arti-

Article XVI.

A Steward fhould ever have a watchful Eye upon all the feveral Farm-Houfes belonging to his Lord within the Manor, and under his Care, to fee they are kept up in good repair. When an Improvement is made upon an Eftate, and new Leafes granted, it is cuftomary that the Lord of the Manor be at the expence of putting the Houfes, *&c.* in Tenantable Repair; but, after that, 'tis highly reafonable that they fhould be kept fo by the Tenants, efpecially being allow'd rough Timber to do the fame ; which yet fhould be affign'd them by the Steward himfelf, and no leave given to the Tenant to haggle and cut where and what he pleafes; as hath been too frequently practis'd under a pretended and miftaken notion, that they ought to have an Allowance for *Ploughboot,*

boot, *Cart-boot*, and *Fire-boot*, &c. a Cuſtom formerly indeed allow'd to ſuch Tenants who had Leaſes for Three Lives, and likewiſe to Copyhold Tenants upon Lives, but very ſeldom to Tenants at *Will*, and ſhort Leaſes for a Term of Years. Theſe Rules being duly obſerv'd by a Steward, will not only be a means to preſerve the Woods, but alſo prevent any Bills for repairs of Houſes for the future, which commonly prove no inconſiderable Burthen, and has been indeed a ſort of *Tax* upon Noblemen's Eſtates.

THE like Reaſoning ſhould take place, and be allow'd with reſpect to Water-Mills and Wind-Mills, which, generally ſpeaking, are the *worſt* part of an Eſtate; eſpecially as the Matter is now order'd, when Cuſtom prevails to oblige the Landlord to find Mill-ſtones, Wheels, and Coggs, with all other Utenſils proper and belonging to Mills, which continually wearing out, are conſtantly one or other of them wanted. To prevent therefore this conſtant Demand and annual Rent-charge, as well

as

as the Repairs of the Mill and Out-Houses,
I have all along (where I have been concern'd in the Valuing and IMPROVING E-
ftates) agreed for the *beft* and *moft* improv'd Rent I could get ; at the fame time
obliging the Miller by Covenant to be at
ALL the abovemention'd Charges, having
firft put the Mills and Appurtenances in
fufficient Repair; after which I fuffer'd
them to take a long Leafe of Twenty-one
years. And, to make Matters ftill eafier,
in fome Parts of the North, where the
Land-Tax is not exceffive, I have agreed
with ALL the Tenants for a clear Rent,
themfelves paying ALL Taxes and Affeffments whatfoever. Such Advice and Practice I founded upon this reafoning; That
thefe and the abovemention'd Disburfements being left out of Accompts, would
prove of great Eafe to Noblemen and Gentlemen in the examining them, as well as
of great Satisfaction to their Minds, when
they fee in one View what their real E-
ftates are, and what they can command upon all Emergencies, without unknown and
endlefs Deductions. Every Steward there-
F fore

fore fhould be perfuaded to govern himfelf
by thefe Rules, as of great Ufe and Eafe
to himfelf in making up his Accompts, ex-
clufive of this Confideration, that it will
recommend his Diligence alfo, by making
it appear, that he ftudies both his Lord's
Eafe and his *Intereft*.

Article XVII.

WHEN a Tenant's Term or Leafe
is out, or that he happens to leave
his Farm, 'tis the Steward's Bufinefs to fee
that he doth not *overftock* his Pafture and
Meadows before the time of Expiration,
whether it be *Lady-day* or *May-day*, by
taking in more Cattle than his own, by way
of JOYSTING; which is a Practice contrary
to both *Law* and *Juftice*. In moft parts of
the North of *England*, and in many others,
May-day is the time of *Entering* and *Leaving*, which makes the Steward's Care to
prevent Abufes the more neceffary, becaufe
over-

overstocking the Meadows at a time when
they should be *growing* and getting head
to defend themselves from the Drought and
scorching Summer's Sun, is a great Injury
to a new Tenant. I have known Meadows so manag'd and left, tho' worth Thirty Shillings an Acre, have been so bare
and scorch'd, that they have not produc'd
above half a Load of Hay from an Acre:
A Loss that bears no comparison to the
unjust Gain of the preceeding greedy Tenant. It were indeed, on all Accounts, much
to be wish'd that the Custom and Practice
of eating the Meadows till *May-day*, so hurtful and inconvenient in itself, and so subject to be abus'd, were broken and alter'd
for the better and more reasonable Term
of *Lady-day*; but till that can be effected
with Prudence, and without Clamour, the
stronger will be the Argument for the Steward's
greater Vigilance and Care to prevent A-
buses.

UNDER this Article it may be proper
to observe, that great Care should be taken
that the Tenants sell off their Farms as little

Hay

Hay and Straw as poffible; on the contra-ry, that they be oblig'd to fpend the fame on the Premifes: But yet if it fhould fo happen, that in a fcarce time a great Demand for Hay is made ; or, that the Tenant lives near *London*, or any other confiderable Market-Town, where the Price of Hay and Straw will make a good Advance in his Rent, the Sale may be permitted ; provided at the fame time the moft diligent Care be taken, by *ftrict* Articles and Covenants, that he fupply the Lofs and Damage, by purchafing at leaft Three Loads of rotten Dung mix'd with Earth, for every One Load of Hay carried off the Premifes, over and above what was made there. But ftill, notwithftanding fome of thefe Exceptions, the general Rule fhould in the main take place, and be obferv'd, (efpecially where there's no Dung to be got but what the Premifes afford) *viz.* To fell no Hay or Straw, but to fpend the fame upon the Premifes. And becaufe 'tis plain and cer-tain, from Experience, that conftant mow-ing of Meadows is not only apt to weaken the Soil, but to produce fowre and coarfe

Grafs ;

Grafs ; the Steward fhould oblige the Tenant to alter the Property, turning fometimes Pafture into Meadow, and Meadow into Pafture ; but yet by no means to fuffer the Tenant to *encreafe* the Meadow and *leffen* the Pafture, efpecially at his leaving the Farm.

NEITHER at fuch a time fhould it be forgot, that the Tenant be oblig'd to leave a fufficient quantity of Tillage (*viz.* about a third part) to the fucceeding Tenant, well fallow'd in a feafonable and Husband-like manner by four Tilts or Ploughings, the fucceeding Tenant being by * Cuftom generally willing to allow about Eight or Nine Shillings an Acre, where 'tis the Cuftom to enter at † *Michaelmas*, for fuch

---

* In fome Parts of the North, where 'tis the Cuftom for new Tenants to enter at **Lady-day**, the departing Tenant requires his *'way-going* **Crop** of Corn ; which is a Hardfhip on the new Tenant ; but in other Parts it is *more reafonable*, the departing Tenant requires but two Thirds of the Crop, for his Charge of Fallowing, Sowing, &*c*. The former Cuftom fhou'd by the Stewards be *abolifh'd*, and the latter *encourag'd*.

† The beft time of all others, both for Landlord and Tenant, becaufe it puts an End to all Difputes about the *'way-going* **Crops**.

F 3   Fal-

Fallows; ſtill ever bearing in mind, that the departing Tenant be oblig'd alſo to leave all the Straw and Dung bred and made the preceding year to the new Tenant, without any Conſideration or Reward for the ſame, as agreeable to Reaſon, and ought to be a General Cuſtom.

Article XVIII.

BECAUSE it is a moſt fatal and too general an *Evil* to ſuffer Mounds and Hedges to decay, either tho Negligence or want of Skill, to the great hurt and ſinking of Eſtates, a Steward, in his Surveys ſhould have a conſtant Eye upon the Tenant's Method of cutting and plaſhing the Hedges, directing them not to chop and haggle them in an unskilful and unſightly manner, as the too common Practice (of the North eſpecially) is, but to lay the

Bran-

Branches * *horizontally* ; which will quickly tend to thicken the Hedge, and fill up
all Vacancies and Gaps : And alſo to cut out
all the larger Wood that can be ſpar'd,
leaving the Part ſmooth and ſloping, twiſt-
ing ſome Bryars on the Top, to keep every thing in its place. A diſcreet and skil-
ful management of Hedges is a conſiderable
Article of a Steward's Care, becauſe it tends
not only to prevent Gaps, and uneaſy Treſ-
paſſes of one Tenant upon one another, but
alſo to the longer Continuance and Duration
of the Stools and Thorns of the Hedge it
ſelf. In cutting off all projecting Branches,
which tend to ſowre the Graſs, the Work-
man ſhould regard that the ſtroke of the
Hatchet go UPWARDS and not DOWNWARDS ;
and that ſuch other Branches as lie convenient for thickening the Hedge, and muſt
be bent downwards, be not cut more than
half through ; wherein careleſs Workmen
are apt to tranſgreſs, to the great Damage
of the Hedge.

* See Fig. II.

F 4   WORK

Workmen alſo, in the Management of Hedges, and plaſhing them, ſhould be advertis'd to drive down * Stakes at about five or ſix Foot diſtance, in all thin Parts of the Hedge, which will much tend both to ſtrengthen and thicken it, till the *horizontal* Branches get Strength and Fulneſs to do that Office themſelves. There ſhould be more than ordinary Care taken in the management of *old* Hedges ; not to cut the Heads entirely off, and leave the Stools like ſo many *Pollards,* as the haſty way in the North is, but rather to cut out as

* It may not be amiſs to relate here the Method which a notable Farmer took to prevent his Hedge-ſtakes from being ſtolen; [and, in a ſcarce Country for Fuel, this is a Grievance which requires their utmoſt Care and Invention to prevent.] His Way was ; By the help of a large Nail-piercer, he bored Holes ſlantwiſe in ſeveral of the faireſt and moſt tempting Stakes, then filling the Holes with Gunpowder, and pegging them up very faſt; and, to prevent any Suſpicion of a Deſign, he dawb'd the Part over with Dirt, and then left them ſtanding in a careleſs manner. The Deſign quickly took, and the Stakes were gone; ſo it may be gueſs'd it was not long before the Rumour of a *Porridge-pot* being like to be blown up was got about the Pariſh. And this Effect was certain, that ever after his Hedges were preſerv'd from Robbers.

much

much of the *old* Wood as is poſſible, and to preſerve ALL the beſt of the *young*.

THIS is a proper Place to advertiſe the Steward, that he be always prepar'd and furniſh'd with a Nurſery of Quicks, that he may not be oblig'd to go to Market when a Demand is made for Quantities upon new Incloſures, or dividing others within his Lord's Manors. His Way is, to provide in Autumn five or ſix Buſhels of *Haws,* letting them lie on a heap in ſome by-place out of Doors till the Autumn following, or rather to dig a Hole in the Earth, and cover them with Sand (for they will not grow till the ſecond Year) and then, in a Nurſery of mellow Ground, about a quarter of an Acre, (more or leſs as there is a Demand for 'em) they may be ſow'd, after the Land is dug up with the Spade, in ſmall Ridges, for the better conveniency of *weeding* ; and in two or three years time, according to the Goodneſs of the Soil, they will be fit for tranſplanting and uſe.

THIS

THIS frugal provident Method fhould be encourag'd, not only as it faves his Lord's Money, but as it anfwers better than the common way of getting *ftunted*, mifhapen Plants out of the Woods. And it is to be remember'd alfo, that the Steward, having a full Stock and Quantity of his own at home, will not fuffer him to think much to allow a fufficient Number for all purpofes. A miftaken Frugality has been of ill Confequence in the North, where they plant only *one Row* of Quicks, becaufe where a Failure happens, there is fure to be a Gap; whereas, where there are *two Rows*, (as there ever fhould be) if either of them hit, that Misfortune is prevented, and the Deficiency is fupply'd either from the *upper* or the *under* Row.

WHEN the provident Steward has furnifh'd himfelf with a Nurfery of Quicks, as above, he fhould endeavour and contrive to *inclofe*, and thereby *leffen*, all fuch large Paftures and Meadows as contain thirty or forty Acres, or more; for by leffening and

dividing

dividing such, they will be much improv'd
every way, especially as they are made capable the better to *winter* their Cattle, and
to defend them from the Extremities of the
cold Winds, Storms, and driving Snows:
For want of such convenient Shelters, I have
known large Tracts of Land, only bound-
ed by distant and extended Hedges by the
Trent side, to suffer very much, because
the Tenants were forced to winter them at
home, which of consequence oblig'd them
to carry the Hay along with 'em, the Produce whereof was commonly forgot to be
brought back in Manure, but rather too often carried and laid upon the *Tillage* nearer home, to the great Damage and Impo-
verishment of the Meadows and Pastures.

IN *Devonshire* they are very extraordinary Husbands in this way, as well as many others, wherein they should be imita-
ted; for it is rare and remarkable there to
find a Pasture or Meadow Ground above
eight or ten Acres: But then they are also
very exemplary and diligent in their exact
laying and plashing their Hedges, in order
to

to make them thick and impenetrable, not
fuffering the large Branches to project and
hang over, which would fpoil and fowre
a good Part of the Ground, where the Inclofures are fmall.

To conclude this Head, I would advife
the Steward, when an Inclofure is to be
made, not to be too *rafh* in † planting
Timber-Trees, of any fort, efpecially *Afhes*,
in the Hedge-rows; for all of them tend to
impoverifh the Land by their fpreading
Roots, and by their projecting Branches
(the Wet dropping from them) do much
hurt to the Hedges, as well as to the Soil,
by fowring the Grafs.

† I hope the latter part of this Article will not be
fo underftood, as if I was for difcouraging the *noble*
Improvements of planting Timber-Trees.
The hint I have given in this Article is only to
fhew the neceffity of planting Timber-Trees by themfelves, becaufe it is now pretty well known, that the
fpreading Branches do no fmall Damage to large Underwoods, as well as Hedge-rows.

Arti-

Article XIX.

A Steward, on his Survey, fhould not be unmindful to enquire, and by proper Marks and Tokens to obferve, whether there be any *Coal, Tin,* or *Lead*-Mines within his Lord's Manors, thefe being ofttimes greater Riches *under* Ground than the beft Improvements *above.* Wherefore a timely and faithful Account of all (even the Probabilities of) thefe Treafures fhould be related, that Tryals may be made, firft by *boring,* and then by *finking* Pits. However, it may be neceffary to add, that the Borer be narrowly watch'd, to prevent the *Coal-Owners* from all parts, and others, whofe Intereft it is to *ftifle* thefe Enquiries, from tampering with him, and ufing fuch indirect and unlawful Arts as tend to make *abortive* all fuch honeft Endeavours both for a publick and private Good. The fame Diligence in the Steward fhould be extended

to

to the Difcovery of all *Quarries* that
happen to lie within his Lord's Manors;
for if they prove to be of a good and fine
fort of Free-ftone, and efpecially if near
the Sea-Coaft or a navigable River, fuch
Quarry frequently tends to no inconfiderable Advancement of his Lord's Eftate.

Article XX.

IT is not only neceffary that a Steward
fhould be a good Accomptant, but alfo
that he fhould have a tolerable Degree of Skill
in *Mathematicks*, Surveying, Mechanicks,
and Architecture; for in every one of thofe
Particulars his Ingenuity and Skill will be
upon many Occafions call'd upon and made
ufe of. And he fhould likewife endeavour
to make himfelf Mafter of the true * Prices
of all forts of Work relating to Husbandry,
that he be not impos'd upon, or oblig'd to

* See the latter End of Steward's Accompts.

I   watch

watch the Day-workmen, which commonly proves the moſt chargeable Method. A
Steward then thus qualified, before he en-
gageth in any Work of Conſequence, relating either to *Incloſures*, or *Architecture*,
or *Draining*, &c. ſhould firſt ſend as exact
an Eſtimate as poſſible, what the ſame will
amount to, that his Lord may *ſit down and
count the Coſt*, and make a deliberate Judgment, whether the Charge will anſwer his
Expectations in the propos'd Benefit. And
becauſe upon every Eſtate lying at ſome
diſtance one from another, it is on many
Accounts very neceſſary that a Villa or
Country-Houſe ſhould be built, the Steward
ſhould uſe his beſt Skill (or by the Aſſiſ-
tance of the beſt * Architect) in drawing out

* The Example of the noted Architect Mr. *Morris*,
and ſome few others, ſhould be a Pattern to the reſt,
to be *punctual*, to make their *Calculations* ſo, as to undertake the building of a Nobleman's or Gentleman's
Seat according to the Deſign firſt made and *calculated*;
and not as too many have done, who have told Noblemen, *&c.* the Charge of building a Seat, according
to their Calculation, for *Twenty thouſand Pounds*; but before the Building was finiſh'd, they found, to their *Sorrow*,
that it coſt them near Fifty thouſand Pounds. *N.B.* I
have known a very neat Country-houſe, juſt fit for a
Nobleman, *&c.* when he comes down to look into his
Affairs, built for leſs than Three thouſand Pounds.

the

the Particulars of the Charge of doing the fame, aiming not fo much at *State* as *Convenience* ; *i. e.* juft fo as to anfwer his Ufe and Diverfion in the Summer.

I cannot but think every Contrivance right, and every Convenience fit to be encourag'd, which tend to *invite* the Lord of the Manor himfelf fometimes to come down and *vifit* his Eftate, that his *Intereft* and his Diverfions may give a Relifh to one another. His own Ingenuity and Contrivance added to his Steward's *Care*, will quickly introduce *Politenefs* into his Country, and tend to fet fuch Examples of *Improvements* and good Husbandry, as will make him *belov'd* and popular, at the fame time when he is furnifh'd with larger Abilities to fupply his *own* and his Country's *Wants*.

Arti-

Article XXI.

AFter a Steward hath diligently furvey'd his Lord's Eftate, and hath
made himfelf mafter of the Method which
every Tenant takes to raife his Rent, and
to provide for his Family, he fhould alfo
carefully obferve the Crops and Stocks of
Cattle that each Tenant hath upon the feveral forts of Land, whether Arable, Pafture or Meadow; by which means (always
fuppofing him to be well vers'd in Country Affairs) he'll be able to judge, not only what Care hath been ufed to *improve*
and advance, and what Neglects have been
fuffer'd to diminifh the Products, but alfo
how many Quarters of the feveral forts of
Grain each Acre one with another on Tillage produces; and how many Loads of
Hay came from the Meadows. He fhould
likewife confider (and, if need be, *direct*)
what ftock of Cattle of all forts each Te-

G   nant's

nant's Farm will maintain, that he may be a conftant Cheque upon them, that they do keep a *fufficient* Stock; for a deficiency in that kind is as fatal and hurtful to the Farmer's Intereft as *overftocking* : Accordingly I have known many a Farmer fink and fail in the World meerly for want of a *fufficient* Stock, altho' they have had very *cheap* Bargains. And indeed a certain Truth it is, confirm'd by Experience, that an *overcheap* Bargain and Farm many times tends to indulge the Farmer in Luxury and Idlenefs, and to make him V I E with Gentlemen, and thofe that have Eftates of their own, in their way of living, and the bringing up their Families: And when thefe Follies and abfurd ways of Living have reduced them to Poverty, the neceffary Confequence is, that the Farm (cheap as it is) is made *poor* too, and the Farmer cannot raife his Rents, becaufe there is a Defeƈt of Stock, both as to Number and Goodnefs.

A careful provident Farmer, that keeps well his Accompts, and wifely balanceth

his

his Gain and Lofs, if he would be affur'd that he gets by his Farm, and thrives in the World, muft fell * *two Rents* at the leaft off the Premifes one year with another. Indeed the Farmers in *Kent, Effex,* and other Southern Counties round *London,* us'd to make it a Maxim, that *three* Rents fhould be fold; the Confequence of which was, that if they rented Two or Three hundred Pounds a year, they quickly purchas'd Eftates of their own, and let them to Tenants, who were forced to be content to fell *two Rents* off the Premifes.

BEFORE a Steward makes his laft Judgment of the Value of a Farm, he fhould be well and exactly inform'd what the neighbouring Gentlemen or Freeholders let *their* Lands for by the Acre, and then the noble Rule of COMPARISON ufed difcreetly, will give a Sanction to his Office and Duty,

---

* 'Tis fuppos'd that the Tenant is to maintain his Family with fuch Provifions as his Farm produceth, and to fell two Rents off the Premifes, but not to fpend in an extravagant manner more than one Rent, as too many have done, to their fudden Failure, altho' they have a good pennyworth.

making

making Allowances on both fides for better and worfe, either on *fome*, or on *many* accounts.

A due Regard had to this and the 'foregoing Rules would, I am perfuaded, be a good Foundation for forming a Judgment of the true Value of Eftates, in order to their being let to the Satisfaction of both Landlord and Tenant, which fhould always be effected, if poffible, that there may be no juft Foundation for Complaint on either fide: For altho' the Lord's Eftate ought to be let to the beft advantage, yet it fhould be let without *racking* the induftrious Tenant; as hath been too frequently done with *Art* and *Cunning* enough in fome Stewards, in order to hide and conceal other unrighteous Practices: But fuch *racking*, on what pretence foever it be done, ever tends to the *Differvice*, as well as to the *Difcredit* of Perfons of Quality, feveral of whom, to my knowledge, have repented of being *led* into that Miftake, as having fuftain'd great Trouble and Lofs in their Rents. Some Inftances I have known (efpecially in the North, where

the

the Farms are fmall) of poor Tenants, who, rather than be turn'd off to feek their Living, will promife more than they are really able to perform.

I have been the longer on this Head with a view of making the *Truth* of thefe *Facts*, founded on Experience, take the deeper Impreffion on all Noblemen and Gentlemen, as of the laft Confequence to their real Intereft, and the Improvement of their Eftates.

MOREOVER, as it hath appeard to be a matter of great Confequence, that proper Methods be ufed by the Steward, in order to let his Lord's Lands to the beft advantage, fo it is likewife proper to take notice here, that if the Steward doth not take care that the Tenants *keep up* the Farms in a due Courfe of Husbandry, there will be no fmall danger of the Rents finking again, even from an Advance made and founded on modern Knowledge and rational Improvements. To prevent therefore this undefirable Circumftance, the Steward fhould fee and infift upon it, that the Tenants do, every one of them, really and punctually perform the Covenants which they themfelves have agreed to in their Leafes. This is a matter of no *inconfiderable* confequence; for I have known Inftances of Gentlemen's Eftates finking very much by irregular and *uncovenanted* Practices, whilft the Tenants (by *neglect* or overfight) have been fuffer'd to plow up frefh Pafture and Meadow, to *pare* and *burn* and *worry* out the Strength of the Land by fowing *Rape*, &c. the confequence whereof hath been, that when they have throughly *impoverifh'd* the Farm, and thus *eat* out the Life and *Heart* of it, they have thrown it back into the Lord's hand, where it commonly *fticks*.

In the * Covenants of their Leafes there fhould therefore be a *Penalty* laid to each Covenant, to be paid *over* and above their

---

* I have always found, where-ever I have been concern'd in agreeing with Tenants and drawing up Covenants, that they have *more readily* agreed to fign fuch Leafes where a Penalty was laid to each Covenant, to be paid over and above the yearly Rent, for Non-performance, than to fign fuch Leafes where they are oblig'd to give Bond, and alfo to find Security.

yearly

yearly Rent, which being intended to pre-vent Abufes, is recoverable by *Law* ; whereas the common way of inferting Co-venants into Leafes (except a Bond is given, and the Tenantsfi nd Security) proves of little or no Ufe, for want of a Power to force and compel the Execution.

As for the Farms of Eight or Ten pounds *per Annum*, I have always found it to be of little moment to *leafe* fuch, becaufe the Tenants that rent them are generally poor and neceffitous: Wherefore the beft way to deal with them, when they do not per-form, or tranfgrefs their Duty, is, firft to *reprove* them for not obferving good Rules, and when there is little hopes of their do-ing better, to get *rid* of them as foon as poffible, always fuppofing that fome Care be taken of their Families, in fetting them to work in fuch ways which they better un-derftand.

ALTHO' I have not yet laid before the Steward and his Lord every part of a Steward's Duty; yet, by what hath been

G 4   already

already faid, it fufficiently appears, that to perform thefe and all the following Articles as they ought to be perform'd, with Fidelity and conftant Care, will take up almoft his whole Time, without much room for Diverfions. I could wifh all Noblemen and Gentlemen, for their own *Honour* and *Intereft*, would be perfuaded to make fomething larger Allowances of Salary than are ufually given : I do not fay that large Wages makes a Man *honeft* ; but I am fatisfied that a *too ftrict*, and therefore *miftaken* Notion of *faving Oeconomy*, with refpect to a Steward's ftanding Wages, hath oft-times been the Occafion of *corrupting* the Steward, and putting him upon indirect means to get where and what he ought not ; which proves in the end the *deareft Bargain* to thofe who think themfelves *wife in their Generation.*

In fhort, there fhould no one Circumftance relating to the Office and Duty of a Steward be made a Gain to Him, but the whole fhould accrue, and ought to be accounted to his Lord, whofe Wifdom it

fhould

ſhould be to make the *Salary* an ample
Reward for his *faithful* Labours.

Article XXII.

A Steward ſhould make ſtrict Enquiry
after all *Poachers*, that deſtroy the
Game within his Lord's Manors; and when
they are found and known, to lay regular
Complaints before the next Juſtice of the
Peace, that they may be proſecuted and
puniſh'd according to Law. And alſo if
there be any found not qualified to keep
Greyhounds, Guns, Setting dogs, Nets, *&c.*
he ſhould be diligent in informing againſt
them, that their Dogs and Guns, *&c.* may
be taken away from 'em; the purſuit of
theſe ſorts of Games being obſerv'd, in the
lower ſort of People, to be the effect of Idleneſs, the Conſequence whereof is neglect of
their proper Buſineſs, which ends in Pover-
ty, and oftentimes ſomething worſe. However, on all accounts, the Game ought to
be

be preferv'd by the Diligence and Care of
the Steward and Game-keeper, for the fake
of their Lord's Diverfion and his Table.
Indeed every Temptation fhould be encourag'd that tends to invite Noblemen and
others to vifit their Eftates in Perfon every
Summer; for, without fuch prefence, whatever others may think who have not a fenfe
of it, I who know the Misfortunes and Loffes that have happen'd by continued Abfence, muft *averr*, That nothing has tended more to the Abufe and Ruin of brave
Eftates, than the Lord's Neglect of looking
himfelf fometimes into his own Affairs:
whereas, on the contrary, I have always
found his Prefence to have been a conftant
Cheque both upon Steward and Tenant, as
to any *unjuftifiable* Connivances or private
Bargains. Where-ever therefore I have been
concern'd, I have, with pretty good fuccefs,
inculcated this Advice and Maxim (fupport-
ed by the 'foregoing Reafons) of *Occafional
Refidence*.

Arti-

Article XXIII.

AGAIN: It is the Duty, and fhould be the Care of a Steward, to make himfelf mafter of all the ancient * Cuftoms belonging to his Lord's Manors; which Knowledge will enable him to keep them up, and to prevent their Oblivion. As for inftance; (1.) It is cuftomary in moft Manors for the Tenants to fend their Teams to lead home the Hay and Corn which comes off the Demefne Lands commonly kept in hand for the ufe of the Lord of the Manor, when he comes in the Summer to live among his Tenants. (2.) It is alfo cuftomary for the Tenants to fend their Teams to lead Timber and Stone, *&c.* whenever there is occafion for Building or Re-

---

* The Steward, at his firft entering upon his Office, fhould get a Copy of the Cuftoms from the Ancienteft Court Rolls, in order to make himfelf mafter of the ancient Cuftoms of the feveral Manors.

pairs.

pairs.   (3.) It is alfo a good-natur'd Cuftom for each Tenant to fend every year,
during their Lord's Refidence, a Prefent of
two fat Capons or Turkeys; or elfe any o-
ther Prefent of Fifh or Fowl, fuch as the
Country produceth, of the like value. (4.) It
is common for each Tenant to keep a cou-
ple of Hounds or Setting-Dogs for the ufe
of the Lord when he comes down, for his
Diverfion.

I t may not be amifs here to advertife
the Steward to take care, where the Free-
hold-Tenants have a Townfhip entire to
themfelves, that they do not encroach upon
the Lord's Wafte, by digging *Stone*, *Sand*,
&c. expofing the fame to fale, when it is
none of their right: And when there is
any want of Submiffion and Acknowledg-
ment of the Offence, to make Examples of
one or two by a Profecution, to deter o-
thers from offending in the like manner.

I have known Inftances, where the Freeholders have inclos'd the Lord's Wafte
down to the Sea-fide, infomuch that in procefs

cefs of time they have gain'd confiderable quantities of Land, and were beginning to difpute even the Privileges of the Lord; nay, and have fometimes claim'd a Right to all the Advantages along the Sea-coaft, fo far as their encroach'd Inclofure reach'd, fuch as *Wrecks* and *Strays*. Herein alfo appears the Neceffity of an *occafional Refidence.*

THE like care fhould be taken by every Steward with relation to fuch Eftates as are let out upon Lives, whether Leafehold or Copyhold, (a Cuftom much ufed in the Weft of *England*) that a ftrict Enquiry be made at the Death of a Tenant, whether the beft Goods, or the beft Beaft which is due to the Lord of the Manor by way of Harriot is not clandeftinely convey'd away by thofe who think it no Sin to cheat either the *Lord* or the *Parfon*, but applaud themfelves for being *witty* in giving it a new Name, and *cunning* in keeping fecret what will not bear the Light. The Steward therefore fhould be as watchful and circumfpect as may be, to prevent Frauds : Not but that,

at

at the fame time, if an honeft and fair Difcovery of the Truth could be obtain'd, I
would advife every Lord of *fuch* Manors
as confift of Copyholders of Inheritance, not
to be too * rigid and exact on the account
of *Harriots*, becaufe the Severity of it dif-
courageth the Tenants in buying and felling
thofe Eftates to one another, and fo confequently leffens a confiderable Income by
Fines and *Surrenders*, which is no fmall
part of the Lord's cafual Profits arifing from
the feveral Manors, efpecially where the
Tenants are numerous, as it moft commonly happens when Lands are held by the
foremention'd Tenure.

To conclude this Article about Cuftoms,
I would advife all Noblemen and Gentlemen, whofe Tenants hold their Lands by
Copy of Court-Roll for three Lives, not to
let them renew, except they will agree to
deliver up their Copy, in order to alter the

---

* I remember an Inftance of a Lord of a Manor that
would always take the Harriots in kind, fuch as Jewels,
Plate, &c. but he found his Miftake in a few years, by
the leffening of the cafual Profits by Surrenders, &c.

Tenure,

Tenure, by converting it to *Leafehold on Lives*. This Method will put a ftop to that *unreafonable Cuftom* of the WIDOW's holding a Life by her *Free-bench*, which is a *fourth* Life, not covenanted for in the Copy, but only pretended to by *Cuftom*; which deprives the Lord of an undoubted Right of making the beft, and *doing what he will with his own*.

Article XXIV.

WHERE the Lord of the Manor is the *Impropriator* of the Livings of the feveral Parifhes, and confequently has the great *Tythes* to difpofe of as he feeth fit, it is the Steward's Wifdom and Care to let the feveral great Tythes, either in *whole* or in *parcels*, to fuch Tenants as have the *worft* Land, or are furtheft remote from the Conveniency of *Dung* and proper Manure, never fuffering them, on any Confideration to be let to the *Freeholders*, tho' Tenants; becaufe

becaufe they will be fure to enrich their own Lands therewith, and let their Farms fhift for themfelves, efpecially when their Leafes are near expiring, that then they intend to get the Heart out of the Land, and afterwards give it up into the hand of the Lord to make the beft of it. If the Parifhes or Townfhips from whence Tythes are due are of any extent, it is hardly to be imagin'd what Riches they will afford to the Impropriator's Farms, difcreetly parcel'd out, by means of the Hay, Straw, &c. brought home from every quarter, and loaded out again in Dung, over and above the ufual quantity made on a Farm. And to prevent any future Lofs or Decay in this advantageous Article of *Tythes*, the Steward fhould ever be upon his watch, to prevent (if poffible) the Freeholders inclofing any part of their Land in the common Fields, which commonly ends in leffening the *Tillage* and encreafing the *Pafture* ; which is a conftant Detriment to the *Impropriator*. This *partial Inclofure* therefore fhould never be fuffer'd without a general Agreement to do the *whole*.

Arti-

👑👑👑👑👑👑👑👑👑👑👑👑

Article XXV.

BEcaufe PARKs are liable to great Abufes and Loffes for want of *Honefty*
and due Care, a Steward fhould have a
watchful Eye, to fee that the *Keeper* performs his Duty, by keeping the Pales or
Walls entire, that the Deer do not * ftray,
and fo give occafion of Complaint, or elfe
of Violence done them : And alfo, that he
be diligent in foddering them in fome dry
parts of the Park, not only in Froft and
Snow, but alfo in a *wet Seafon*, at which
time they want it almoft as much as in
harder Weather, chiefly to prevent the *Rot* ;
for a Neglect in this Article has been the
occafion of the Ruin of many a Park.

* I am forry to fay that too many Landlords (who are
fond of out-lying Deer) are carelefs in this Affair, and
don't confider the great Damage done to the induftrious
Tenant, by not keeping the Deer from the Tenant's
Corn, *&c.* and alfo the great Damage done to the young
Woods kept in hand.

H THE

THE Park-keeper fhould alfo contrive, in *hard Weather*, to beat down the *Haws*, which are a great *Delicacy* and Nourifh-ment to the Deer; for it is obferv'd, that they will *eagerly* follow the Perfon who beats 'em down, from one Thorn-pollard to another, in order to *lick* them up and feed upon them. I have feen this practis'd with a great deal of Pleafure, and have of-ten wonder'd it is fo much omitted in moft Noblemen's Parks. Since therefore this Method is found to anfwer both *Pleafure* and *Profit*, it is very advifable that the Steward fhould preferve and propagate thefe *White-thorn* Pollards. The fame might be faid with refpect to the planting the true * *Chefnuts*, which, after a few years, are apt to bear great quantities of Fruit, which the Deer are *ftrangely* fond of; and it is obferv'd, they will very readily *fhell* the Fruit from its prickly Husk or outward Coat.

* This Method of propagating White-thorn Pollards and Chefnuts has been found to fave not a little Fodder in the Winter.

MORE-

MOREOVER, in the Management of a Park it fhould not be forgot always to preferve a fufficient number of *male Deer*, gelt at about a year old, one under another; by which means they will be fat at five years old the latter end of *September*, in *rutting* time, when the other Bucks are out of feafon. Thefe *male Deer*, fo order'd, are call'd HAVIORS, and are accounted a great Rarity between Buck and Doe Seafons. Neither fhould the Keeper forget this feafonable piece of Wifdom, (known to be right by all who are nice and curious) *viz.* to order the Skin of the Deer to be got off the very *minute*, if it is poffible, after he's fhot; which not only caufes the Venifon to have a *richer* tafte, but is a means to preferve it and keep it fweet much the longer: A Circumftance to be much regarded by thofe who have frequent Occafions to fend them at a diftance in hot Weather.

UNDER this Article it may not be a-mifs to advertife the Steward to fee (as much

as

as in him lieth) that the Park-keepers do
not abufe the Truft repos'd in them, by
killing too many of the female Fawns at
the time when the Does drop them; for
the number of thefe preferv'd fhould be
nearly the fame with the number of Does
intended to be killed in the Winter Seafon :
And no lefs care fhould be taken that the
Keeper (for the *lucre* of Gain both in the
Fawns and their Skins) do not fuffer them
to live too long ; for indeed the proper number fhould be kill'd as foon as poffible after the Does have dropt them, left by fuck-
ing too long, the Does have not time to gather Fat againft the Winter feafon.

It is alfo advifable that the Steward
fhould be careful every Year to fee that the
Park be *drove*; *i. e*, that he take an exact
Account of the number of male and female
Deer, entering them down in a Book kept
for that purpofe, expreffing how many
Fawns, Male and Female, there are re-
ferv'd, as well as the number of both kinds,
from one year old to five, together with
the number of Bucks and Does kill'd each
year.

year. The doing of this (and to a faithful diligent Servant it is not much work, especially where the Parks are small) will not a little recommend the Steward's Diligence, and will at the same time be a great Satisfaction to his Lord, to see whether, or how much, his Park every year encreases or decreases: And this Knowledge will be a constant Cheque upon the Keepers, that they do not dare to abuse their Truft.

An

An Example of the Method of keeping a Book for this, is as followeth.

Years when the Park was drove.	Fawns 1 year old.		2 years old.		3 years old.		4 years old.		5 years old.		Total Number of Deer.	Nº kill'd each year.	
Anno	males.	females.	Males or Prickets.	Females.	Males, or Sorels.	Females.	Males, or Sores.	Females.	Bucks.	Does.		Bucks.	Does.
1724	172	168	147	139	130	127	139	138	210	195	1565	86	48
1725	182	190	159	128	140	120	148	170	225	170	1632	80	40
1726	195	170	149	135	160	134	170	160	240	165	1658	70	35
1727	183	148	153	148	170	130	180	165	247	179	1703	76	30

If Order and Accuracy in this Affair be intended, the Park ought to be divided into

two

two other Parts ; the *firſt* of which ſhould
ſerve to *drive* a ſmall Herd into, in order to
be *told over* exactly; and the *ſecond* part, to
keep thoſe *told together* till the whole is taken an account of.

Article XXVI.

BEcauſe the WOODS belonging to ſome
Noblemen's Eſtates are ſo conſiderable and valuable a part of them, it would
not be prudent to let the whole Care and
Profit of them depend ſolely upon the Honeſty and Care of the *Wood-keeper* ; and
therefore *here alſo* will be expected a little
Watchfulneſs and Diligence in a Steward,
to ſee that the Keeper performs his Duty in
the following particulars :

(1.) THAT he doth keep and preſerve
the Fences, whether Pales or Hedges, in
ſuch a manner that no Cattle may be able
to get into the Woods, whereby great and
incredible Miſchief would quickly be done,
eſpecially among the young Underwoods
H 4 newly

newly fprung out, of which moft forts of Cattle are very greedy : Wherefore a conftant Care in this Article will be a great means to accelerate their Growth and Encreafe ; whereas, on the contrary, the Time for the repeated Sale of fuch Woods, by Indolence and Neglect, will be (according to conftant Experience) poftpon'd and retarded, to the great Lofs and Damage of the Lord.

(2.) THAT the Keeper do clear off all the Trumpery that grow and cleave to the Timber-Trees, efpecially Ivy, which being a Robber and Sucker, much retards their Growth and Encreafe.

(3.) If by the Force of Winds any of the larger Branches happen to be broken off, that Care be taken to cut the remaining part within a few Inches of the Body of the Tree, flopewife and fmooth, the better to caft off the Wet, left it get into the Body of the Tree, which in time would corrupt it either in whole or in part.

(4.)

(4.) GREAT care fhould be alfo taken when Underwoods are to be cut for fale, that the Workmen do not *haggle* them at the place of Amputation; neither fhould they be cut too clofe to the Ground, rather four or five inches from it, with a fharp Tool flopewife, and the Stroke of the Hatchet *upward*, fo as to leave the Surface fmooth, and not fplit, the better to caft off the Wet, and to preferve them from rotting.

IT is the Cuftom in many Parts of the North, not to cut their Underwoods till they have grown Thirty or Forty Years; but that Cuftom is by no means for the Owner's Intereft; becaufe, upon long Obfervation and Experience, I cannot find that the laft Ten or Fifteen Years anfwers fo well as a quicker return of only * Twenty or Twenty-five years growth, which yet, if care and diligence hath been us'd, fufficiently anfwers all the Ends and Purpofes of thofe who purchafe them.

* Underwoods above Twenty years growth in moft places pay no Tythe.

AFTER

AFTER Twenty or Twenty-five Years growth therefore, when a Sale of Wood is determin'd, the firſt thing a Steward hath to do, is to have the Lands exactly ſurvey'd, plotted, and laid out into Acres *parallel* to one another, taking care to view every Acre diſtinctly and throughly, in order to conſider the Uſes every part of the ſaid Acre may be apply'd to. For inſtance; if there be any fine, tall, ſtreight *Aſh's*, they will turn to the beſt account for Coopers uſe : The *Hazles* in the North, and where Coals are found, are profitably imploy'd to make Baskets for the Coal-trade : The *Oak* is uſeful for Spars for ordinary Buildings, and alſo for Poſts and Rails, for Fences and Hedges to preſerve the young Quicks, *&c.* It is obſervable, that the Underwoods in the North run moſtly upon *Oak*, which is by much the beſt, and brings moſt Profit, by reaſon of the Bark, ſo uſeful to the Tanners ; for tho' there may be ſuppos'd to be about an eighth part of *Aſh* and other ſoft Wood intermix'd, yet the Bark of the Underwood that runs chiefly upon *Oak*, commonly ſells for half the Value of the Underwood.

THE

THE beſt Method a Steward can take to guide himſelf in ſelling Timber and Underwood, and to know the Market-price, is to be well inform'd how the neighbouring Gentlemen ſell theirs, always allowing for a difference in Goodneſs; as ſuch there will be, on account either of the Sort of the Wood, or of the Nature of the Soil and Situation, or of the accidental Misfortunes that have attended it during its time of Growth: The Steward muſt therefore (as I ſaid before) uſe that noble Rule of COMPARISON, which if rightly and diſcreetly apply'd, will be of no ſmall Advantage to him, in this part, as well as moſt of his other Country Affairs.

MOREOVER, a Steward, at his firſt entring into Buſineſs, ſhould take an exact * Account of every *ſingle* Timber-Tree, as well

---

* The following Account and Table has given greater Satisfaction than the common Method uſed by ſome Surveyors, who pretend to a Nicety by inſerting each Timber-tree in their Map; which is not practicable, except in *very* ſmall Farms, and where the Scale is *very* large. I would deſire ſuch Surveyors to conſider how the Map will be defac'd by altering of it when ſuch Timber-trees are cut down and ſold. Therefore the following Table anſwers much the beſt, by reaſon the Dimenſions and *Value* are there given. This Method puts Noblemen and Gentlemen to leſs Expence, becauſe the other

well as others likely to become Timber, in
all the Woods within his Lord's Manors:
And in doing this with advantage, and to
purpofe, he fhould have a Book ruled with
proper Columns, in order (1.) to infert the
fourth part of the Girt of each Tree in inches; (2.) the Length of each Tree in Feet;
(3.) the number of folid Feet in each Tree;
(4.) the value *per* Foot that each Tree is
worth, according to its Dimenfions and Goodnefs; (5.) the Value of the Body of each
Tree, in proportion to the aforefaid Price;
(6.) the Value of the *Head* of each Tree;
(7.) the Value of the *Bark* of each Oak-
tree, which generally holds to be about a
third part of the Value of the Body and
Head; and (laftly) a Column for the Value
of the Body, the Head, and Bark added together; an Example whereof is exhibited
in a following Page.

A N D it may be obferv'd, that a Book
put into this Method will not fail to give

other is very tedious, to put each Tree in its proper
place; and I fuppofe the Cuftom was brought up by
fuch as wanted to fpin out Time, and to be paid accordingly.

great Satisfaction to his Lord, who hath now something to depend upon, whenever his Neceſſities or his Inclinations call for a *certain* Sum of Money. However, after ſuch Sale, the Book muſt be alter'd, and ſuch Trees ſtruck out of it.

It ſhould alſo be remembred that, when an Account is taken of the ſeveral Timber-trees, they be mark'd with Iron-ſtamps made on purpoſe: Only before the Stamp is apply'd, the rough part of the Bark ſhould be taken off with a Hatchet, that the Impreſſion may be made eaſy and viſible: And, to make it *laſting*, the Stamp ſhould not go deeper than the Bark, becauſe in ſuch caſe the number will ſoon grow up; but otherwiſe it may laſt ſeveral years by renewing, which is no undeſirable Circumſtance.

To treat of the beſt Methods of cultivating and dreſſing all ſorts of Timber-trees, ſo as beſt and ſooneſt to anſwer the End of the Planter, would carry me beyond the Limits of this intended ſhort Eſſay; and it

may

may better be deferred to a Treatife of Husbandry, as practis'd in feveral parts of the Kingdom, of which I have already given the Publick notice, and which I intend (GOD willing) to finifh in due time. However, before I leave this Article, I would advife every Steward throughly to confider the beft Advantage that even the worft of Land may be turn'd to. For inftance; On my Surveys I have feen, to my great furprize, a great number of Acres, (not capable of being drain'd, except by a Sum of Money, by no means equal to the Profit) lain quite wafte; whereas *Willows* and Oziers planted *very* thick would, even in the moifteft Bogs, grow and bear good Lop, and by their encreafe make a good return of Rent, by reafon of the great and conftant demand for them, chiefly on the account of Baskets for the Coal-trade, and for many other Ufes.

I T may not be amifs in this Article to fhew the Ufe of the Table of Timber-meafure (which is placed at the end of *The Duty of a Steward*) ready caft up, from 3

inches

inches fquare to 7 5 ; and from 1 foot to 4 5
in length.

FIRST gird the Tree with a String about
the middle, then double the String twice,
which is call'd a fourth part of the Girt,
which you muft exactly meafure upon your
Rule; as, fuppofe it is 19 Inches, a Method
that reduces round Timber to fquare the cuftomary way : but if the Tree is full grown
with a thick Bark, it muft be call'd but
18 inches, whereas in others half an inch is
fufficient, as every Practitioner will eafily
judge : Then meafure the height of the
Tree by the help of a Ladder and a long
Pole, and fuppofe it to be 36 foot high ;
look then in the Table for 18 inches at the
top, and caft your Eye downwards to 36
foot length, and at the angle of meeting
you'll find juft 81 foot for the number of
folid feet which the Tree contains : And fo
the fame for any other number. *N.B.* The
parts of a foot for the Content is given in
tenths, which is nearer than the Dimenfions
can be taken.

THERE

THERE hath been great pains taken by
feveral Authors upon this Subject, endeavouring to fet afide this cuftomary way of
meafuring, which indeed (ftrictly fpeaking)
is falfe, and gives the Content in feet above
a fifth part too little; but fince a cuftomary
Price is fettled accordingly, it is but a *vain*
and *fruitlefs* Attempt; becaufe if the one
is alter'd, the other muft be alter'd alfo,
which comes to the fame thing.

N.B. IT may not be amifs to obferve
under this *Article*, that it fometimes happens, in a fale of Underwood, that the Perfons who buy it cannot lead the whole off
the premifes before the latter end of the
Summer, when the new Shoots are got to
a confiderable height : But this, if poffible,
fhould be avoided ; becaufe the treading of
the Horfes, and the impreffion of the Wag-
gon-wheels, do a great deal of damage to
the young Springs: However, to prevent as
much mifchief as may be, the Steward
fhould fee that the Wain Horfes and Oxen
be *muzzled,* to prevent their *cropping* the

young Springs, which they are very fond of, whereby the Underwood hath often fuftained incredible Damage.

IT hath been often the wonder of an Agent, who hath been fent down to view and value the Woods, why they were not fo good as thofe of the neighbouring Gentlemen refiding in the Country, at the fame number of years growth. The Anfwer to which is obvious : The Gentlemen take care to prevent the Mifchief above, and the Steward, either by *Abfence* or *Indolence* or *Neglect*, fuffers it; and fometimes alfo, for a * *valuable* Confideration, connives at the turning of the Woodward's and Tenants Cattle into the young Springs; which, to my knowledge, in a few years has done at leaft a Hundred pound Damage in a Wood of Eight or Nine hundred pound value.

* I know of feveral Inftances where Woodwards have rais'd a great deal of Money in breeding up young Cattle in the Woods and young Springs; but when the Nobleman came down to look into his Affairs, he foon put a ftop to it, by difcharging both Steward and Woodward.

I   *A*

A particular Account of the Number of OAK *Timber-Trees, and such others as are likely to be Timber, in* SKITSCREW-WOOD.

Numb. of the Trees.	The 4th part of the Girt of each Tree in Inches.	The length of each Tree in feet.	Numb. of solid feet in each Tree.	Value per foot of the several Trees.	Value of the Body of each Tree.			Value of the Head of each Tree.			Value of the Bark of each Tree, which is commonly about a third of the Head and Body.			Total Value of each Tree.		
				s. d.	l.	s.	d.	l.	s.	d.	l.	s.	d.	l.	s.	d.
1	15	25	39	1:4	2	12	0	0	4	6	0	18	10	3	15	4
2	11	22	18½	1:2	1	1	7	0	1	6	0	7	8	1	10	9
3	12	23	23	1:4	1	10	8	0	2	6	0	11	1	2	4	3
4	11½	27	25	1:2	1	9	2	0	2	0	0	10	5	2	1	7
5	11½	19	17½	1:3	1	1	10	0	2	6	0	8	1	1	12	5
6	9½	25	15½	1:2	0	18	1	0	1	0	0	6	4	1	5	5
7	15	25	39	1:6	2	18	6	0	3	0	1	0	6	4	2	0
8	12	23	23	1:4	1	10	8	0	2	6	0	11	1	2	4	3
9	15	17	26½	1:2	1	10	11	0	3	6	0	11	6	2	5	11
10	11	25	21	1:4	1	8	0	0	2	6	0	10	2	2	0	8
11	13	29	34	1:4	2	5	4	0	4	6	0	16	7	3	6	5
12	12½	24	26	1:6	1	19	0	0	3	0	0	14	0	2	16	0
13	13	24	28	1:6	2	2	0	0	3	6	0	15	2	3	0	8
14	13	38	44½	1:6	3	6	9	0	3	0	1	3	3	4	13	0
15	13	23	27	1:2	1	11	6	0	3	0	0	11	6	2	6	0
16	12	23	23	1:3	1	8	9	0	5	6	0	10	9	2	3	0
17	11½	25	23	1:0	1	3	0	0	2	0	0	8	4	1	13	0
18	9½	24	15	1:0	0	15	0	0	1	6	0	5	6	1	2	0
19	11½	20	18	1:2	1	1	0	0	4	6	0	8	6	1	14	0
20	11½	27	24½	1:2	1	8	7	0	3	0	0	10	6	2	2	1
21	10½	27	20½	1:2	1	3	11	0	2	0	0	8	8	1	14	7
22	14½	23	33½	1:6	2	10	3	0	4	0	0	18	1	3	12	4
23	15½	32	53	1:6	3	19	6	0	4	0	1	7	10	5	11	4
24	15	24	37½	1:6	2	16	3	0	5	6	1	0	7	4	2	4
Total			655½		43	11	3	3	12	6	16	4	11	62	19	4

Arti-

Article XXVII.

IN the 'foregoing Article I have hinted how Lands that are fubject to Wet, are boggy, and cannot eafily be drain'd without great Charge, may be improv'd; yet neverthelefs, where Drains can be made at a tolerable Charge, it is advifeable to fet about it, efpecially if it fo happens that the fame Paffage that brings it in from Rivers and Brooks may alfo carry it off. The Improvement of Land by *floating* with muddy Water is now pretty well underftood, and frequently practis'd : But yet there are many Inftances of low boggy Lands, that are fuffer'd to lie under Water half the Year, by which means they are ftarv'd, and worth little; which yet, with fome Expence in making frequent and deep Drains, might be made to have communication with the neighbouring Brooks and Rivers, whereby they

will

will receive *vaft* Improvements, even to three times the former Value: For as thefe Drains will occafionally bring up the muddy Water to enrich the Land, fo they will carry the Water back when it is clear.

BUT before a Steward begins this Work, he muft by the help of a *Spirit-Level* find out whether the River or Brook is higher or lower than the Lands on each fide, and how much. In the next place, he muft level all the other Parts, in order to find where the Water can be carried off at pleafure: After which, by the help of Sluices placed in the feveral parts of the feveral Trenches, each part may eafily be flooded, and fo the muddy Water may be continued, and convey'd from one part to another. I have known Inftances of low Lands lying near a Market-Town frequented by *Tanners*, the very Liquor of whofe *Tann-vats*, being made to find its way into the low Grounds, hath ftrangely enrich'd them: And it hardly need be faid, that if their Refufe-Bark be alfo fuperinduced, no greater Riches can well be defir'd.

Arti-

Article XXVIII.

I Have known great Improvements made
on large and extended Parcels of Land
lying uninclos'd, and on a warm Soil well
fhelter'd with Trees and Hills, by having
moveable Hurdles, or Pofts and Rails; by
which means the Cattle were mov'd from
one *frefh* Pafture to another, and by which
Management more Cattle were kept, and
thofe better fed ; for as a Succeffion of *frefh*
Food gave them better nourifhment, fo they
were conftantly obferv'd to be fat much the
fooner. This is taken notice of as an Ad-
vertifement to the Steward, that in cafe
large Parks and Forefts happen to be kept
in hand for his Lord's ufe, he may have
regard to it, as a thing that will turn to good
advantage with a little Charge : And by
this means his Lord may have his Beef and
Mutton fent up alive to *London,* at a cheaper Rate than to go to Market. And, to do

I 3   this

this to the beſt advantage, the Steward
ſhould be advis'd to ſtock the Ground with
Scotch Keylys or *Welch Runts* at Midſummer *half-fat*, that they may be *made up*,
and their Improvement compleated, before
the hard Weather comes on; for if they are
bought in *lean*, or later, they will, in the
Grazier's Phraſe, *eat off their Heads* with
* Hay in the Winter.   The *Sheep* proper
to be bought in for ſuch Lands are thoſe
fetch'd from *Norfolk*, or ſome other diſtant
barren Country : But it is to be remember'd,
that Care be taken that they be not immediately put into the beſt *Park-Land*, but
rather into ſome *Fallows*, or ordinary breeding Paſtures, for about a Week before they
are put into the *beſt*, where they are to be
made fat : Not forgetting alſo a piece of
excellent and ſeaſonable Advice, given by
a † ſkilful and experienc'd Grazier, To bleed
them in the Vein juſt under their Eye, a day

---

* If Noblemen or Gentlemen are deſirous to have
this curious ſort of Beef ſent up to *London*, &c. all the
Year round, then Proviſions for Hay or Rye-flower
muſt be made in the Winter accordingly. [See the
Appendix.]

† The famous Merchant *Morley*.

after

after they come off their Journey. A neglect of these two material points relating
to Sheep, has been obferv'd to be the
occafion of feveral Diftempers amongft
them, fome of which have ended in their
Death foon after.

Upon the whole, it is very advifeable
for all Noblemen and Gentlemen, whofe E-
ftates are not too far from *London,* to keep
Lands in hand to the value of Three or
Four hundred a year, more or lefs; not only to fupply them with Neceffaries whilft
they are in the Country, but in *London* alfo; which, if manag'd by the Steward a-
broad, and by the Dairy-Woman at home,
to the *beft* Advantage, may be made to anfwer, and to turn to a very good account,
by having almoft every thing fent up to
London in feafon, and at the *beft* hand.
This is not a matter of *Theory* only; but I
have known feveral Inftances of thofe who
are reckon'd the beft *Oeconomifts,* who have
practis'd it with great Satisfaction, and as
they find it to anfwer their End, are refolv'd
to continue the Practice.

I 4 BUT

BUT as the Succeſs of this whole Affair is owing to the Steward's *Skill* in Husbandry, ſo that Knowledge is here taken for granted; and his Lord will have ſtill a more *feeling* Senſe of it, when he comes to find that the Steward is able to direct a Tenant, upon occaſion, to manage his Farm, or even his *whole* Eſtate, to the beſt advantage.

Article XXIX.

IN a Country where Slate and Tyle and Lime are not *extreamly* dear, a Steward ſhould uſe his beſt Endeavours to oblige all his Lord's Tenants to cover their Houſes with Slate or Tyle, not only as a better Security againſt Accidents and the Misfortune of * Fire, but alſo as it prevents that great

* The dreadful Fires which happen'd at *Thrapſton, Wooburn* and *Graveſend,* and ſeveral other Places, have chiefly been increas'd by the *multitude* of *Thatch'd* Houſes.

conſump-

confumption of Straw, the conftant Demand
for Thatch and Covering, too much ufed
in moft Country Villages, *robbing* the Land
of fuch quantities of Manure ; which is felt
very *feverely* in fuch places, and on fuch
Farms, where little elfe is to be got but
what the Premifes afford. This Advice of
the Steward fhould alfo extend itfelf to the
Freehold Tenants round about, that they
may be made fenfible how much it is for
their own, as well as their Country's Good.

Article XXX.

A Steward, when he draws out proper
Covenants, to oblige Tenants to
keep up their Farms in a due Courfe of
Husbandry, fhould not forget this material
one, viz. *Not to commit Wafte in any
fort*, and efpecially by erecting Brick-kilns,
and by digging Clay in order to make
Bricks for fale, without giving a *valuable*
Confideration for the fame. This I have
found

found practis'd, to the great Injury of some
of the best Land; and the whole has been
kept a Secret from the Lord. Nay, for
want of such a Covenant, I have known
that the Freehold Tenants have pared the
Turf off from extraordinary good Land, and
carried the rich Mould for eight or ten inches deep away, in order to improve *their
own* Lands, laying the Turf down again:
And when they have committed this *Waste*,
I have known the Land thrown up into the
Lord's hand, to make the best of it.

Article XXXI.

IN letting Pasture-Lands to such Tenants
as breed or have a *great* stock of *Horses*, some Caution should be used, that the
best Land be not allotted for such purposes;
forasmuch as a constant feeding with such
Cattle only, is known to breed coarse sowre
Grass, and in time, greatly to hurt and much
diminish

diminiſh the Value of ſuch Land. And indeed, where-ever Horſes feed, there ſhould
be an allowance of conſiderable *Superinductions* every year, of all ſuch Dungs and
Manures as the Country affords.

Article XXXII.

A Steward, upon his Surveys, ſhould obſerve whether the Tenants keep the
Bye-roads leading thro' their Grounds in
good Repair, eſpecially the Gate-ways and
Bridges ; for want of which, great Damage
hath been done by Travellers breaking the
Hedges, and riding over good Land on each
ſide the way. It would be too much beſide
my preſent Purpoſe to direct the beſt Method for mending Roads ; and it may perhaps hereafter be done by one who has
promis'd it : But it may not be amiſs here to
obſerve, that the great Myſtery of making
Roads good, is to lay and keep them *dry* ;

3   for

for which purpofe they fhould ever lie *round* and *high* in the middle ; which may be eafily fo order'd, by throwing on what comes out of the Ditches into the middle, and afterwards, when the Earth is well fet. tled, at Midfummer, the beft Gravel, Stones, or Rubbifh which the Country affords fhould be laid upon it. When this hath been done with Judgment and Skill, even thofe Roads which (by means of ftagnating Water) have been almoft unpaffable at Midfummer, have become fit for a galloping Horfe in the Winter.

Article XXXIII.

THERE is a great deal of Difcretion, as well as Judgment, to be ufed by a Steward when he enters upon that *difficult* Work of letting his Lord's Farms, efpecially if he finds there is a good deal of reafon for raifing the Rents : But becaufe there is one Circumftance which I I think may tend to miflead him, I fhall here adver-

advertife him never to parcel out Lands to *fmall* Freeholders in Townſhips where there are large Commons without STINT, tho' they would give (as ſometimes they will offer) double the Value of what the Land is really worth to a large Farm; which would prove in the end a manifeſt Prejudice to the Lord's Tenants, becauſe thoſe ſmall Freeholders only make uſe of thoſe Lands rented *dear* to put their Cattle into at ſuch times as the Commons are under Water, or in the Winter, when 'tis ſo cold and open that the Cattle are ready to ſtarve. By which it may appear, that a Freeholder who hath only an Houſe and Homeſted of Twenty ſhillings a year, may improve it to Ten pounds a year, or more: But then, by ſuch a Contrivance, the Commons would be ſo full ſtock'd, that the Lord's Tenants, who rent large Farms, would not receive their proportion of Advantage, which was one Motive that put them upon taking their Farms: So that the Steward's well-intended Aim of getting an advanced Rent, hath prov'd in the end a real Hindrance to the Improvement of the whole.

3

THUS

THUS again, in other *Townships*, where 'tis the Cuftom to STINT the Commons and Common-Fields, the Steward fhould take care that the Richer Tenants do not *ftock* them beyond the Cuftom of the Manor. This is what I have too often found abufed to a *very great* degree, to the no fmall Damage of the poorer Tenants, who are not always in a Condition to buy fuch a Stock as is their due to put in. In fuch Cafes the Steward fhould oblige the Richer Tenants not to put in beyond their STINT, without making an Allowanee to the poorer fort for the Sheep, *&c.* that they put in above their number in their ftead; and by no means to fuffer the whole to be over-ftock'd. Thefe Abufes ufed formerly to be *ftrictly* obferv'd at the Court-BARON, but of late years have been little regarded, except in fome Manors, where the diligent *Steward* would *exert* himfelf, by *prefenting* them that had offended; and the more when he found the fubftantial Tenants had agreed together not to *prefent* one another, and to *crufh* thofe poorer Tenants that fhould offer to do it.

Arti

Article XXXIV.

A Steward, before he lets any confiderable Farm to a feeming-good Advantage of an advanc'd Rent, fhould be well fatisfied of the *Ability* of the Tenant; for want of which he manifeftly, and of courfe, muft run behind-hand, tho' he hath no ill Bargain. A Farm of a Hundred pounds a year requires at the leaft Three hundred pounds Stock; and if 'tis a grazing Farm, above Four hundred pounds. The want of fuch a Subftance either forces them to be content to *breed* upon fuch *good* Land as would make their Cattle fat, or elfe to take in *Joifts* at any rate they can get, till they can raife a Stock of their own: Which is a Method that often proves the Ruin of a Tenant, except he has the good fortune to rent a Farm at half the Value.

THE

THE like may be said when a Tenant firſt enters upon his Farm, that he ſtocks it with Cattle ſuitable to the nature of the Land: Paſture and Meadow Grounds in the Northern Parts of *England,* worth about Twenty or Twenty-five ſhillings an Acre, ſhould be ſtock'd with the beſt and largeſt Cattle; the middling Paſture or Meadow, worth about Ten or Twelve ſhillings an Acre, with a leſſer ſize; and the more barren, with the ſmaller ſort, chiefly for *Breeding,* in order to be ſold off to better Land to be made fat.

Article XXXV.

AS it ought to be the conſtant Study and Endeavour of a Steward to promote the Eaſe and comfortable Subſiſtance of his Lord's Tenants, ſo in a particular manner he ſhould endeavour to prevent *all* Loads and Incumbrances upon their honeſt Endea-

Endeavours, fuch efpecially as are wont to
arife from Strangers and Vagrants harbour-
ing amongft them, fometimes fo long till
they or their Children obtain Settlements,
and when they are difabled or *fuperannua-
ted*, demand Relief. And this of confequence
muft be a means, time after time, of increa-
fing the Poor's Seffes, and loading the Parifh with a more than ordinary Tax, *more*
fometimes than they are able to bear, which
proves the occafion of ARREARS in Rent.
Our Laws have well guarded againft this
Evil; but the Indolence of *Parifhes* (where
Every-body's Bufinefs is No-body's) is commonly fo great, that little or no Care is taken in this Affair: Wherefore the *Steward's
Care* and Vigilance are the more neceffary
to put the Laws in execution, and to have
recourfe to Juftice, to prevent the Mifchief
and Burthen which, in the end, would o-
therwife fall upon the Lord of the Manor.

UNDER this Article it is alfo proper to
obferve, that a Steward, in order to prevent
Law-fuits, unneceffary Expences, and lofs
of Time, fhould endeavour (as much as in

K

him

him lieth) to act as a *Mediator* between
one Tenant and another, when they happen to quarrel and diſpute about *Trifles*; or
indeed in any other Affair, where any real
Difficulty ariſes about Property.   The Uſe-
fulneſs of this Office of a Steward is ſo ap-
parent, that I need not paint it in any other
or more words.

A N D altho' poſſibly there might be o-
ther and further Enlargements made on the
Office and Duty of a Steward, yet foraſmuch as I apprehend I have touch'd upon
the moſt neceſſary and moſt material Parts
of the Office; and as I intend to avoid Pro-
lixity in repeating any Apology which the
Freedom I have uſed might be ſuppos'd to
want; I ſhall, in this and the next Article,
conclude this Part of my Treatiſe by perſuading *Stewards,* and others, to obſerve and
practiſe ſome ſuch following rational Method of *ſurveying* and drawing up the Particulars of Eſtates, before they begin to
make *Improvements* from the *old* Rents,
that each Tenant's Farm may be ſettled in
a due *Proportion* of Rent, and that they
may

may keep their Accompts fo, as to diftinguifh the feveral *kinds* of *Articles* feparate-
ly made ; which will prove no fmall Satif-
faction to their Lord.

THE following Accompts are intended
to be in great meafure Examples ; but the
Steward is to take notice, that 'tis his **Duty**
to bring what was formerly a Perquifite
(*i. e.* every thing which the Eftate produceth) to Accompt, and to content himfelf
with a handfome Salary ; which I am perfuaded, both from their own Inclination,
and from what hath been here faid, *moft*
Noblemen will think it their *Intereft* to
allow.

Article XXXVI.

AS a Steward fhould know the Quanti-ty as well as Quality of every Parcel of Land occupied by the feveral Tenants; fo likewife he fhould have a Map of the whole drawn out in the moft perfect Me-thod; which may ferve to fhew, not only the Quantity, but alfo the true *Figure* of the Parts as well as the Whole; wherein ought to be reprefented all the Bends in the Hedges or other Boundaries fo nearly, that any Fraud in alienating even the leaft part may quickly be detected: And by feeing in the Map the Pofition which every Parcel in the Eftate hath with refpect to one another, he will be able to judge what Parcels are proper to lay to one Farm, and what to another, in cafe any Change of Te-nants fhould happen by Death, or other-wife.

I t

I T will not therefore, I hope, be thought improper here to propose to the Surveyor the most perfect Method now used by my self and Agents to take such a Survey, whereby with care he may do his Work so correct, that it may answer the abovemention'd End, which the common Methods will not.

FOR this purpose he should provide himself with a good THEODOLITE well graduated, with a *Telescope* and a *Spirit-Level* fixed thereto, the whole to be so united and made stedfast, that it may not be liable to *shake* on turning round the *Index*, when the Angles are taken.

FOR the more perfect understanding of what I would say on this head, it will be requisite that I give a Description of one of the best sort of *Theodolites* ever yet invented for the use of a *Surveyor* in measuring and mapping, made and contrived by Mr. JONATHAN SISSON at the Corner of *Beaufort-Buildings* in the *Strand*; (a Figure

K 3 whereof

whereof is exhibited in the Map fronting the Title-Page of this Book.)

THE Ball and Socket of this Inſtrument are ſo contrived, that by the help of four Screws placed at Right Angles to one ano-ther, below the Center, the whole is very readily fix'd *horizontal* as well as *ſteady*; and thereby not liable to any Motion or Variation upon moving the *Index*. There is a double *Sextant* of Equal Radius to the Limb, (with a *Spirit-Level* fix'd in it, and a *Teleſcope* above it) that moves in a Cir-cle at Right Angles to the *Index* on the Limb; whereby the *vertical* Angles may be taken as readily as the *horizontal*, and at the ſame time; and ſo the *hypotenuſal* Lines may be reduced to *horizontal*, which are thoſe that ſhould always be laid down in *plotting* any Survey.

THE Head of the three-legg'd Staff is of Braſs, and not ſo liable to *ſhake* as the wooden ones: The Needle in the *Compaſs-box* hangs on a Pin of temper'd Steel (turn'd and poliſh'd in a Lath) on which it moves

very

very freely; and the Limb is fo curioufly
divided, (by a new Method) that tho' there
be three *Indexes* at 120° from each other,
with *Nonus*'s Divifions on them, to fhew
the decimal Parts of a Degree; yet you
fhall perceive no Inequality in the Divifions
on any part of the whole Circle. There is
alfo a Spring and Screw to the *Index* under the *Telefcope* to fix it to any Degree of
the Limb. The whole is nicely framed,
very portable and well contrived for difpatch of Bufinefs.

BY way of Direction therefore to one
who enters on a Survey with one of thefe
Theodolites, it may be proper to add, That
his beft way will be, at his firft Station,
(after having fix'd it *horizontal*) to place
the *Index* at 360° on the Limb, and the
Needle alfo at the fame in the *Compafs-box*,
and then to take the Angle of the firft
Line on the Limb, which will be the fame with
the *Needle*. Having fet this down in his
Field-book, let him then do the fame with
his fecond Line, and there fix the *Index* to
the *Limb:* And then his *Theodolite* may

K 4 be

be carried to a fecond Station, where having fix'd it *horizontal*, he muft turn the
whole *Limb* about, till the vertical Hair
in the *Telefcope* cuts the Object, which he
left at his firft Station; then loofening the
Index-fcrew, he muft turn the *Index* itfelf,
till the fame Hair in his *Telefcope* cuts the
Object for his third Station, and then he
muft fix the *Index* as before : And if he
thus proceeds on to never fo many Stations,
he will always find that either one end or
the other of his *Needle* will correfpond with
the *Index*, fo nearly as even to detect all
Errors that may happen in fetting down
the Angles taken on the Limb : By this Method, when he comes to *plot* the Survey,
he may fet off as many Angles as he pleafes at once, laying down and fixing his
Protractor, (which by the way fhould be
that of a whole Circle, well graduated, and
at leaft fix inches diameter) by which the
ftationary Lines may be much exacter
drawn than by the common way of fetting
off each fucceffive Angle.

N o w

N o w if by this Method the Surveyor will go round the *Plot* to be furveyed, and will take all the Angles, as well as mea-fure all the *Stationary Lines*, if the Summe of thofe Lines doth not exceed four Miles, then a Miftake made of one Chain in any one of the *Stationary Lines* may be difcovered (efpecially if he is careful in fetting off the Angles, and the Lengths of his *Stationary Lines*) and a fmaller Scale than 4 of *Gunter*'s Chains to an Inch will not readily do it.

T h e r e f o r e by this way the careful Surveyor may be fure of avoiding any ma-terial Error ; whereas by the common Me-thods hitherto ufed, the Surveyor is not fure he comes within one Acre in forty, tho' he has been fo fortunate as to make no Miftake in his meafured Lines; and if he hath made any fuch, he doth not always know it ; by means whereof it may fo happen that he may err more than after the rate of one in twenty, without fufpecting any Error at all.

As

As for the common *Theodolites* with wooden Heads at the top of the three-legg'd Staff and plain Sights only, without a *Telescope* or *Spirit-Level*, they cannot be depended on in going round a large Survey ; for with *plain* Sights, your Eye not being fix'd, (as it muft be allowed the Image of an Object is in a *Telescope*) whatever your Eye varies from the true Line clofe by, is increafed at a diftance in proportion to the Length thereof ; fo that an Angle cannot *exactly* be taken to a few Minutes, tho' the *Theodolite* fhould happen to be fix'd *horizontal* : But without a *Spirit-Level* the fixing it fo can only be guefs'd at ; and where the Ground is *hilly*, you can't be fure of being right within two or three Degrees ; by which I fhall demonftrate the Surveyor is liable to a very great Error, which fhould ever be induftrioufly avoided, by ufing fuch Inftruments as will not lead them into it. Large Surveys done by the *plain Table* cannot, ought not to be depended on ; for befides all the Inconveniencies attending the *common Theodolites*, the *plain Table* is fubject to many others: as for
in-

inftance, there is no remedy if the *Table*
alters by moving the *Index*, without drawing new Lines by the erroneous ones, which
will caufe Confufion. And befides, the
Paper will extend or fhrink up, as the Weather alters to *moift* or *dry ;* by which the
ftationary Lines will be unavoidably *en-
creafed* or *leffened*. Neither can you fuppofe that a Surveyor will ftrictly attend
the Exactnefs neceffary in ftationary Lines
in the open Field, when his Affiftants are
by him, efpecially if the Weather be fharp
and cold, as he would with pleafure do in
a warm Room *by himfelf.* And then, if on
coming round to the Place he began at, he
finds his Work doth not clofe on the Point
it fhould do, (which yet in a large quantity there is no reafon to expect from the
ufe of that Inftrument) he muft either alter
the Angle or Length of the laft Line, or
both, to make it *clofe, i. e.* the End of the
laft Line to touch the beginning of the firft,
to conceal the Error: For if he difcovers it,
and no Error is found in the meafured Lines,
his Inftrument or his Judgment muft be con-
demned; becaufe he can be liable to no
material

material Error in the Angles, but by a real Fault or Defect in the Inftrument.

NEITHER fhould this Obfervation be omitted, That by the Method which Surveyors are wont to follow in cafting up the quantity of the Lands meafured, they are alfo liable to feveral Errors, as they are obliged to form and caft up as many Triangles as the Field has Sides, abating two, which in fome irregular Fields are very many : and if *halfing* the Bafe, Perpendicular or Product of any of them fhould be forgot, there might infenfibly be a great Error committed, or one of the many little Triangles might be forgot.   This, befides the Errors in every one of thofe Lines which form the Triangles, would make the whole Miftakes very confiderable.   Whereas thefe Errors are prevented in the Method ufed by myfelf and Agents in reducing all irregular Figures to *one Triangle*, and in as little time as the Lines that form their Triangles can well be drawn, if they be done correctly ; and in fuch cafe, there is but one Triangle to be caft up, equal to the whole Field.

Now

No w therefore to prevent Errors, and to fhew you the Neceffity of the *Theodolite's* being fix'd horizontal, I fhall give one Example. Suppofe you were to meafure (in the following Figure) from A to B, which is a ftrait Line, but a Hill being between, you could fee no further than C near the Top of the Hill; at which place you fix your *Theodolite* (of the common fort) with the Addition of a *Telefcope*, but no *Spirit-Level*; then C being on the Edge of the Hill (firft declining to A and B, and then growing fteep and higher even to D it will then be very likely that the Plane of the Limb of the *Theodolite* would be nearer to the Plane of the Superficies of the Ground between C and D than two Degrees *from* the horizontal Plane, when you fhall have fix'd it as near as you can *to* it.

But allowing it to be juft two Degrees, then fuppofe you fix your *Index* at 360, and direct your *Telefcope* down to A by depreffing it 10 Degrees, then you turn it to look at B, where it is ftill depreffed 10 Degrees, in this Cafe your *Index* will

will cut 179° : 18′ : 38″ very nearly; for A by calculation is taken 20′ : 41″ out of its true place on one side, and B the same on the other side, which together (the whole being thrown upon B) puts B 41′ : 22″ out of its true Place, which is full twelve Links, if the length of the Line be 10 Chains from C to B; and if 20 Chains, it will be double, *viz.* 24 Links.

Now this is better and more to be depended on by the help of a *Spirit-Level* and *Telescope* than can possibly be imagin'd in any other way without them; because in that case you cannot know when any Object is *cut* nearer than to about 20′: And therefore very considerable Errors may be committed by a *plain Table,* whose Plane on the like occasion, if there should be any Observation made at D, (the Surveyor not knowing better) would place the Plane of his *plain Table* nearer to the Plane of the Superficies of the Ground between C and D than *two* or even *ten* Degrees from the horizontal Plane; which last Case would throw B out of its true place 3° : 30′ : 27″ ; which

if

if B is but 10 Chains from C is near $61\frac{1}{4}$ Links; and if 20 Chains, it will be $122\frac{1}{2}$ Links out of its true place. This, added to all other Errors which may be committed by that very incorrect Inftrument, fhould difcourage all Perfons, that know it, from depending on the *plain Table* in any large Survey. But to make ftill a ftronger Impreffion on the Mind, I have added an exact Calculation of Errors in the two aforementioned Cafes.

(1.)

As Rad. to S. $\sqrt{}$ 10° = Log. 9.2396702

So is Tang. $\sqrt{}$ 2° — = Log. — 8.5430838

To Tang. 20′. 41″ nearly Log. 7.7827540

then

As Rad. to 1000 Links = Log. 3.0000000

So is S. $\sqrt{}$ 20′. 41″ nearly Log. 7.7827462

to 6.06382 Links — = Log. 0.7827462

(2.)

As Rad. to S. $\sqrt{}$ 10° = Log. 9.2396702

So is Tang. $\sqrt{}$ 10° — = Log. 9.2463188

to Tang. $\sqrt{}$ 1°. 45′. 13″. $\frac{5}{8}$ = Log. 8.4859890

then

then

As Rad. to 1000 Links = Log. 3.0000000
So is S. √ 1°. 45′. 13″ ⅝ = Log. 8.4857856

to 30.6045 Links — = Log. 1.4857856

(1) then 6.06382 being doubled 12.12764 Links being what B is put out of his place, when the Limb of the *Theodolite* is inclined but 2° to the horizontal Plane, and the Telescope depressed 10° below the Horizon, and that A and B are at right Angles to the greatest Declination of the Plane of the Limb,

then (2)

30.60545 being doubled is 61.209 Links being what B is put out of his true place, when the *Plain-Table* is inclined to the horizontal Plane in an Angle of 10°, and each Object at A and B depressed 10° below the Horizon, and are at right Angles to the greatest Declination of the Plane of the *Plain-Table*.

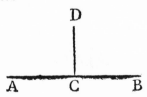

N.B.

N.B. ALTHO' I approve of the Needle, as being of great Ufe, and as it is a fure Checque upon any Error that may be committed thro' miftaking a number on the Limb; yet it is by no means to be depended on alone, as too many Surveyors do, by reafon of its great Difpatch; for we can't be certain it gives every particular Angle true within a few Degrees.

L   A

A
SURVEY

OF

𝕿𝖍𝖊 𝕸𝖆𝖓𝖔𝖗 of K—, in the County of H—

C O N T A I N I N G

The Particulars of the feveral FARMS following, *now* in the poffeffion of his Grace the
Duke of *K*——, Lord of the faid Manor.

Survey'd, *Valued*, and *Improv'd* by
EDWARD LAURENCE, Land-Surveyor.

N.B. The Defign of drawing up thefe Particulars, is,
to fhew the neceffity of every Steward or Agent's having a Survey drawn out in this manner following, before he begins to make an Improvement from an *old-
rented* Eftate, in order to fettle each Tenant's Farm in a
due Proportion of Rent; becaufe it plainly appears by
the following Particulars, that the old Rents were not
fo : And had the common Method of Poundage been
ufed, 'twould have been a means to have prevented fo
good an Improvement as has *now* been made in this
proper way, to the Tenants Satisfaction, *i. e.* being *equal-
ly* ferv'd *all* alike.

L 2

Tenant's Name, and Lands.	Arable inclosed. (a r p)	Common Arable. (a r p)	Pasture. (a r p)	Meadow. (a r p)	Total Number of Acres. (a r p)	Yearly Value per Acre. at (s. d.)	Yearly Value of the several Parcels. (l. s. d.)
Robert Hunt for the **Priory** Farm.							
N° (1) { Old Rent — 80:0:0 / New Rent — 105:0:0							
A *Messuage*, with Barn, Stable, Yard, &c. and Garth adjoining	—	—	1 3 7	—	—	20: 0	1 15 6
Priory Closes in two parcels	—	—	25 1 5	—	—	18: 0	22 14 6
Monks Meadow	—	—	—	10 1 7	—	25: 0	12 17 0
Chantry Croft	—	—	14 3 15	—	—	15: 0	11 0 0
Priest Croft	—	—	9 2 9	—	—	15: 0	7 3 6
Apple-tree Close	7 2 11	—	—	—	—	12: 0	4 11 6
Crab-tree Close	9 1 5	—	—	—	—	10: 0	4 13 6
Castle Close	—	—	15 0 16	—	—	13: 0	8 16 6
Castle Ings	—	—	—	9 0 25	—	25: 0	11 8 0
Broad Field	10 0 18	—	—	—	—	8: 0	4 1 0
The Banks, in three parcels	16 2 9	—	—	—	—	6: 0	5 0 6
The Back of Peal	—	—	18 3 38	—	—	11: 0	10 9 6
30 Lands in *Thisto* Common-Field	—	21 1 30	—	—	—	6: 0	6 8 6
N.B. The whole is Tythe-free.							
Total	43 2 3	21 1 30	85 2 10	19 1 32	169 3 3		L. 110 17 6

N.B. The Abatement of Five Pounds a Year less than the value, is in consideration of this Tenant's being oblig'd to divide the larger parcels of the Pasture into smaller ones, in order to improve them.

Tenant's Name, and Lands.	Arable incloſed. a	r	p	Common Arable. a	r	p	Paſture. a	r	p	Meadow. a	r	p	Total Number of Acres. a	r	p	Yearly Value per Acre. at s.	d.	Yearly Value of the ſeveral Parcels. l.	s.	d.
Thomas Newton, for Blyth Farm.																				
Nº (2) { Old Rent — 68:6:8 / New Rent — 82:0:0 }																				
A *Meſſuage,* with Barns, Stables, Yard, and Homeſtead adjoining,							2	3	12							20:	0	2	17	0
The Shaws, in two parcels	17	3	20													8:	0	7	2	6
Cow Cloſe							9	1	0							12:	0	5	11	0
Oldby Cloſe							5	1	5							11:	0	4	17	10
Kirkhow Cloſe	11	0	0													7:	0	2	17	
Barton-holds, in two parcels	9	3	38													9:	0	4	10	
Bull-ings, in three parcels										18	1	12				15:	0	12		
Far-field							10	2	12							15:	0	7		
Oldbyhead Cloſe							11	0	19							10:	0	5	11	
The Whinny Field							20	1	11							10:	0	6	1	
Long Meadow										16	1	0				20:	0	16	5	6
26 Lands in *Tküſlo* Common-Field				30	2	10										6:	0	9	3	6
Total	38	3	18	30	2	10	55	1	19	34	2	12	162	1	19			L. 85		4

L 3

N.B. The Abatement of 3 *l.* 8 *s.* 4 *d.* a year leſs than the Value, is in conſideration of this Tenant's being oblig'd to divide the larger Parcels of the Paſture and Meadow into ſmaller ones, in order to improve them.

Tenant's Name, and Lands.	Arable inclosed. (a r p)	Common Arable. (a r p)	Pasture. (a r p)	Meadow. (a r p)	Total Number of Acres. (a r p)	Yearly Value per Acre. (at s. d.)	Yearly Value of the several Parcels. (l. s. d.)
John Hill, for the Castle Farm.							
Nº (3) { Old Rent — 69 : 13 : 4 ; New Rent — 88 : 0 : 0 (l. s. d.)							
A Messuage, with Barns, Stable, Yard, &c. and a Croft adjoining —			2 1 0			20 : 0	2 5 0
Oldby Closes, in two parcels —	19 0 11					15 : 0	14 6 6
Odus Field —	11 1 13					13 : 0	7 2 0
Stoney Field —	7 0 5					6 : 0	2 2 0
Smales Closes, in three parcels —			24 0 30			12 : 0	14 9 0
Long Close —			6 1 12			15 : 0	4 14 0
Long Meadow —				9 0 31		25 : 0	13 7 0
Kirkhow Close —			5 3 21			11 : 0	5 3 0
The Launder Flats, in three parcels —			12 1 10			15 : 0	11 5 4
Bull Meadow —				1 1 0		20 : 0	11 0
26 Lands in Castle-Common-Field —		18 0 29				5 : 0	4 10 6
Total	37 1 29	18 0 29	50 3 5	3 20 0 31	130 3 12	L.	88 12 6

Tenant's Name, and Lands.	Arable inclofed. a	r	p	Common Arable. a	r	p	Pasture. a	r	p	Meadow. a	r	p	Total Number of Acres. a	r	p	Yearly Value per Acre. at s. d.	Yearly Value of the feveral Parcels. l. s. d.
John Scot, for Ecclefwal Farm. l. s. d.																
No (4) { Old Rent — 80:6:8 / New Rent — 110:0:0 }																
A Meſſuage, with Barns, Stable, Yard and Garden, and a Home-Clofe adjoining							3	0	0							25:0	3 15 0
Church Clofe							7	3	38							15:0	6 0 0
Priors Clofe							9	1	21							15:0	7 1 6
St. Peter's Field	8	2	10													12:0	5 2 6
Nuns Clofes, in four parcels							28	2	5							11:0	17 4 0
Snout-end Clofe							9	0	15							10:0	4 11 6
The Park Clofes, in two parcels							15	0	0							15:0	11 5 0
Dale Croft, in three parcels	27	0	7													9:0	12 3 0
Cow-hill Field	9	1	3													8:0	3 14 0
Laith Clofe							3	0	5							17:0	2 11 0
Ecclefwal Meadows, in four parcels										24	1	11				25:0	30 7 0
35 Lands in Caftle Common-Field				29	3	9										5:0	7 9 0
Total	44	3	20	29	3	9	76	0	4	24	1	11	175	0	4		L.111 3 0

N B. The whole is Tythe-free.

L 4

Tenant's Name, and Lands.	Arable Inclosed.			Common Arable.			Pasture.			Meadow.			Total Number of Acres.			Yearly Value per Acre. at		Yearly Value of the several Parcels.		
	a	r	p	a	r	p	a	r	p	a	r	p	a	r	p	s.	d.	l.	s.	d.
Robert Ravens, for Bagmoor Farm																				
N° (5) Old Rent —— 56:13:4 New Rent —— 65: 0:0																				
A Messuage, with Barns, Stable, Yard, &c. and a Garth adjoining		3	0				1	2	37							20:	0	1	15	0
The Dial Banks ——	7	3	10													7:	0	2	13	6
The Cliff Hills ——	5	1	5				17	2	30							6:	0	2	19	0
The Boor Flats ——	12	3					1	1	15							11:	0	6	15	0
Abraham Closes, in two parcels ——							10	0	0							15:	0	13	6	0
Nether Close ——							13	3	11							12:	0	2	12	0
Far Close ——																9:	0	4	10	0
Laith Close ——										18	0	9				10:	0	9	8	0
Bull Ings ——																20:	0	18	0	0
31 Lands in Castle Common-Field				13	0	10										5:	0	3	5	0
Total	29	2	25	13	0	10	52	2	13	18	0	9	113	2	20			L. 65	3	6

Tenant's Name, and Lands.	Arable Inclosed. a r p	Common Arable. a r p	Pasture. a r p	Meadow. a r p	Total Number of Acres. a r p	Yearly Value per Acre. at s. d.	Yearly Value of the several Parcels. l. s. d.
William Vaux, for Thistlo Farm.							
N° (6) ⎰ Old Rent —— —— 80:0:0 ⎱ New Rent —— —— 89:0:0							
A Messuage, with Barns, Stable, Yard, &c. and Garth adjoining			3 1 21			20:0	3 3 6
Twin-yates, in two parcels ——	15 0 0					11:0	8 7 0
Rye Close ——	9 1 10					10:0	4 11 0
Howle-Horkham Close ——	8 3 15					9:0	3 15 6
Eel-pye Close ——			12 1 18			15:0	9 5 0
Broad Close ——			11 3 27			14:0	8 7 0
The High Close ——			6 2 16			17:0	8 3 6
The Mill Butts ——			8 3 13			20:0	8 16 0
Casket Ings ——				13 3 35		25:0	17 9 0
Wood Meadow ——				9 2 15		25:0	11 18 0
20 Lands in Thisto Common-Field ——		17 3 10				6:0	5 5 0
Total	33 0 25	17 3 10	46 0 16	33 2 10	120 2 20	L.	89 8 6

Tenant's Name, and Lands.	Arable Inclofed. a	r	p	Common Arable. a	r	p	Pafture. a	r	p	Meadow a	r	p	Total Number of Acres. a	r	p	Yearly Value per Acre. at	Yearly Value of the feveral Parcels. l	s	d
David Robinfon for Roft-hill Farm.																			
$l.\ s.\ d.$ No (4) { Old Rent — — 40:13:4 New Rent — — 72: 0:0																s. d.			
A Meffuage, with Barns, Stables, Yard, &c. and Garth adjoining —																20:0	2		0
Roft-hill Clofes, in two parcels —	27	3	11				2		0							7:0	9	15	0
Calice Clofe —	9	1	19													8:0	3	14	0
Nettle Dale —							12	0	0							13:0	7	16	0
The Ridings, in two parcels —							21	3	39							12:0	13	14	0
Ownfow Clofe —							11	3	38							10:0	6	0	0
Cliff Clofe —							8	1	18							8:0	3	6	0
Cutler Ings, in two parcels —										19	2	7				20:0	19	10	0
24 Lands in the Priory Common-Field —				20	1	17										7:0	7	2	0
Total	37	0	30	20	1	17	56	1	15	19	2	7	133	1	29	L.	72	18	0

N.B. The 24 Lands in Priory Common-Field are Tythe-free.

Tenant's Name, and Lands.	Arable Inclofed. a r p	Common Arable. a r p	Pafture. a r p	Meadow. a r p	Total Number of Acres. a r p	Yearly Value per Acre. at s. d.	Yearly Value of the feveral Parcels. l. s. d.
Daniel Cole, for **Dale-Houfe** Farm. *l. s. d.* No (8) { Old Rent — 40:13:4 { New Rent — 74: 0:0							
A *Meffuage*, with Barns, Stables, Yard, &c. and a Garth adjoining	—	—	—	—	—	20:0	1 15 0
Pipers Clofes, in two parcels	17 1 15	—	—	—	—	9:0	7 15 6
Raffle-Ridge Clofe	8 0 0	—	—	—	—	8:0	3 4 6
Lay-Field	6 1 13	—	—	—	—	9:0	3 0 6
The Sweet-heads, in two parcels	—	—	30 0 0	—	—	12:0	18 0 0
Well Clofe	—	—	11 3 7	—	—	15:0	8 17 6
The Bents, in two parcels	—	—	8 2 14	—	—	13:0	5 11 6
The Weft Ings, in two parcels	—	—	—	21 0 0	—	20:0	21 0 0
27 Lands in Priory Common-Field	—	16 3 10	—	—	—	7:0	5 17 6
Total	31 2 28	16 3 10	52 0 26	21 0 0	121 2 24	L.	75 7 0

N.B. The 27 Lands in Priory Common-Field are Tythe-free.

Tenant's Name, and Lands.	Arable inclosed. a r p	Common Arable. a r p	Pasture. a r p	Meadow. a r p	Total Number of Acres. a r p	Yearly Value per Acre. at s. d.	Yearly Value of the several Parcels. l. s. d.
John Cox, for Weather-hill Farm.							
N° (9) { Old Rent — 38 : 0 : 0 / New Rent — 40 : 0 : 0 }							
A Messuage, with Barns, Stables, Yard, &c. and a Garth adjoining			1 3 0			20 : 0	1 15 0
Cock-line Close	5 3 17					10 : 0	2 18 6
Breary Close	8 1 5					11 : 0	4 11 0
Barton-hold Close	3 0 24					12 : 0	1 17 6
The Dun-Bogs Closes, in two parcels			17 2 21			11 : 0	9 13 6
The Lay Closes, in two parcels			12 0 15			10 : 0	6 1 0
The Low-Ings Closes, in two parcels				11 3 39		20 : 0	12 0 0
20 Lands in Cogdale Common-Field		10 1 21				5 : 0	2 12 0
Total	17 1 6	10 1 21	31 1 36	11 3 39	71 0 22	L	3 14 0

N.B. This Farm was advanc'd Twenty years since ; as appears by an old Rental.

Tenant's Name, and Lands.	Arable inclosed.			Common Arable.			Pasture.			Meadow.			Total Number of Acres.			Yearly Value per Acre. at		Yearly Value of the several Parcels.		
	a	r	p	a	r	p	a	r	p	a	r	p	a	r	p	s.	d.	l.	s.	d.
Richard Bland, for *Blakes* Farm.																				
N° {10} Old Rent — 70:0:0 New Rent — 74:0:0																				
A *Messuage*, with Barn, Stable, Yard, &c. and Garth adjoining,	8	1	33				3	1	0							20	0	3	5	0
The Hill Close, in two parcels,	9	3	31													8	0	3	8	0
Lakes Field	7	0	0													12	0	3	6	0
The High Field							11	3	11							11	0	3	17	0
The Low Field							21	1	12							15	0	8	17	0
Barton-Holds, in two parcels																12	0	12	16	0
Cogdale Ings, in two parcels										19	3	7				25	0	24	14	0
22 Lands in Cogdale Common-Field				10	1	17										5	0	2	11	0
Total	25	1	24	10	1	17	36	1	23	19	3	7	91	3	31			L. 75	8	0

N.B. This Farm also was advanced Twenty years since; as appears by an old Rental.

An ABSTRACT from all the 'foregoing Particulars.

N°	Tenants Names, and Farms.	Arable inclofed.			Common Arable.			Pasture.			Meadow.			Total Number of Acres.			Old Rents.			New Rents agreed on for Leafes.			Yearly Value on lue of the feveral Farms.		
		a	r	p	a	r	p	a	r	p	a	r	p	a	r	p	l	s	d	l	s	d	l	s	d
1	Robert Hunt, for the Priory Farm.	43	2	3	21	1	30	85	1	10	19	2	32	169	3	35	80	0	0	105	0	0	110	17	6
2	Thomas Newton, for Blyth Farm.	38	3	18	30	2	10	59	1	19	34	2	12	163	1	19	68	6	8	82	0	0	85	8	4
3	John Hill for the Castle Farm. —	37	1	29	18	0	29	55	0	3	20	0	31	130	3	12	69	13	4	88	0	0	88	12	6
4	John Scot, for Ecclefwal Farm. —	44	3	20	29	3	9	76	0	4	24	1	11	175	0	4	80	6	8	111	0	0	111	3	0
5	Robert Ravens, for Bagmoor Farm	29	3	28	13	0	10	52	2	13	18	0	9	113	2	20	56	13	4	65	0	0	65	3	6
6	William Vaux, for Thiflo Farm —	33	0	25	17	3	10	46	0	15	23	2	10	120	2	20	80	0	0	89	0	0	89	8	6
7	David Robinfon, for Rott-hill Farm	37	0	30	20	1	17	56	1	15	19	2	7	133	1	29	40	13	4	72	0	0	72	18	0
8	Daniel Cole, for Dale-houfe Farm	31	2	28	16	3	10	52	0	26	21	0	0	121	2	24	40	13	4	74	0	0	75	7	0
9	John Cox, for Weather-hill Farm	17	1	6	10	1	21	31	1	36	11	3	39	71	0	22	38	0	0	40	0	0	41	8	0
10	Richard Bland, for Blakes Farm	25	1	24	10	1	17	36	1	23	19	3	7	91	3	31	70	0	0	74	0	0	75	8	0
	Total Amount of this Manor.	339	1	11	188	3		355	1	0	212	1	38	1291	2	16	624	6	8	799	0	0	815	14	4

```
                                            l.    s.  d.
N.B. { New Rents agreed on — 799:  0: 0
      { Old Rents       — 624:  6: 8
Total Improvement in this Manor- 174: 13: 4
```

An ABSTRACT of

GENERAL COVENANTS

To be obferved by

A LL the 'forefaid Tenants in the aforefaid
Manor of *K——*, which I left with the Steward
of the Court, in order to be inferted in all the
aforemention'd Tenants Leafes.

N.B. *Thefe* Covenants *will prove of general Ufe to moft
Eftates.*

Covenant I.

THAT ALL the Tenants in the faid
Manor fhall be oblig'd not to *pare*
and *burn* any Part or Parcel of the
Lands in their Farms; the practifing of this
having been found by long Experince to be
very

very prejudicial to Lands, becaufe it draws out moſt of the *Nitrous Particles* fit for Vegetation. Therefore any one of the Tenants, that ſhall be Guilty of this Offence, ſhall pay (over and above his yearly Rent) the Sum of Twenty pounds for every Acre pared and burnt as aforeſaid.

Covenant II.

THAT ALL the ſaid Tenants ſhall be oblig'd not to ſow any *Rape*, *Hemp*, *Flax*, *Woad*, *Weld*, *Madder*, &c. on any Part or Parcel of their Lands ; nor to plant any *Potatoes*, or *Hops*, (except in ſmall quantities for their own uſe) on the Penalty of paying, *over* and *above* their *yearly* Rent the Sum of Ten pounds for every Acre of Land on which they ſhall *ſow* or *plant* any of the abovemention'd Vegetables, without further Covenants, in order to pay a
valuable

valuable Confideration for the fame, and alfo
to lay down the Lands for Pafture in a good
* Condition.

****

Covenant III.

THAT ALL the faid Tenants fhall be
oblig'd not to plow up, nor convert
into Tillage, any Part or Parcels of any Inclofure, as is fpecified in the Particulars under the proper Columns of Pafture and Meadow, on Penalty of paying Ten pound for
every Acre fo plow'd, to be paid *over*
and *above* their yearly Rent. And if any
part of the faid Inclofures fhall happen to
grow over with *Mofs*, *Prie*, or other
Coarfe Grafs, then the faid Tenants (Leave

---

* As thefe Vegetables breed no Manure, fo great
Care (by a ftrict Covenant) fhould be taken that the
Lands are laid down in a good condition, *i. e.* by re-
enriching them with Twenty Load of Dung (over and
above what the Farm produces) or a Hundred Bufhels
of Lime, upon an Acre. If fuch a Covenant is not duly obferv'd, 'twill be the fame prejudice to the Lands,
as felling the Hay and Straw off the Premifes.

M

being

being firſt granted) may plow up the ſame, or convert it into Tillage, in order to improve the ſame, for the ſpace of three years only : Provided always that the ſaid Tenants ſhall, the Spring following, be oblig'd to lay down the ſaid Lands with *Clover, Rey-graſs,* or other proper *Graſs-Seeds,* as ſhall be thought moſt agreeable to the nature of the Land. But before the ſaid Tenants begin to plow up the ſaid Paſtures or Meadows, *timely* Notice before-hand ſhall be given to the proper *Agent* or *Steward* appointed by the Lord of the Manor, that they may be Judges whether the ſaid Paſtures or Meadows will not ſuffer Damage by a *moderate* plowing. And alſo the ſaid Tenants (before they begin to plow the aforeſaid Paſture and Meadow) ſhall conſent to pay a *valuable* Conſideration (according to the Goodneſs of the Land) to be paid *over* and *above* their yearly Rent, for the advantage of plowing up freſh Paſture or Meadow-ground, to be agreed on firſt by the Steward and Tenant.

Covenant **IV.**

THAT ALL the faid Tenants fhall be oblig'd not to cut down any Timber-trees, Saplins, Pollards, or Under-woods on any part of their Farms, on Penalty of paying *over* and *above* their yearly Rent ten times the Value of the fame, except only what is neceffary for Repairs of their Houfes; and this to be affign'd them by the proper Agent or Steward.

Cove

Covenant V.

THAT ALL the faid Tenants fhall be oblig'd to obferve and practife the following due Courfe of Husbandry in the inclos'd Lands, *viz.* the *firft* year after the fallow, to fow Wheat, Rye or Barley; the *fecond*, to fow Beans or Peafe, or rather Both 𝕯𝖓𝖉𝖊𝖗-𝕱𝖚𝖗𝖗𝖔𝖜; the *third*, to fow Barley or Oats; and the *fourth* year, to let the Land lie for Fallow: which Covenant is calculated for the good both of the Farms and the Farmer. And, that the faid Tenants fhall be oblig'd to lay upon their Pafture and Meadow-ground at leaft one half of the Dung which their Farms produce, and the other half upon the Tillage-Land. And, to reftore the Riches of the Tillage, each Tenant, every year, fhall be obliged to lay Forty Bufhels of Lime upon every Acre of *their* Land lying fallow,

which,

which, * according to the 'foregoing Courſe of Husbandry, muſt be a fourth part of what is allotted them for Tillage, ſpecified under the proper Columns of *Arable Inclos'd* and *Common Arable*. And alſo, that each Tenant ſhall be oblig'd, every year, to feed or Summer-paſture about one fourth part of their Meadows; ſo that the whole quantity of Meadowing may be Summer-eaten once in four years: The due obſerving of this, will eſtabliſh that known *Maxim* amongſt the moſt experienc'd Farmers, that *mowing of Lands too often and too long*, is as great a Prejudice to them, as *too often and too long plowing them is to Tillage*, except plenty of *Superinductions* of Dungs, *&c.* can be had with eaſe. Any one of the Tenants not performing every part of this Fifth Covenant, ſhall be oblig'd to pay, *over* and *above* his yearly Rent, the Sum of Twenty pounds.

---

* Where 'tis the Cuſtom for new Tenants to enter at *Michaelmas*, then the old Tenant ſhould be oblig'd to leave a fourth part of his Tillage well fallow'd (by giving the ſame four tilts or plowings) to the new Tenant, he paying a reaſonable price for the ſame, according to cuſtom.

Cove-

Covenant VI.

THAT ALL the faid Tenants fhall be oblig'd to fpend *all* the Hay and Straw upon the Premifes; and at the end of their Leafes or Term of years, to leave all, both Dung and Straw, to the fucceeding Tenant, without any confideration for the fame. And the better to perform this Article, tho' their Leafes expire at *Lady-day*, yet neverthelefs the faid Tenants (if they leave their Farms) may have liberty till *May-day* following to make ufe of the Barns to thrafh out their Corn, and alfo to make ufe of the Fold-yard. The faid Tenants not performing every part of this Article, fhall be oblig'd to pay, *over* and *above* their yearly Rent, the Sum of Twenty pounds.

Cove-

Covenant VII.

THAT ALL the said Tenants shall be oblig'd to cleanse and scowre up their Ditches in a Husbandlike manner, in order to carry off the Water in such manner, as (if possible) not to let the Water *settle* or *stagnate* any where in the *lower* part of the Grounds, on Penalty of paying Ten pounds for such neglect.

Covenant VIII.

THAT ALL the said Tenants shall be oblig'd, at their own proper Cost and Charge, to keep up their Messuages or Dwelling-Houses in good and tenantable Repair, and to leave the same to the succeeding

M 4 Tenant

Tenant without any Confideration for the fame, they being allow'd rough Timber, and Stone from the Quarries, fuch as the Eftate produces.

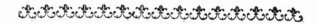

Covenant IX.

THAT ALL the faid Tenants fhall be oblig'd to yoke and ring their Hogs, to prevent Damage to the Fences, and rooting up the Pafture-Grounds, on the Penalty of paying Ten fhillings, for each Hog fuffer'd to be unrung or unyoked.

Cove-

Covenant X.

THAT ALL the faid Tenants fhall be oblig'd to fow their Winter Corn (if poffible) rather before than after *Michael-mas*, (which by Experience is found to be moft fuitable to the Northern parts.) In like manner the Summer Corn (if poffible) to be fown *before Lady-day*, in order to *forward* the Harveft. Alfo the faid Tenants fhall be oblig'd to *Hayn* (*i. e.* clear their Meadows of the Cattle) at *Lady-day*, on the Penalty of paying Ten pounds for this and the 'foregoing Neglect.

Covenant XI.

THAT ALL the faid Tenants fhall be oblig'd not to let out any part of their Farms to any *Under-Tenant*, the doing of which having been found to be very *prejudicial* to moft Eftates. The faid Tenants therefore fhall pay *over* and *above* their yearly Rents, the Sum of Twenty pounds for every part or parcel fo let out as above-mention'd.

Covenant XII.

THAT ALL the faid Tenants fhall be oblig'd to cut and plafh their Hedges in a Husband-like manner, at about twelve years growth from the time of their firft planting ; and alfo to nurfe up the fame by weeding.

weeding. The neglect of doing these has been the Ruin of most Fences in the North of *England*; therefore any Tenant that neglects the doing of this *great* piece of service to *Himself*, as well as the *Lord of the Manor*, shall pay, *over* and *above* his yearly Rent, the Sum of Twenty pounds.

Covenant XIII.

THAT ALL the said Tenants shall be oblig'd not to stock any part of their Farm with Rabbits, the doing of this having been found by long Experience to be very prejudicial to Estates, especially upon a dry sandy Soil ; therefore any one of the Tenants, that shall be guilty of this, shall pay, *over* and *above* his yearly Rent, the Sum of Two hundred pounds for such Offence.

Cove-

Covenant XIV.

THAT ALL the faid Tenants fhall be oblig'd not to gather the Cow-dung together on Heaps, firft to dry it, and then to burn it inftead of Wood and Coal; the doing of this alfo having been found to be very prejudicial to Eftates, becaufe it robs the Land of one of the beft forts of Manures: Therefore any one of the Tenants that fhall be guilty of this, fhall pay, *over* and *above* his yearly Rent, the Sum of Ten pounds for fuch Offence.

Covenant XV.

THAT ALL the faid Tenants fhall be oblig'd to pay the *Mole-catcher* after the rate of 1 2 *d.* a dozen for what he deftroys; and, that *each Tenant* do pay in proportion

to

to the bignefs of his Farm, which is to be
adjufted by the Steward. If one of the Tenants refufes to pay his Dividend, then it fhall
be in the power of the Steward to charge it
to his yearly Rent.

Covenant XVI.

THAT ALL the faid Tenants fhall be
oblig'd (at their own proper coft and
charge) to keep the Bye-roads leading
through their Grounds in good and fufficient
repair, by laying and keeping them *dry*;
and afterwards to make them lie *round* and
high in the middle; and, when the Earth
is well fettled at Midfummer, to lay all the
Gravel-ftones that can be got upon it: This
will be a means to prevent Travellers from
poaching on each fide, to the no fmall detriment of a Farm. Any one of the Tenants
not performing this Article, fhall pay, *over*
and *above* his yearly Rent, the Sum of Ten
pounds for fuch Neglect.

Cove-

Covenant XVII.

THAT ALL the said Tenants shall be oblig'd not to keep any Greyhounds, Guns, *&c.* nor to set any Snares, Ginns, *&c.* so as to destroy the Lord's Game in any sort; nor to trace any Hares in the Snow. Any one of the Tenants that is guilty of this Offence shall pay, *over* and *above* his yearly Rent, the Sum of Five pounds.

Covenant XVIII.

THAT ALL the said Tenants shall be oblig'd not to commit waste in any sort upon any part of their Farms, especially by erecting Brick-kilns, and by digging Clay in order to make Bricks for sale, without further Covenants, in order

I   to

to pay a valuable Confideration for the fame. Any one of the Tenants, not duly performing this Covenant, fhall pay, *over* and *above* his yearly Rent, the Sum of Five hundred pounds.

Covenant XIX.

THAT ALL the faid Tenants fhall be oblig'd (whenever the Lord of the Manor or his Steward demands it) to fend their Teams to lead home the Hay and Corn which comes off the Demefne Lands only, kept in hand for the Lord's Ufe; and alfo to lead home Stone or Timber whenever he has occafion for Building or Repairs. Any one of the Tenants not performing this Covenant, fhall pay, *over* and *above* his yearly Rent, the Sum of Five pounds for fuch Neglect.

Cove-

Covenant XX.

AS the Lord of the Manor has been at an extraordinary Charge in covering the Farm-houfe and Out houfes with Slate and Tile, inftead of thatching them with *Straw*; fo ALL the faid Tenants fhall be oblig'd, at their own coft and charge for the future, to keep them up in the like Repair; not only as a better Security againft the Accidents and Misfortunes by Fire, but that it robs the Land of great quantities of Manure that the faid thatching with Straw would produce.   Any one of the Tenants not duly performing this Covenant, fhall pay *over* and *above* his yearly Rent, the Sum of Twenty pounds for fuch Neglect.

Cove-

Covenant XXI.

THAT ALL the said Tenants in the said Manor shall be oblig'd to pay the Church, Poor, and Constable's Assessments, and *all* other Taxes and Assessments whatsoever, except the Land-Tax.

Covenant XXII.

THAT ALL the said Tenants shall be oblig'd every *Christmas*, or some other time of the Year (as shall be adjudg'd most acceptable) to send a Present to his Lord of two fat Capons, or two fat Turkeys, or two fat Geese, or any other Fowl,

N or

or Fish of the like Value; on Penalty of paying Ten shillings *over* and *above* their yearly Rent for such Neglect.

N. B. It may be objected by *many*, that several of these Covenants might have been omitted, because they are *presentable* at the Court-Baron; but let such consider how *little* these matters of *consequence* have been regarded of late years at these Courts, because too many Stewards are indolent, and the Tenants *combine* together, and will not present one another: Therefore the most effectual Remedy to have Covenants strictly observ'd, is to have recourse to Common Law.

THE afore-going Articles are only Heads of Covenants; and tho' the Reasons of them are there assign'd, yet the putting them in proper Forms of Law, and wording them, is left to the Discretion of the Lawyer.

Note also, 'Twou'd be very proper to have a Plan annex'd to each Lease, with the

Par-

Particulars in the manner 'foregoing; and like-wife an ABSTRACT of the Covenants join'd with the faid Particulars, that they may be more readily look'd into upon occafion.

AND for the greater Satisfaction of every Nobleman and Gentleman, 'tis advifeable to have three parts of the Leafes executed, each by the Leafor and Leafee, one to be kept by the Lord of the Manor, another by the Steward, and the third by the Te-nant. This will moft certainly prevent ma-ny wilful Miftakes, which otherwife in an ill-difpos'd Steward may impofe upon the Lord of the Manor by FORGERY, *&c.*

A

A

Plain and Easy Method

To be practis'd by every

STEWARD

IN

Keeping his ACCOMPTS in such a
manner as to be readily examin'd.

𝕱𝖎𝖗𝖘𝖙, By Entering down ALL the *Articles*
of the several Kinds for Money Receiv'd
distinctly by themselves, with the Sum
Total of each Kind.

𝕾𝖊𝖈𝖔𝖓𝖉𝖑𝖞, By Entering down ALL the Articles of the several Kinds of Disbursements distinctly by themselves, with the
Sum Total of each Kind.

𝕿𝖍𝖎𝖗𝖉𝖑𝖞, and lastly, By Drawing up an Abstract, or an Accompt-Current by way of
Debtor and Creditor, from ALL the 'foremention'd Particulars, in order to shew the
exact Balance.

N.B. I publish these Accompts, not only for the Use of such Stewards who are *better* qualified in Country Business than in Accompts, but also to shew an Example of what Articles shou'd be charg'd as Receiv'd for the Lord's Use, which was formerly thought to be a Steward's Perquisite.

It may be very proper the Steward shou'd keep a Cash-book and Journal, according to the Common Method, for his own private Use and Satisfaction; but some such following Methods should always be deliver'd to his Lord, in order to their more easy Examination by him.

AN

An Account

*Of the several Sums of Money Recei-
ved from the four several Manors
of* G, H, I, K, *in the* County *of* H,
by A. B. *Steward to his Grace the
Duke of* K.

For One whole Year.

From *Lady-day* 1725, *to Lady-day* 1726.

A Rental for the Manor of *G.* in the County of *H.* Receiv'd by *A. B.* Steward to His Grace the Duke of *K.* Being One whole Year's Rent from *Lady-day* 1725, to *Lady-day* 1726.	Yearly Rents.		
N°	*l.*	*s.*	*d.*
1 Roger Cooper, for the 𝔐anor of 𝔎. Farm and Demesnes	210	0	0
2 William Rogers, for the 𝔚ell-house Farm	95	10	0
3 George Atkinson, for 𝔎idley's Farm	82	10	0
4 Robert Atkinson, for 𝔎obottom's Farm	65	0	0
5 Lawrence Davidson, for 𝔠rowley's Farm	48	10	0
6 Abraham Jackson for 𝔅road Farm	37	0	0
7 Abraham Cooling, for the 𝔠old-𝔅ath Farm	36	10	0
8 Jonathan Caverly, for 𝔅lacksmith's Farm	31	0	0
9 Gabriel Badcock, for the 𝔊ill Farm	28	10	0
10 John Reynolds, for the 𝔅usky Farm	20	15	0
11 David Bigg, for the 𝔓ark-pond Farm	20	10	0
12 Nathaniel Bigg, for 𝔇ovehouse Farm	17	15	0
13 Mary Goodchild, for her House in *Crowley,* and *Lake's* Lands	8	5	0
14 *Tho. North,* for a House and Close in *Crowley*	3	10	0
15 *Geo. Caverly,* for a House and Close in *Crowley*	2	5	0
16 *Tho. Caverly,* for a House and Close in *Crowley*	2	0	0
17 Jane Goodchild, for a House and Close in *Crowley*	1	15	0
18 Mary Cooper, for a House and Close in *Crowley*	1	10	0
19 John Davidson, for a House and Close in *Crowley*	1	5	0
20 John Blackburn, for a House and Close in *Crowley*	1	5	0
21 David Robinson, for a House and Close in *Crowley*	1	0	0
Receiv'd of the several *Copyholders of Inheritance* their Quit-Rents, as appears yearly in the Copy of Court-roll for this Manor	18	17	5
Total Amount of this Manor	735	2	5

		l.	s.	d
A Rental for the Manor of *H.* in the County of *H.* receiv'd by *A. B.* Steward to His Grace the Duke of *K.* *Being one whole Year's Rent, from Lady-day 1725 to Lady-day 1726.*	Yearly Rents.			
Nº		l.	s.	d
1	*John Hill,* for the 𝔥all Farm and Demesnes	170	0	0
2	*Roger Hill,* for 𝔅ernard's Farm ———	65	10	0
3	*John Manners,* for the 𝔯idge=house Farm	62	0	0
4	*William Stonehouse,* for 𝔭aradise Farm	60	10	0
5	*Edward Barlow,* for the 𝔣enn Farm ——	47	0	0
6	*Benjamin Butler,* for the ℭalbot=𝔦nn Farm	43	10	0
7	*Mary Johnson,* for the 𝔚ilderness Farm	38	0	0
8	*Mary Scott,* for 𝔣letcher's Farm ———	24	10	0
9	*Elizabeth Marygold,* for the 𝔇ale Farm —	20	15	0
10	*Christopher Thompson,* for 𝔬loby's Farm	20	0	0
11	*Margery Rogers,* for 𝔯abie's Farm ——	18	0	0
12	*Thomas Masterman,* for 𝔊regory's Farm	16	10	0
13	*Thomas Ball,* for 𝔫utt's Farm ———	15	15	0
14	*William Bernard,* for 𝔅lake's Farm ——	12	0	0
15	*John Gill,* for the 𝔩ow Farm ———	11	0	0
16	*Jane Hansel,* for *Tanner's* Lands ———	9	5	0
17	*Roger Mason,* for the Road-lands ———	9	0	0
18	*Margery Snell,* for a House and Close in *Denton* ——— ———	2	10	0
	Total Amount of this Manor—	645	15	0

A Ren-

A Rental for the Manor of *I.* in the County of *H.* Receiv'd by *A. B.* Steward to His Grace the Duke of *K.* Being One whole Year's Rent from *Lady-day* 1725 to *Lady-day* 1726.	Yearly Rents.		
N°	*l.*	*s.*	*d*
1 *James Wilson*, for 𝕽ougbp Farm ———	130	0	0
2 *Roger Vaux*, for 𝕾kelton's Farm ———	100	0	0
3 *John Turner*, for 𝕸anwaring's Farm —	100	0	0
4 *William Moss*, for 𝕭og-houſe Farm —	85	0	0
5 *Thomas Mason*, for 𝕯ove-houſe Farm —	82	0	0
6 *Abraham Johnson*, for the 𝕳all Farm —	80	0	0
7 *John Forster*, for the 𝕱enn Farm ———	76	0	0
8 *James Fyſh*, for 𝕸ath Farm ———	75	0	0
9 *John Fyſh*, for 𝕬thome Farm ———	73	0	0
10 *Edward Trotter*, for 𝕷ake's Farm —	71	0	0
11 *Edward Taylor*, for 𝕲efferſon's Farm —	70	10	0
12 *William Williams*, for 𝕮overdale Farm —	67	0	0
13 *John Younger*, for 𝕷aith Farm ——	66	0	0
14 *William Lawrence*, for 𝕲rimsbp Farm —	62	10	0
15 *Thomas Keld*, for the 𝕮ap-houſe Farm —	60	10	0
16 *John Thompson*, for 𝕬ngel Farm ———	52	0	0
17 *James Badcock*, for 𝕭ingley's Farm —	41	10	0
18 *Robert Jennens*, for the 𝕯ale Farm —	32	0	0
19 *James Noakes*, for 𝕱ogg Farm ———	21	10	0
Total of this Manor——	1345	10	0

A

A Rental for the Manor of *K.* in the County of *H.* Receiv'd by *A.B.* Steward to His Grace the Duke of *K.* Being One whole Year's Rent from *Lady-day* 1725, to *Lady-day* 1726.	Yearly Rents.		
N°	*l.*	*s.*	*d*
1 *Robert Hunt*, for the Priory Farm ——	105	0	0
2 *Thomas Newton*, for Blyth's Farm ——	82	0	0
3 *John Hill*, for the Castle Farm ——	88	0	0
4 *John Scot*, for Ecclefwal Farm ——	110	0	0
5 *Robert Ravens*, for Bag Moor Farm —	65	0	0
6 *William Vaux*, for Childo Farm ——	80	0	0
7 *David Robinson*, for Roft-Hill Farm —	72	0	0
8 *Daniel Cole*, for Dale-Houfe Farm —	74	0	0
9 *John Cox*, for Weather-hill Farm ——	40	0	0
10 *Richard Bland*, for Blake's Farm ——	74	0	0
Total of this Manor —	799	0	0

An ABSTRACT of the Rentals from thefe four Manors, *viz.*

	l.	*s.*	*d*
1. The Manor of G. —— ——	735	2	5
2. The Manor of H. ——	645	15	0
3. The Manor of I. —— ——	1345	10	0
4. The Manor of K. ——	799	0	0
Total Amount of the certain Rents from thefe 4 Manors	3525	7	5

An Account of Cafual Profits of Courts by Fines, Hariots, and Surrenders, &c. from the feveral *Copyholders of Inheritance* within the Manor of *G.* in the County of *H.*

(At a Court-Baron held the 27th of *March*, 1725.)

	l.	*s.*	*d.*
REceiv'd of *John Todd*, a Compofition for Five Hariots, inftead of his Five beft Beafts or Goods, due to the Lord of the Manor, at the Death of his Father *John Todd*	56	0	0
REceiv'd of the aforefaid *John Todd*, a Fine for his being admitted Tenant to his Father's Eftate Mr. *Thomas Todd*. The Fine formerly accepted by the Lord of the Manor for this Eftate ufed to be but 80 Pounds ; but, in confideration that the value of Money is decreas'd very much of late years, the faid *John Todd* agrees to pay —	110	0	0
REceiv'd of *Jonathan Cooper*, a Compofition for a Hariot inftead of his beft Beaft or Goods, due (as aforefaid) at the Death of his Father *Jonathan Cooper* —	10	0	0
REceiv'd of the faid *Jonathan Cooper*, a Fine for his being admitted Tenant to his Father's Eftate aforefaid. The Fine formerly ufed to be but 15 Pounds ; but, for the reafon aforemention'd, the faid *Jonathan Cooper* agrees to pay —	20	0	0
REceiv'd of *Robert Hunt*, for an eftray Gelding fold to him, which was due to the Lord of the Manor, the faid *Robert Hunt* being at *all* Charges of keeping a Year and a Day, and alfo for crying at the feveral Market-Towns — —	7	8	3
Continued—	203	8	3

Profits of Court continued.

(At a Court-Baron held the 9th of *October*, 1725.)

	l.	s.	d.
Brought over ——— —— —— —	203	8	3

R Eceiv'd of *Tho. Giles*, a Fine on account of a Surrender made to him of an Eſtate of Mr. *Tho. Hart*. The Fine formerly accepted by the Lord of the Manor uſed to be but 60 pounds, but on the Conſideration aforemention'd, the ſaid *Tho. Giles* agrees to pay ——— —— —— **82 0 0**

R Eceiv'd of the aforeſaid *Tho. Giles* a Fine for his being admitted Tenant to the aforeſaid *Thomas Hart's* Eſtate. The Fine formerly accepted by the Lord of the Manor for an admittance to the aforeſaid Eſtate uſed to be but 15 Pounds; but, for the reaſon aforemention'd, the ſaid *Thomas Giles* agrees to pay —— — —— —— **20 0 0**

R Eceiv'd of *Robert Williams*, a Fine on account of a Surrender of an Eſtate made to him by *William Rachel*. The Fine formerly accepted by the Lord of the Manor, for the aforeſaid Eſtate, uſed to be but 30 pounds, but for the reaſon aforemention'd the ſaid *Robert Williams* agrees to pay **40 0 0**

R Eceiv'd of the aforeſaid *Robert Williams*, a Fine for his being admitted Tenant to the aforeſaid *William Rachel's* Eſtate. The Fine formerly for admittance to this Eſtate uſed to be but 15 Pounds; but for the reaſon aforemention'd the ſaid *Robert Williams* agrees to pay —— —— **20 0 0**

| Total Amount of this Manor— | 365 | 8 | 3 |

I

An Account of Cafual Profits receiv'd *over* and *above* the Yearly Rents from the feveral Tenants following, by their entring into *New Covenants* for plowing up *Frefh* Pafture-Grounds, in order to fow *Woad*, *Weld*, and plant *Madder* for the Dyers ufe, for three Years only, and then to lay down the faid Pafture for *Grafs* the fourth Year, by fowing the natural *Hay-feeds*, or *Rye-grafs* and *Clover* together. And, to reftore the Riches that the 'forefaid *Woad*, *Weld*, &c. may have taken from the faid Pafture, the faid Tenants alfo are oblig'd by this *New Covenant* to lay on 100 Bufhels of Lime, or 20 Loads of Dung, upon every Acre, at the time of laying down the faid Grounds.

	l.	*s.*	*d.*
Received of *Robert Hunt*, Tenant for the Priory Farm in the Manor of *K.* for liberty of plowing up two Parcels of Pafture-grounds in his Farm, call'd the *Priory Clofes*, containing acres R. P. 25 : 1 : 5 for 3 years only, for fowing *Woad* thereon, at the rate of 6*l.* 10*s.* per Acre for the faid 3 years	163	7	6
Received of *John Scot*, Tenant for Ecclefiwal Farm, in the aforefaid Manor, for the like liberty of plowing up four parcels of Pafture-grounds call'd *The Nuns Clofes*, containing acres R. P. 28 : 2 : 5 for 3 years only, for fowing *Weld* thereon, at the rate of 5 *l.* 10 *s.* per Acre, for the faid 3 years	156	15	0
Received of *Daniel Cole*, Tenant for Dale Houfe Farm, in the aforefaid Manor, for the like liberty of plowing up two parcels of Pafture-ground in his Farm call'd *The Sweet-heads*, containing 30 Acres, for 3 years only, for planting *Madder* thereon, at the rate of 5 *l.* 15 *s.* per Acre for the faid 3 years	172	10	0
Total of cafual Profits for plowing up frefh Pafture-	4 2	12	6

N.B.

N.B. The 'foremention'd Articles are not always by
Stewards brought to Accompt, becaufe they look up-
on them as Perquifites to themfelves: Which is one way
that *unjuft* Stewards take to acquire large Eftates. If
Tenants break up Frefh Pafture for fowing common
Grain for Three Years, the like Covenants ought to
be obferv'd, and the Steward fhould make the beft
Bargain he can with them: And if the Pafture is good,
it may be worth about Five pounds an Acre for Three
Years *over* and *above* their yearly Rent; and this the
Steward fhould bring to Accompt. In moft Manors
where there are large Commons and Waftes, the
Waftes are much fubject to grow over with *Fern*,
which if mow'd down and burnt in a dry feafon, the
Afhes turn to a good account for the Soap-boilers ufe.
This ought alfo to be brought to Accompt, with every
thing elfe that the Eftate produceth.

An

An Account of the Sale of the Underwood in the Wood call'd 𝕻𝖗𝖎𝖔𝖗's 𝖂𝖔𝖔𝖉, in the Manor of *K.* in the County of *H.* containing in the whole 22 Acres, the Underwood of which being 25 Years growth.

[The Sale-day *November* 28th, 1724.]

N° of Acres.		*l.*	*s.*	*d*
1	Sold to *Robert Hunt* —— —— for—	14	0	0
2	Sold to *Ditto* —— —— for—	15	10	0
3	Sold to *Thomas Newton* —— for—	11	10	0
4	Sold to *Ditto* —— —— for—	16	0	0
5	Sold to *Ditto* —— —— for—	16	10	0
6	Sold to *John Hill* —— —— for—	10	15	0
7	Sold to *Ditto* —— —— for—	13	15	0
8	Sold to *John Scott* —— —— for—	17	0	0
9	Sold to *Robert Ravens* —— for—	18	0	0
10	Sold to *Ditto* —— —— for—	16	15	0
11	Sold to *Ditto* —— —— for—	15	15	0
12	Sold to *William Vaux* —— —— for—	13	10	0
13	Sold to *David Robinson* —— for—	11	15	0
14	Sold to *Ditto* —— —— for—	12	0	0
15	Sold to *Daniel Cole* —— —— for—	12	0	0
16	Sold to *John Cox* —— —— for—	12	0	0
17	Sold to *Richard Johnson* —— for—	13	15	0
18	Sold to *Edward Jackson* —— for—	19	10	0
19	Sold to *James Wilson* —— for—	20	0	0
20	Sold to *Ditto* —— —— for—	20	10	0
21	Sold to *Mary Knowles* —— for—	20	10	0
22	Sold to *Ditto* —— —— for—	18	15	0
	Total for the Sale of this Underwood——	339	15	0

N.B. 'Tis the Custom in the North of *England* to sell the Underwood by the Statute-Acre, Bark and all standing, and the Person that buys it to be at all Charges of felling, &c.

An

An Account of the Bodies of the several Timber-Trees sold out of the aforesaid Prior's Wood, containing in the whole 274 Timber-Trees.

[The Sale-day being the 30th of *November* 1724.]

Nº of Trees	Persons Names sold to.	Nº of solid Feet.	Value *per* Foot.	Value of the several parcels of Timb. trees.		
				l.	s.	d.
13	sold to *Jo. Cotterel,* containing	489	at 1 : 0 *per* foot	24	9	0
29	sold to *Will. Rogers,* containing	1456	at 1 : 2 *per* foot	84	18	8
52	sold to *Ja. Wells,* containing	1920	at 1 : 6 *per* foot	145	10	0
24	sold to *Thomas Cox,* containing	969	at 1 : 0 *per* foot	48	9	0
17	sold to *Tho. Law,* containing	1029	at 1 : 4 *per* foot	63	12	0
18	sold to *Roger Leng,* containing	720	at 1 : 2 *per* foot	42	0	0
39	sold to *Wil. Adams,* containing	1574	at 1 : 3 *per* foot	98	7	6
43	sold to *Ed. Johnson,* containing	2150	at 1 : 6 *per* foot	161	5	0
28	sold to *E. Norwood,* containing	1673	at 1 : 5 *per* foot	118	0	0
31	sold to *Job. Rogers,* containing	1865	at 1 : 6 *per* foot	139	17	6
274	Total.	Total- 13845	Total *l.*	926	8	8

N.B. The aforemention'd Persons that bought this Timber were at all Charges of felling them.

O

An

An Account of the 𝕳𝖊𝖆𝖉𝖘 of the 'foregoing
Timber-Trees fold to the feveral Perfons
following, for Faggoting only : Moft of the
faid Timber-Trees being tall and ftrait, the
Heads were not of great value.

Nᵒ ofthe Heads of Trees	(The Sale-Day being *December* the 1ft, 1724.)	l.	s.	d
			s. d.	
43	Sold to *Dorothy Johnfon*- at 5 : 6 each-	11	16	6
32	Sold to *John Ridley* —— at 7 : 6 each-	12	0	0
28	Sold to *Richard Alleley* --at 8 : 0 each-	10	4	0
29	Sold to *Robert Holmes* -·-at 7 : 6 each-	10	17	0
31	Sold to *Mary Rogers* —— at 10 : 0 each-	15	10	0
39	Sold to *Jane Hooper*——at 11 : 0 each-	21	9	0
13	Sold to *Elizabeth Market* at 12 : 6 each-	8	2	6
24	Sold to *Thomas Cox* -·-- at 13 : 0 each-	15	12	0
18	Sold to *MargeryGoodchild* at 11 : 0 each-	9	18	0
17	Sold to *John Robinfon* —— at 9 : 0 each-	7	13	0
274	Total for the Heads fold-	123	2	0

N.B. The Bark is excepted out of the Sale of the Heads of the
faid Trees, as well as the Bodies.

An

An Account of the Sale of the 𝕭𝖆𝖗𝖐 from the
'forefaid Timber-Trees and Heads, to the feveral
Perfons following, by the yard, the faid Bark
being placed a yard wide at the bottom, and a
yard high, meeting in a point at top in the form of
a triangular Prifm, the better to caft off the Wet.

(The Sale-Day being the 24th of *April*, 1725.)

N° of yards.		l.	s.	d.
2970	yards fold to *Abraham Wilks*, at 13 *d. per* yard	160	17	6
604	yards fold to *Daniel Roper*, at 13 *d. per* yard.	32	14	2
1500	yards fold to *Tho. Fairchild*, at 13 *d. per* yard	81	5	0
1370	yards fold to *John Whimp*, at 13 *d. per* yard	74	4	2
	(*NB.* Thefe Perfons were at all Charges of ftripping, *&c.*)			
6444	Total	349	0	10

An 𝕬𝖇𝖋𝖙𝖗𝖆𝖈𝖙 of the Sale of the Underwood,
Timber, Heads and Barks, in 𝕻𝖗𝖎𝖔𝖗's 𝖂𝖔𝖔𝖉.

	l.	s.	d.
Sold the Underwood to the feveral Perfons mention'd.	339	15	0
Sold the Timber-trees to the feveral Perfons mention'd	926	8	0
Sold the Heads of the Trees to the feveral Perfons mention'd	123	2	0
Sold the Bark of the Trees to the feveral Perfons mention'd	349	0	10
Total Amount for Underwood, Timber, Heads and Bark-	1738	5	10

An

An ACCOMPT *of*

Disburſements *or* Out-goings,

From the Four ſeveral Manors of G, H, I, K, *in the County of* H, *paid by* A. B. *Steward to His Grace the Duke of* K.

(for one whole Year)
From *Lady-day* 1725, *to Lady-day* 1726.

N.B. Every Steward that is curious ſhou'd take particular Care to have *all* his Bills and Vouchers drawn out upon a ſheet or half-ſheet of Paper, according to the bigneſs of the Bill, and to fold them *all* up *exactly* of an equal Bigneſs, and to *indorſe* them on the back-ſide, and alſo to number 'em as to anſwer the Nº in the following Disburſements, in the firſt Column. The being exact in this, will make eaſy the examining all ſorts of Accompts.

An Account of Disbursements for the Land-Tax.

Nᵒ		l.	s.	d.
1	Paid Mr. *John Collins*, Collector, for the four Quarterly Payments of the Land-Tax, from *Lady-day* 1725, to *Lady-day* 1726, for the Manor of *G*; as appears by his Receipts	17	0	0
2	Paid Mr. *John Collins*, Collector, for the four Quarterly Payments of the Land-Tax, from *Lady-day* 1725, to *Lady-day* 1726, for the Manor of *H*; as appears by his Receipts	27	0	0
3	Paid Mr *John Collins*, Collector, for the four Quarterly Payments of the Land-Tax, from *Lady-day* 1725, to *Lady-day* 1726, for the Manor of *I*; as appears by his Receipts	57	0	0
4	Paid Mr. *John Collins*, Collector, for the four Quarterly Payments of the Land Tax, from *Lady-day* 1725, to *Lady-day* 1726, for the Manor of *K*; as appears by his Receipts	30	0	0
	Total for the Land-Tax ——	131	0	0

Disbursements for the *Church*, *Poor*, and *Constable*'s Assessments for Lands in hand.

Nᵒ		l.	s.	d.
5	Paid *John Trolop*, Churchwarden, for four Quarterly Assessments for the *Church* from *Lady-day* 1725, to *Lady-day* 1726, for the Manor of *K*. House, Park, and Gardens and Woods in hand	4	10	0
6	Paid *Robert Hunt*, for four Quarterly Assessments for the *Poor*, from *Lady-day* 1725, to *Lady-day* 1726, for *ditto* Lands	5	10	0
7	Paid *Thomas Newton*, for 4 Quarterly Assessments for the *Constable* from *Lady-day* 1725, to *Lady-day* 1726, for *ditto* Lands ——	0	10	6
	Total for the Church, Poor, and Constable's Assessments	10	10	6

Disbursements for the Repairs of several Farm-Houses, by agreement at the time an Improvement in
the Manor of *K.* was made ; but for the future
there is to be no Allowance made on this account,
all the Tenants being oblig'd to build and repair
at their proper Cost and Charge, they being allow'd rough Timber and Stone to do the same.

N°		*l.*	*s.*	*d*
8	Paid *John Clark's* Bill for Masons Work done for *Robert Hunt*, Tenant for the Priory Farm, as appears by his Receipt	19	15	0
9	Paid *Robert Gefferson's* Bill for Carpenters Work done for *ditto Hunt* for *ditto* Farm, as appears by his Receipt ——	13	10	0
10	Paid *Thomas Clark's* Bill for Masons Work done for *John Scot*, Tenant for Eccleswall Farm, as appears by his Receipt	24	5	0
11	Paid *John Gregory's* Bill for Carpenters Work done for *ditto Scot* for *ditto* Farm-house, as appears by his Receipt	15	10	0
12	Paid *John Scarth's* Bill for Masons Work done for *John Hill's* Farm at the Castle, as appears by his Receipt	34	10	0
13	Paid *Robert Gefferson's* Bill for Carpenters Work done for *ditto Hill* at *ditto* Farm, as appears by his Receipt —	19	15	0
14	Paid *John Clark's* Bill for Masons Work done for *Richard Bland*, Tenant for Blake's Farm, as appears by his Receipt	17	0	0
15	Paid *Robert Gregory's* Bill for Carpenters Work done for *ditto Bland* for *ditto* Farm, as appears by his Receipt --	9	15	0
	Total for Repairs of Farm-Houses——	154	0	0

N.B. The Glazier's, *&c.* Bills were paid by the Tenants by agreement.

Disbursements for repairing and fitting up the Manor-house against the time Your Grace comes down to look into your Affairs.

[Done by Your Grace's Order.]

N°		*l.*	*s.*	*d.*
16	Paid *John Clark*'s Bill for Masons Work done by him in the several parts of the House, as appears by his Bill and Receipt	74	10	0
17	Paid *John Gregory*'s Bill for Carpenters Work done by him in several parts of the House, as appears by his Bill and Receipt	36	0	0
18	Paid *John Commins*'s Bill for Joyners Work done by him in several parts of the House, as appears by his Bill and Receipt	42	0	0
19	Paid *John Blunt*'s Bill for Bricklayers Work done by him in several parts of the House, as appears by his Bill and Receipt	19	10	0
20	Paid *Jonathan Cox*'s Bill for Glaziers Work done by him in several parts of the House, as appears by his Bill and Receipt	7	15	0
21	Paid *Jonathan Roberts*'s Bill for Plaisterers Work done by him in several parts of the House, as appears by his Bill and Receipt	7	10	0
	Total for Repairing the Manor-house——	187	5	0

N.B. The Bills for Furniture, and putting them up, were paid by the Groom of the Chambers, by your Grace's Order.

Disburfements for the Repairs and fitting up the Gardens.

[By your Grace's Order.]

		l.	s.	d.
N°				
22	PAid *John Blunt*'s Bill for Bricklayers Work done by him, in building a South-Eaft and South-Weft Wall, in order to plant the choiceft Fruit againft the fame, as appears by his Bill and Receipt	59	10	0
23	PAid *Nicholas Parker*'s Bill the Nurfery-man, for feveral forts of Fruit-Trees fent from *London*, as appears by his Bill and Receipt	23	18	0
24	PAid *John Gregory*'s Bill for Carpenters Work done by him in feveral parts of the Green-houfes, &c. and other Out-houfes belonging to the Garden, as appears by his Bill and Receipt	15	10	0
25	PAid *Jonathan Cox*'s Bill for Glaziers Work and Glafs done by him, for Glafs Frames for the Melon-ground, &c. as appears by his Bill and Receipt	8	17	0
26	PAid *John Wyld*'s Bill for Bell-glaffes for the ufe of the feveral parts of the Kitchen-garden, as appears by his Bill and Receipt	2	15	0
27	PAid *John Fletcher* the Gardener's Bill for feveral Garden-Tools which he bought ; alfo for feveral forts of Seeds he bought in *London*, and alfo for the feveral Labourers he employ'd in the Gardens, the Particulars of which may be feen in his Accompt, which I have examin'd	73	16	0
	Total for the Garden Account——	184	6	0

Disburfe-

Disbursements for the several forts of Work done in the Park.

No.		l.	s.	d.
28	Paid *John Gregory's* Bill for Carpenters Work done by him, in making Pales to divide the Park into 3 parts, in order to *drive* the Park once a year, as appears by his Bill and Receipt —	175	0	0
29	Paid *John Lacy* the Park-keeper's Bill for the several *Labourers* he employ'd in doing odd Jobbs in the Park, and also for mowing and making Hay in the Park-bottoms for the use of the Deer and House; all which Particulars appears by his Bill, which I have examin'd — —	49	15	6
30	Paid *Robert Clay's* Bill for Smiths Work done by him, for making new Locks and Keys for the several Park-gates, as appears by his Bill and Receipt	3	15	0
31	Paid *John Gregory's* Bill for Carpenters Work done by him, for making 3 new Swing-gates for the Park, he finding Nails and other Iron-work, as appears by his Bill and Receipt — —	4	15	0
32	Paid *Tho. Bowman's* Bill for Work done by him in painting the 'foremention'd Gates and other Pales fronting the Manor house, as appears by his Bill and Receipt — —	6	18	0
	Total for the Park Account—	240	3	6

N.B. I might have enter'd more variety of Disbursements, but these are sufficient to shew the Method of being Particular in such Accounts. As for Arrears, I have taken no notice of, hoping the Industrious Steward will make it his Study, for his Lord's Interest, to prevent them.

Disburse-

Disbursements and Allowances for Salary and Servants-wages.	*l.*	*s.*	*d.*
N° 33 **P**Aid myself my year's Salary allow'd by Your Grace for collecting the Rents and riding over the whole Estate once a Month, to see that the Tenants perform their *Covenants*, and that they manage their Farms to the best advantage, for themselves as well as the Lord of the Manor ——— ———	150	0	0
34 **P**Aid Mrs. *Mary Chambers*, the House-keeper, her year's Wages, according to agreement with my Lady Dutchess	15	0	0
35 **P**Aid *Eliz. Cox*, one of the House-Maids, her yearly Wages, according to agreement with the House-keeper —	3	15	0
36 **P**Aid *Jane Long*, the other House-Maid and Dairy-Maid, her yearly Wages, according to agreement with the House-keeper ——— ——— ———	3	15	0
37 **P**Aid *John Fletcher* the Gardener his yearly Wages, according to agreement with your Grace ——— ———	15	0	0
38 **P**Aid *John Lacy*, the Park-keeper, his yearly Wages according to agreement with your Grace, besides the Perquisites of the Skins, Shoulders, Humbles, Fat, and Ten Shillings Fees for every Buck, and Five Shillings for every Doe kill'd out of the Park, that are sent as *Presents* to Country Gentlemen round ——— ———	5	0	0
Total for Servants Wages———	192	10	0

N.B. There are several other Disbursements relating to Board-wages, &c. that might have been enter'd, but these are sufficient to shew the Method of entering the several Kinds by themselves. The Bills and Vouchers are suppos'd to shew more Particulars, which are to be perused at the time of examining these Accounts.

An

An 𝕬𝖇𝖘𝖙𝖗𝖆𝖈𝖙; or, an 𝕬𝖈𝖈𝖔𝖒𝖕𝖙-𝕮𝖚𝖗𝖗𝖊𝖓𝖙 ſtat
going Particulars, in or

From *Lady-da*

A. B. *Steward to His Grace the Duke of* K——, 𝕯𝖊𝖇𝖙𝖔𝖗.	*l.*	*s.*	*d.*
R Eceiv'd the whole certain Rents from the four ſeveral Manors of *G, H, I, K*; as appears by the Rentals, *Page* 187. —— ——	3525	7	5
R Eceiv'd the Caſual Profits of Courts by Fines, Hariots, and Surrenders, as appears by that Accompt, *p.* 188, 189. ——	365	8	3
R Eceiv'd the Three Years Caſual Profits by the Tenants plowing up freſh Paſture-Land, as appears by that Accompt, *p.* 190.—	492	12	6
R Eceiv'd for the Sale of the Underwood, Timber-Trees, Heads and Bark in 𝕻𝖗𝖎𝖔𝖗'𝖘 𝖂𝖔𝖔𝖉 in the Manor of *K.* as appears by that Accompt *p.* 192, 193, 194, 195. ——	1738	5	10
Total of what I have receiv'd *L.*	6121	14	0

Debtor and *Creditor* from all the 'fore-
e exact Balance.
day 1726.

per Contra —— — — — —**Creditor.**	*l.*	*s.*	*d.*
PAid the four Quarterly Payments of the Land-Tax for the Manors of *G, H, I, K*; as appears by that Accompt, *Page* 198. ——	131	0	0
PAid the four Quarterly Assessments for the *Church, Poor,* and *Constable,* for the Manor of *K.* House, Park, and Gardens, and Woods kept in hand ; as appears by that Accompt, *p.* 198.	10	10	6
PAid the several Bills for the Repairs of the several Farm-houses by agreement, as appears by that Accompt, *p.* 199.	154	0	0
PAid the several Bills for repairing and fitting up the Manor-House against the time your Grace comes down to look into your Affairs ; done by your Grace's Order, *p.* 200.	187	5	0
PAid the several Bills for the Repairs and fitting up the Gardens, by your Grace's Order, *p.* 201.	184	6	0
PAid the several Bills for the several sorts of Work done in the Park, as appears by those Accompts, *p.* 202.	240	3	6
PAid the several Servants-wages, as appears by that Accompt and Vouchers, *p.* 203.	192	10	0
Total Disbursements——	1099	15	0
REturn'd and paid to *Francis Child* Esq; your Grace's Banker, by several Bills, as will appear by his Accompt, to balance this whole Year's Accompt from *Lady-day* 1725, to *Lady-day* 1726.	5021	19	0
Total of what I have paid L.	6121	14	0

This is a True Accompt, (Errors excepted) witness my Hand,

A B.

A Particular Account of the

Prices of the feveral Artificers Works,

Which relate to

Ordinary Buildings, and the Repairs
of Farm-Houfes, Mills, &c.

A L S O

The Prices of the feveral forts of *Works* relating to *Husbandry*, computed according
to *Labourers Wages* in moft Parts of the
North, at Twelve-pence a Day in *Summer*,
and Nine-pence in the *Winter*.

N.B. As Labourers Wages are fomething more in the
South of *England*, and fomething lefs in the more
Northern Parts, fo 'tis eafy for every Steward to
adjuft a Price in proportion to Labourers Wages in
the feveral Parts.

Alfo if any new fort of Work is to be done, not mention'd
in the following Particulars, the Steward's beft way
is to hire a good Labourer, and to ftand by him the
whole Day, to fee that he does a good Day's-Work,
and then to meafure the fame, in order to know what
it is worth.

The Prices of Ordinary Buildings, and Repairs of Farm-Houses *in the* Northern Parts *of* England.

N.B. A Rod is fuppos'd to contain 21 foot in length, which is the Dimenfions in moft parts of the *North* ; but if in other parts of *England* the cuftomary Rod fhou'd be more or lefs, then the Rule of Proportion muft be ufed.

'Tis alfo fuppos'd that all Materials are found, and laid at hand for the Workmen, (except the Glazier's) which is *much* the beft way, becaufe the Workmen fometimes are apt to *impofe*, and ufe bad Materials.

Mafons Work.

Hammer'd Double-walling 22 **Inches** thick, of middling Freeftone, containing a Rod in length, and 3 Foot high, which is called a Rod of *Mafons Work*, may be done for 5 *s.* 6 *d.*

Coarfe Flagging of the 'foremention'd Stone, being rough hammer'd, may be done for 1 *s.* 4 *d.* a fuperficial Yard.

3

Door-

Door-Jaumes and Window-Jaumes, of Hewn-work of the 'foremention'd Stone, may be done for 3 *d.* a superficial Foot.

The Price for carrying up Chimneys is conformable to the height of the Building; which, if of a middling height, may be done for about 5 *s.* a Story for each Chimney, and 3 *d.* a Foot for the Chimney-tops of hewn Stone.

Paving-work of Flint or Pebble-stones for Stables or Court-yards, *&c.* may be done for 2 *d.* half-penny a superficial Yard.

Bricklayers Work.

WAlls of a Brick in length may be done for 2 *s.* a Rod.

Walls of a Brick and half may be done for 2 *s.* 10 *d.* a Rod.

P   Partition-

Partition-Walls a Brick in breadth, which often are ufed in low Houfes, may be done for 1 *s.* 6 *d.* a Rod.

Lathing, Tyling, and pointing the Tyles, may be done for 6 *d.* a Rod.

Plaiftering the infides of Brick or Stone-walls with Lime and Hair, two Coats, the one coarfe, the other fine, may be done for 2 *d.* a Yard; but if plaifter'd with three Coats, the Price is 3 *d.* a Yard.

Lathing and Plaiftering for Ceiling-Stair-cafes may be done for 4 *d.* a Yard.

N.B. Seven hundred Bricks will make a Rod of Walling of a Brick thick; and fo in proportion for every thicknefs.

In digging Foundations, the Price is according to the nature of the Earth : If upon a Rock, it will coft 6 *d.* a folid Yard ; but if upon a Clay or other light Soil, it may be done for 4 *d.* a folid Yard.

Car-

Carpenters Work.

ROofing for plain Tyling, may be done for 6 ſhillings a Square, *i. e.* One hundred ſquare Feet.

Flooring with Joyce and Dorments ; and laying the Floors, which is call'd Double Meaſure, may be done for 12 ſhillings a Square.

Single Poſts and Rails for ſecuring Quick-wood, may be done for 4 *d.* a Rod running meaſure.

Plain Wainſcotting, and making Doors and Windows, may be done for 1 *s.* 6 *d.* a ſuperficial Yard.

Park-paling eight foot high, with Poſts and three Rails, may be done for 12 *d.* a Yard running meaſure, or 7 *s.* a Rod.

Gla-

Glaziers Work.

COmmon Windows (with *Newcastle* or *Sunderland* Glaſs) the Glazier finding Glaſs, Lead, and *all* other Materials, may be done for 5 *d.* a Foot.

Millwrights Work.

BEcauſe *over-ſhot* Water-Mills are be-come moſt general, (eſpecially in the Northern parts of *England*) and indeed do the leaſt hurt to the Publick, (as they are generally placed) I ſhall in the firſt place give the Prices as perform'd by Mr. *Ralph Fowler*, Millwright to the Right Honoura-ble the Earl of *Carliſle*, at *Caſtle-Howard*

in

in *Yorkſhire.* If other Noblemen or Gentlemen are pleas'd to employ him, I am ſatis-
fied they will be faithfully ſerv'd at reaſonable Rates.

For making a Water-wheel, 4 pounds.
For making a Cogg-wheel, 2 pounds.
For making the Axletree, 1 pound.
For Flooring a pair of new Mill-ſtones,
   2 pounds.

N.B. I have given theſe Particulars in caſe of Repairs,
where any one is wanting to be made new.

An *over-ſhot* Water-Mill (and making all
the Utenſils belonging) which takes water
about the Centre of the Axletree, may be
built for about 25 pounds, for the Millwright's Work only: As for the Roofing,
&c. which comes under the head of Car-
penters and Maſons work, 'tis already given
in the 'foregoing Pages.

A *Windmill* (with all the Utenſils belonging) for grinding Corn may be made

P 3   for

for about 30 pounds, for the Millwright's
Work only.

An *Horſe-Mill* for grinding Malt and
ſhelling Oats may be made for about 8
pounds for the Millwright's work only.

Becauſe the *blue* Stones from *Holland* are
become moſt general, they being *cheaper*,
on the account of laſting 40 or 50 years, I
ſhall give the Prices as they are commonly
ſold at the Sea-ſide upon the *Northern*
Coaſts, according to the ſeveral Dimenſions
following.

Inches diameter.	Inches thick.	*l.*	*s.*	*d.*	
54	15	at 20 :	0 :	0	a pair.
48	14	at 15 :	0 :	0	a pair.
46 and	13	at 11 :	10 :	0	a pair.
44	13	at 10 :	10 :	0	a pair.
40	12	at 8 :	10 :	0	a pair.

For the ſake of ſuch as are not willing to
go to the Price of the abovemention'd *blue*
Stones, it may not be amiſs to give the Prices of the *grey* Stones, as they are ſold at
Bautry

Bautry in *York-fhire*, according to the feveral Dimenfions following.

		l.	*s.*	*d.*	
20 hands diameter— at		11	: 10	: 0	a pair.
19 ditto ——— — at		10	: 0	: 0	a pair.
18 ditto ——— — at		9	: 0	: 0	a pair.
17 ditto ——— —— at		8	: 0	: 0	a pair.
16 ditto ——— —— at		7	: 0	: 0	a pair.
15 ditto —— — — at		6	: 0	: 0	a pair.
14 ditto — — — at		5	: 0	: 0	a pair.

N.B. The Hand is $3\frac{5}{8}$ Inches.

Works relating to Husbandry.

HEdging, Ditching, and planting double Rows of white-Thorn Quickfetts,
may be done for 3 pence a Rod running
meafure.

> *N.B.* 150 Plants will plant a Rod, which will coft about
> 4 Shillings a Thoufand, if rais'd from Berries, which
> are much the beft.

P 4   For

For plaſhing a Hedge in the beſt manner, and alſo ditching along the ſame, may be done for 7 *d.* a Rod.

For digging a Ditch ten foot wide at top, and ſix foot wide at the bottom, and four foot deep, (which Dimenſions is commonly practiſ'd in the Marſhes and Fenns) 2 *s.* a Rod.

Plowing the firſt time on a ſtiff Clay Stubble, may be done for 3 *s.* 6 *d.* an Acre.
Plowing the ſecond time the 'foreſaid Land at 2 *s.* 9 *d.* an Acre.
Plowing, harrowing, and ſowing the third time the 'foreſaid Land, at 3 *s.* 9 *d.* an Acre.

Plowing the firſt time on a light gravelly Soil, at 2 *s.* 9 *d. per* Acre.
Plowing the ſecond time of the 'foreſaid Land, at 2 *s.* 4 *d.* an Acre.
Plowing, harrowing, and ſowing the third time on the aforeſaid Lands, at 3 *s. per* Acre.

Plow-

Plowing the firſt time on a light ſandy Soil at 2 *s.* an Acre.

Plowing the ſecond time on the afore-ſaid Lands, at 1 *s.* 10 *d.* an Acre.

Plowing, harrowing, and ſowing the third time on *ditto* Lands, at 2 *s.* 6 *d.* an Acre.

Reaping and binding of Wheat and Rye, may be done for 4 *s.* an Acre.

Mowing of Barley, Oates, and cocking, and raking with a Sweath-rake, at 3 *s. per* Acre.

Mowing, raking, and cocking of Hay in Meadows where 'tis pretty rank, at 3 *s.* an Acre.

Mowing, raking, and cocking of Hay in Uplands, where 'tis pretty thin, at 2 *s.* 6 *d.* an Acre.

Thraſh-

Thrashing and winnowing of *Wheat* or *Rye* may be done for 2 *s.* 8 *d.* a quarter.

Thrashing and winnowing of *Barley*, at 1 *s.* 10 *d.* a quarter.

Thrashing and winnowing of *Oates*, at 1 *s.* 6 *d.* a quarter.

Thrashing and winnowing of *Beans* and *Pease*, at 2 *s.* a quarter.

A

A

New and Concise Table

OF THE

Solid Measure of *Timber*, *Stone*, &c. ready caft up in Feet and Tenths of a Foot, to the greateft exactnefs poffible in the firft place of DECIMALS, anfwering to every half-Inch from 3 Inches to 75, for the fourth part of the Girt, (which in Round Timber is cuftomarily taken as a Side of the Square) and from 1 Foot to 40 in length; withan Explanation of its Ufe in feveral Cafes, fhewing how to take readily the Quantity anfwering to any length of Feet, and Tenths of a Foot, under 41 Foot long: Very eafy to be underftood by any Perfon the leaft converfant in Numbers.

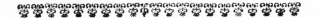

The Explanation and Use of the following Table.

CASE I. THere is a piece of round Timber, whose 4th part of the Girt is 18 Inches, and length 32 Feet : Look for 18 in the top Column, under which, even with 32 in the left-hand Column, is 72 Feet for the solid Content.

> *N.B.* If it had been squared Timber of 18 Inches each side, the Solution would be the Geometrical Truth. *Note also*, This first Case is agreeable to the Custom of general Use in measuring Timber, *viz.* to reckon the Length only to even Feet, and to half an Inch in the 4th part of the Girt, and the Quantity but to a quarter of a Foot; therefore to have this Table answer thereto, 1 or 2 in the Tenths place may be neglected, 3 or 4 may be express'd $\frac{1}{4}$; 5, 6, or 7, $\frac{1}{2}$; and 8 or 9, $\frac{3}{4}$ of a Foot: But for such as would be more exact, I proceed.

CASE II. There is a piece of Timber whose fourth part of the Girt is 18 Inches, and length 32.4 Feet ; then look, as above, for the quantity answering 32 Foot long, but for the .4 equal to $\frac{4}{10}$ of a Foot look down in the same 18 inches Column for the quantity even with 4 in the left-hand Column, which you will find to be 9 feet, but must

be

be made .9 equal to $\frac{9}{10}$ of a folid foot, which in this Cafe may be placed thus:

32.0 Feet in length is —— ——72.0
.4 equal to $\frac{4}{10}$ of a Foot is   .9 } folid Feet.
————————————
32.4 equal to 32 $\frac{4}{10}$ Feet is—72.9

72	.0
72	.9
141	.9
630	.1
144	.0
204	.0
226	.9
592	.1
2083	.9

N.B. That thofe who do not underftand *Decimal Fractions* in general, may underftand thofe in this Table, I think proper not only to mention, that any Figure placed on the right hand of a Point denotes it to be Tenths of an Integer, as .1 is $\frac{1}{10}$, .2 is $\frac{2}{10}$, *&c.* therefore .9 added to 72 Feet, will be 72.9, equal to $72\frac{9}{10}$ Feet; but alfo to place in the Margin the Solutions of thefe feveral Cafes, with their Sum-Total, as a Specimen to fhew the manner of their Addition, which is the fame as whole Numbers.

CASE III. There is a piece of Timber to be meafur'd of 37 foot long, which is taper, (*i. e.* bigger at one end than the other) the Cuftom is to take the Girt at the middle; then look as before in the top Column for $\frac{1}{4}$ of the Girt, which fuppofe $23\frac{1}{4}$ inches, and below, even with 37, is 141.9 folid feet for the quantity.

N.B. This Table is continued to fo great a fpace for one fourth of the Girt, that the quantity of *Stone* or *Marble-blocks* (which are often very large) may be taken out at once, they being generally hewn out in the rough not much differing in form from a piece of fquared Tim-ber;

ber; and if a Stone or Marble-block should be in form of a *Parallelopipedon*, 'tis customary to take a Mean between the Dimension of the two Sides, as a Side of the Square, whereby the quantity is given near enough, unless the two Sides are much different from one another.

CASE IV. There is a Stone or Marble-block in form of a *Parallelopipedon*, whose one side is 69, t'other 73 inches, and 18 foot long; to find the mean side add 69 and 73 together, the sum is 142, half whereof is the mean side, *viz.* 71, which look for in the top Column, and below even with 18 the length in feet is 630.1 feet for the quantity, which differs *little* from the truth.

CASE V. There is a Stone or Marble-block in form of a *Parallelopipedon*, whose one side is 24, t'other 72 inches, and 12 foot long; here the mean side would be 48, under which even with 12 is 192 feet for the quantity, which is a deal too much.

N.B. In this Case it is necessary to enquire how many times 24 is in 72, which being 3 times, it may be suppos'd three Stones of 24 inches for a Side of the Square, and 12 foot long; or else one Stone of 3 times that length, (*i.e.* 36 foot long) whose quantity is but 144 feet.

CASE

CASE VI. There is a Stone or Marble-block in form of a *Parallelopipedon*, whose one side is 23, t'other 75 inches, and length 17 feet; here a third part of 75 is 25, and the mean between 23 and 25 is 24, which must be taken, and the Stone counted 3 Stones; then under 24, even with 17, is 68 feet for quantity of each, which *multiplied* by 3, make 204 for the whole.

CASE VII. There is a Stone or Marble-block in form of a *Parallelopipedon*, whose one side is 36, t'other 60 inches, and 15 foot long; here half 60 is 30, and a Mean between 30 and 36 is 33, which may be taken, and the length suppos'd double, *viz.* 30 feet; then under 33, even with 30, is 226.9 feet for quantity.

> *N.B.* The best way in this Case would be to suppose it one Stone of 60 inches for a side of the Square, and thrice 36 inches long, *viz.* 9 feet, because 60 inches measures at thrice exactly 15 feet; thus the quantity would be but 225 feet, which is the Geometrical Truth.

CASE VIII. There is a Stone whose every side is unequal, or it may be near to round; the Custom is to gird it as Timber, and

and take a 4th of it, which fuppofe 73 inches, and length·16 feet; under 73, even with the length, is 592.1 feet the quantity.

N.B. In meafuring *Timber*, *Stone*, &c. 'tis convenient to have a ten-foot Rod in 2 parts, which can flide into 5 Feet, divided into Feet and Tenths throughout; but in meafuring Timber ftanding, 'tis fufficient to have a very long Pole divided into Feet only (befide a pocket Foot-Rule divided into Inches) and a Ladder to get up with readily, to meafure the Girt of the Tree at the middle height to which it runs Timber; and if the Tree to be meafur'd is an old thick-bark'd Tree, fomething confiderable muft be abated in a fourth part of the Girt for the Bark; but in young growing Timber half an Inch may be fufficient.

The

Len. in Feet.	The Fourth part of the Girt in Inches.									
	3	3½	4	4½	5	5½	6	6½	7	7½
1	.1	.1	.1	.1	.2	.2	.3	.3	.5	.4
2	.1	.2	.2	.3	.3	.4	.5	.6	.7	.8
3	.2	.3	.3	.4	.5	.6	.8	.9	1.0	1.2
4	.3	.3	.4	.6	.7	.8	1.0	1.2	1.4	1.6
5	.3	.4	.6	.7	.9	1.1	1.3	1.5	1.7	2.0
6	.4	.5	.7	.8	1.0	1.3	1.5	1.8	2.0	2.3
7	.4	.6	.8	1.0	1.2	1.5	1.8	2.1	2.4	2.7
8	.5	.7	.9	1.1	1.4	1.7	2.0	2.3	2.7	3.1
9	.6	.8	1.0	1.3	1.6	1.9	2.3	2.6	3.1	3.5
10	.6	.9	1.1	1.4	1.7	2.1	2.5	2.9	3.4	3.9
11	.7	.9	1.2	1.5	1.9	2.3	2.8	3.2	3.7	4.3
12	.8	1.0	1.3	1.7	2.1	2.5	3.0	3.5	4.1	4.7
13	.8	1.1	1.4	1.8	2.3	2.7	3.3	3.8	4.4	5.1
14	.9	1.2	1.6	2.0	2.4	2.9	3.5	4.1	4.8	5.5
15	.9	1.3	1.7	2.1	2.6	3.2	3.8	4.4	5.1	5.9
16	1.0	1.4	1.8	2.3	2.8	3.4	4.0	4.7	5.4	6.3
17	1.1	1.4	1.9	2.4	3.0	3.6	4.3	5.0	5.8	6.6
18	1.1	1.5	2.0	2.5	3.1	3.8	4.5	5.3	6.1	7.0
19	1.2	1.6	2.1	2.7	3.3	4.0	4.8	5.6	6.5	7.4
20	1.3	1.7	2.2	2.8	3.5	4.2	5.0	5.9	6.8	7.8
21	1.3	1.8	2.3	3.0	3.6	4.4	5.3	6.2	7.1	8.2
22	1.4	1.9	2.4	3.1	3.8	4.6	5.5	6.5	7.5	8.6
23	1.4	2.0	2.6	3.2	4.0	4.8	5.8	6.7	7.8	9.0
24	1.5	2.0	2.7	3.4	4.2	5.0	6.0	7.0	8.2	9.4
25	1.6	2.1	2.8	3.5	4.3	5.3	6.3	7.3	8.5	9.8
26	1.6	2.2	2.9	3.7	4.5	5.5	6.5	7.6	8.8	10.2
27	1.7	2.3	3.0	3.8	4.7	5.7	6.8	7.9	9.2	10.5
28	1.8	2.4	3.1	3.9	4.9	5.9	7.0	8.2	9.5	10.9
29	1.8	2.5	3.2	4.1	5.0	6.1	7.3	8.5	9.9	11.3
30	1.9	2.6	3.3	4.2	5.2	6.3	7.5	8.8	10.2	11.7
31	1.9	2.6	3.4	4.4	5.4	6.5	7.8	9.1	10.5	12.1
32	2.0	2.7	3.6	4.5	5.6	6.7	8.0	9.4	10.9	12.5
33	2.1	2.8	3.7	4.6	5.7	6.9	8.3	9.7	11.2	12.9
34	2.1	2.9	3.8	4.8	5.9	7.1	8.5	10.0	11.6	13.3
35	2.2	3.0	3.9	4.9	6.1	7.4	8.8	10.3	11.9	13.7
36	2.3	3.1	4.0	5.1	6.3	7.6	9.0	10.6	12.3	14.1
37	2.3	3.1	4.1	5.2	6.4	7.8	9.3	10.9	12.6	14.5
38	2.4	3.2	4.2	5.3	6.6	8.0	9.5	11.1	12.9	14.8
39	2.4	3.3	4.3	5.5	6.8	8.2	9.8	11.4	13.3	15.2
40	2.5	3.4	4.4	5.6	6.9	8.4	10.0	11.7	13.6	15.6

Q

Len. in Feet.	8	8½	9	9½	10	10½	11	11½	12
	\multicolumn{9}{c}{The Fourth part of the Girt in Inches.}								
1	.4	.5	.6	.6	.7	.8	.8	.9	1 .0
2	.9	1 .0	1 .1	1 .3	1 .4	1 .5	1 .7	1 .8	2 .0
3	1 .3	1 .5	1 .7	1 .9	2 .1	2 .3	2 .5	2 .8	3 .0
4	1 .8	2 .0	2 .3	2 .5	2 .8	3 .1	3 .4	3 .7	4 .0
5	2 .2	2 .5	2 .8	3 .1	3 .5	3 .8	4 .2	4 .6	5 .0
6	2 .7	3 .0	3 .4	3 .8	4 .2	4 .6	5 .0	5 .5	6 .0
7	3 .1	3 .5	3 .9	4 .4	4 .9	5 .4	5 .9	6 .4	7 .0
8	3 .6	4 .0	4 .5	5 .0	5 .6	6 .1	6 .7	7 .3	8 .0
9	4 .0	4 .5	5 .1	5 .6	6 .3	6 .9	7 .6	8 .3	9 .0
10	4 .4	5 .0	5 .6	6 .3	6 .9	7 .7	8 .4	9 .2	10 .0
11	4 .9	5 .5	6 .2	6 .9	7 .6	8 .4	9 .2	10 .1	11 .0
12	5 .3	6 .0	6 .8	7 .5	8 .3	9 .2	10 .1	11 .0	12 .0
13	5 .8	6 .5	7 .3	8 .1	9 .0	10 .0	10 .9	11 .9	13 .0
14	6 .2	7 .0	7 .9	8 .8	9 .7	10 .7	11 .8	12 .9	14 .0
15	6 .7	7 .5	8 .4	9 .4	10 .4	11 .5	12 .6	13 .8	15 .0
16	7 .1	8 .0	9 .0	10 .0	11 .1	12 .3	13 .4	14 .7	16 .0
17	7 .6	8 .5	9 .6	10 .6	11 .8	13 .0	14 .3	15 .6	17 .0
18	8 .0	9 .0	10 .1	11 .3	12 .5	13 .8	15 .1	16 .5	18 .0
19	8 .4	9 .5	10 .7	11 .9	13 .2	14 .5	16 .0	17 .4	19 .0
20	8 .9	10 .0	11 .3	12 .5	13 .9	15 .3	16 .8	18 .4	20 .0
21	9 .3	10 .5	11 .8	13 .2	14 .6	16 .1	17 .6	19 .3	21 .0
22	9 .8	11 .0	12 .4	13 .8	15 .3	16 .8	18 .5	20 .2	22 .0
23	10 .2	11 .5	12 .9	14 .4	16 .0	17 .6	19 .3	21 .1	23 .0
24	10 .7	12 .0	13 .5	15 .0	16 .7	18 .4	20 .2	22 .0	24 .0
25	11 .1	12 .5	14 .1	15 .7	17 .4	19 .1	21 .0	23 .0	25 .0
26	11 .6	13 .0	14 .6	16 .3	18 .1	19 .9	21 .8	23 .9	26 .0
27	12 .0	13 .5	15 .2	16 .9	18 .8	20 .7	22 .7	24 .8	27 .0
28	12 .4	14 .0	15 .8	17 .5	19 .4	21 .4	23 .5	25 .7	28 .0
29	12 .9	14 .6	16 .3	18 .2	20 .1	22 .2	24 .4	26 .6	29 .0
30	13 .3	15 .1	16 .9	18 .8	20 .8	23 .0	25 .2	27 .6	30 .0
31	13 .8	15 .6	17 .4	19 .4	21 .5	23 .7	26 .0	28 .5	31 .0
32	14 .2	16 .1	18 .0	20 .1	22 .2	24 .5	26 .9	29 .4	32 .0
33	14 .7	16 .6	18 .6	20 .7	22 .9	25 .3	27 .7	30 .3	33 .0
34	15 .1	17 .1	19 .1	21 .3	23 .6	26 .0	28 .6	31 .2	34 .0
35	15 .6	17 .6	19 .7	21 .9	24 .3	26 .8	29 .4	32 .1	35 .0
36	16 .0	18 .1	20 .3	22 .6	25 .0	27 .6	30 .3	33 .1	36 .0
37	16 .4	18 .6	20 .8	23 .2	25 .7	28 .3	31 .1	34 .0	37 .0
38	16 .9	19 .1	21 .4	23 .8	26 .4	29 .1	31 .9	34 .9	38 .0
39	17 .3	19 .6	21 .9	24 .4	27 .1	29 .9	32 .8	35 .8	39 .0
40	17 .8	20 .1	22 .5	25 .1	27 .8	30 .6	33 .6	36 .7	40 .0

Len. in Feet.	The Fourth part of the Girt in Inches.								
	12½	13	13½	14	14½	15	15½	16	16½
1	1 .1	1 .2	1 .3	1 .4	1 .5	1 .6	1 .7	1 .8	1 .9
2	2 .2	2 .3	2 .5	2 .7	2 .9	3 .1	3 .3	3 .6	3 .8
3	3 .3	3 .5	3 .8	4 .1	4 .4	4 .7	5 .0	5 .3	5 .7
4	4 .3	4 .7	5 .1	5 .4	5 .8	6 .3	6 .7	7 .1	7 .6
5	5 .4	5 .9	6 .3	6 .8	7 .3	7 .8	8 .3	8 .9	9 .5
6	6 .5	7 .0	7 .6	8 .2	8 .8	9 .4	10 .0	10 .7	11 .3
7	7 .6	8 .2	8 .9	9 .5	10 .2	10 .9	11 .7	12 .4	13 .2
8	8 .7	9 .4	10 .1	10 .9	11 .7	12 .5	13 .3	14 .2	15 .1
9	9 .8	10 .6	11 .4	12 .3	13 .1	14 .1	15 .0	16 .0	17 .0
10	10 .9	11 .7	12 .7	13 .6	14 .6	15 .6	16 .7	17 .8	18 .9
11	11 .9	12 .9	13 .9	15 .0	16 .1	17 .2	18 .4	19 .6	20 .8
12	13 .0	14 .1	15 .2	16 .3	17 .5	18 .8	20 .0	21 .3	22 .7
13	14 .1	15 .3	16 .5	17 .7	19 .0	20 .3	21 .7	23 .1	24 .6
14	15 .2	16 .4	17 .7	19 .1	20 .4	21 .9	23 .4	24 .9	26 .5
15	16 .3	17 .6	19 .0	20 .4	21 .9	23 .4	25 .0	26 .7	28 .4
16	17 .4	18 .8	20 .3	21 .8	23 .4	25 .0	26 .7	28 .4	30 .3
17	18 .4	20 .0	21 .5	23 .1	24 .8	26 .6	28 .4	30 .2	32 .1
18	19 .5	21 .1	22 .8	24 .5	26 .3	28 .1	30 .0	32 .0	34 .0
19	20 .6	22 .3	24 .0	25 .9	27 .7	29 .7	31 .7	33 .8	35 .9
20	21 .7	23 .5	25 .3	27 .2	29 .2	31 .3	33 .4	35 .6	37 .8
21	22 .8	24 .6	26 .6	28 .6	30 .7	32 .8	35 .0	37 .3	39 .7
22	23 .9	25 .8	27 .8	29 .9	32 .1	34 .4	36 .7	39 .1	41 .6
23	25 .0	27 .0	29 .1	31 .3	33 .6	35 .9	38 .4	40 .9	43 .5
24	26 .0	28 .2	30 .4	32 .7	35 .0	37 .5	40 .0	42 .7	45 .4
25	27 .1	29 .3	31 .6	34 .0	36 .5	39 .1	41 .7	44 .4	47 .3
26	28 .2	30 .5	32 .9	35 .4	38 .0	40 .6	43 .4	46 .2	49 .2
27	29 .3	31 .7	34 .2	36 .8	39 .4	42 .2	45 .0	48 .0	51 .0
28	30 .4	32 .9	35 .4	38 .1	40 .9	43 .8	46 .7	49 .8	52 .9
29	31 .5	34 .0	36 .7	39 .5	42 .3	45 .3	48 .4	51 .6	54 .8
30	32 .6	35 .2	38 .0	40 .8	43 .8	46 .9	50 .1	53 .3	56 .7
31	33 .6	36 .4	39 .2	42 .2	45 .3	48 .4	51 .7	55 .1	58 .6
32	34 .7	37 .6	40 .5	43 .6	46 .7	50 .0	53 .4	56 .9	60 .5
33	35 .8	38 .7	41 .8	44 .9	48 .2	51 .6	55 .1	58 .7	62 .4
34	36 .9	39 .9	43 .0	46 .3	49 .6	53 .1	56 .7	60 .4	64 .3
35	38 .0	41 .1	44 .3	47 .6	51 .1	54 .7	58 .4	62 .2	66 .2
36	39 .1	42 .3	45 .6	49 .0	52 .6	56 .3	60 .1	64 .0	68 .1
37	40 .1	43 .4	46 .8	50 .4	54 .0	57 .8	61 .7	65 .8	70 .0
38	41 .2	44 .6	48 .1	51 .7	55 .5	59 .4	63 .4	67 .6	71 .8
39	42 .3	45 .8	49 .4	53 .1	56 .9	60 .9	65 .1	69 .3	73 .7
40	43 .4	46 .9	50 .6	54 .4	58 .4	62 .5	66 .7	71 .1	75 .6

Len. in Feet	17	17½	18	18½	19	19½	20	20½
	The Fourth part of the Girt in Inches.							
1	2 .0	2 .1	2 .3	2 .4	2 .5	2 .6	2 .8	2 .9
2	4 .0	4 .3	4 .5	4 .8	5 .0	5 .3	5 .6	5 .8
3	6 .0	6 .4	6 .8	7 .1	7 .5	7 .9	8 .3	8 .8
4	8 .0	8 .5	9 .0	9 .5	10 .0	10 .6	11 .1	11 .7
5	10 .0	10 .6	11 .3	11 .9	12 .5	13 .2	13 .9	14 .6
6	12 .0	12 .8	13 .5	14 .3	15 .0	15 .8	16 .7	17 .5
7	14 .0	14 .9	15 .8	16 .6	17 .5	18 .5	19 .4	20 .4
8	16 .1	17 .0	18 .0	19 .0	20 .1	21 .1	22 .2	23 .3
9	18 .1	19 .1	20 .3	21 .4	22 .6	23 .8	25 .0	26 .3
10	20 .1	21 .3	22 .5	23 .8	25 .1	26 .4	27 .8	29 .2
11	22 .1	23 .4	24 .8	26 .1	27 .6	29 .0	30 .6	32 .1
12	24 .1	25 .5	27 .0	28 .5	30 .1	31 .7	33 .3	35 .0
13	26 .1	27 .6	29 .3	30 .9	32 .6	34 .3	36 .1	37 .9
14	28 .1	29 .8	31 .5	33 .3	35 .1	37 .0	38 .9	40 .9
15	30 .1	31 .9	33 .8	35 .7	37 .6	39 .6	41 .7	43 .8
16	32 .1	34 .0	36 .0	38 .0	40 .1	42 .3	44 .4	46 .7
17	34 .1	36 .2	38 .3	40 .4	42 .6	44 .9	47 .2	49 .6
18	36 .1	38 .3	40 .5	42 .8	45 .1	47 .5	50 .0	52 .5
19	38 .1	40 .4	42 .8	45 .2	47 .6	50 .2	52 .8	55 .4
20	40 .1	42 .5	45 .0	47 .5	50 .1	52 .8	55 .6	58 .4
21	42 .1	44 .7	47 .3	49 .9	52 .6	55 .5	58 .3	61 .3
22	44 .2	46 .8	49 .5	52 .3	55 .2	58 .1	61 .1	64 .2
23	46 .2	48 .9	51 .8	54 .7	57 .7	60 .7	63 .9	67 .1
24	48 .2	51 .0	54 .0	57 .0	60 .2	63 .4	66 .7	70 .0
25	50 .2	53 .2	56 .3	59 .4	62 .7	66 .0	69 .4	73 .0
26	52 .2	55 .3	58 .5	61 .8	65 .2	68 .7	72 .2	75 .9
27	54 .2	57 .4	60 .8	64 .2	67 .7	71 .3	75 .0	78 .8
28	56 .2	59 .5	63 .0	66 .5	70 .2	73 .9	77 .8	81 .7
29	58 .2	61 .7	65 .3	68 .9	72 .7	76 .6	80 .6	84 .6
30	60 .2	63 .8	67 .5	71 .3	75 .2	79 .2	83 .3	87 .6
31	62 .2	65 .9	69 .8	73 .7	77 .7	81 .9	86 .1	90 .5
32	64 .2	68 .1	72 .0	76 .1	80 .2	84 .5	88 .9	93 .4
33	66 .2	70 .2	74 .3	78 .4	82 .7	87 .1	91 .7	96 .3
34	68 2	72 .3	76 .5	80 .8	85 .2	89 .8	94 .4	99 .2
35	70 .2	74 .4	78 .8	83 .2	87 .7	92 .4	97 .2	102 .1
36	72 .3	76 .6	81 .0	85 .6	90 .3	95 .1	100 .0	105 .1
37	74 .3	78 .7	83 .3	87 .9	92 .8	97 .7	102 .8	108 .0
38	76 .3	80 .8	85 .5	90 .3	95 .3	100 .3	105 .6	110 .9
39	78 .3	82 .9	87 .8	92 .7	97 .8	103 .0	108 .3	113 .8
40	80 .3	85 .1	90 .0	95 .1	100 .3	105 .6	111 .1	116 .7

Len. in Feet.	The Fourth part of the Girt in Inches.							
	21	21½	22	22½	23	23½	24	24½
1	3 .1	3 .2	3 .4	3 .5	3 .7	3 .8	4 .0	4 .2
2	6 .1	6 .4	6 .7	7 .0	7 .3	7 .7	8 .0	8 .3
3	9 .2	9 .6	10 .1	10 .5	11 .0	11 .5	12 .0	12 .5
4	12 .3	12 .8	13 .4	14 .1	14 .7	15 .3	16 .0	16 .7
5	15 .3	16 .1	16 .8	17 .6	18 .4	19 .2	20 .0	20 .8
6	18 .4	19 .3	20 .2	21 .1	22 .0	23 .0	24 .0	25 .0
7	21 .4	22 .5	23 .5	24 .6	25 .7	26 .8	28 .0	29 .2
8	24 .5	25 .7	26 .9	28 .1	29 .4	30 .7	32 .0	33 .3
9	27 .6	28 .9	30 .3	31 .6	33 .1	34 .5	36 .0	37 .5
10	30 .6	32 .1	33 .6	35 .2	36 .7	38 .4	40 .0	41 .7
11	33 .7	35 .3	37 .0	38 .7	40 .4	42 .2	44 .0	45 .9
12	36 .8	38 .5	40 .3	42 .2	44 .1	46 .0	48 .0	50 .0
13	39 .8	41 .7	43 .7	45 .7	47 .8	49 .9	52 .0	54 .2
14	42 .9	44 .9	47 .1	49 .2	51 .4	53 .7	56 .0	58 .4
15	45 .9	48 .2	50 .4	52 .7	55 .1	57 .5	60 .0	62 .5
16	49 .0	51 .4	53 .8	56 .3	58 .8	61 .4	64 .0	66 .7
17	52 .1	54 .6	57 .1	59 .8	62 .5	65 .2	68 .0	70 .9
18	55 .1	57 .8	60 .5	63 .3	66 .1	69 .0	72 .0	75 .0
19	58 .2	61 .0	63 .9	66 .8	69 .8	72 .9	76 .0	79 .2
20	61 .3	64 .2	67 .2	70 .3	73 .5	76 .7	80 .0	83 .4
21	64 .3	67 .4	70 .6	73 .8	77 .1	80 .5	84 .0	87 .5
22	67 .4	70 .6	73 .9	77 .3	80 .8	84 .4	88 .0	91 .7
23	70 .4	73 .8	77 .3	80 .9	84 .5	88 .2	92 .0	95 .9
24	73 .5	77 .0	80 .7	84 .4	88 .2	92 .0	96 .0	100 .0
25	76 .6	80 .3	84 .0	87 .9	91 .8	95 .9	100 .0	104 .2
26	79 .6	83 .5	87 .4	91 .4	95 .5	99 .7	104 .0	108 .4
27	82 .7	86 .7	90 .8	94 .9	99 .2	103 .5	108 .0	112 .5
28	85 .8	89 .9	94 .1	98 .4	102 .9	107 .4	112 .0	116 .7
29	88 .8	93 .1	97 .5	102 .0	106 .5	111 .2	116 .0	120 .9
30	91 .9	96 .3	100 .8	105 .5	110 .2	115 .1	120 .0	125 .1
31	94 .9	99 .5	104 .2	109 .0	113 .9	118 .9	124 .0	129 .2
32	98 .0	102 .7	107 .6	112 .5	117 .6	122 .7	128 .0	133 .4
33	101 .1	105 .9	110 .9	116 .0	121 .2	126 .6	132 .0	137 .6
34	104 .1	109 .1	114 .3	119 .5	124 .9	130 .4	136 .0	141 .7
35	107 .2	112 .4	117 .6	123 .0	128 .6	134 .2	140 .0	145 .9
36	110 .3	115 .6	121 .0	126 .6	132 .3	138 .1	144 .0	150 .1
37	113 .3	118 .8	124 .4	130 .1	135 .9	141 .9	148 .0	154 .2
38	116 .4	122 .0	127 .7	133 .6	139 .6	145 .7	152 .0	158 .4
39	119 .4	125 .2	131 .1	137 .1	143 .3	149 .6	156 .0	162 .6
40	122 .5	128 .4	134 .4	140 .6	146 .9	153 .4	160 .0	166 .7

Len. in Feet	The Fourth part of the Girt in Inches.							
	25	25½	26	26½	27	27½	28	28½
1	4.3	4.5	4.7	4.9	5.1	5.3	5.4	5.6
2	8.7	9.0	9.4	9.8	10.1	10.5	10.9	11.3
3	13.0	13.5	14.1	14.6	15.2	15.8	16.3	16.9
4	17.4	18.1	18.8	19.5	20.3	21.0	21.8	22.6
5	21.7	22.6	23.5	24.4	25.3	26.3	27.2	28.2
6	26.0	27.1	28.2	29.3	30.4	31.5	32.7	33.8
7	30.4	31.6	32.9	34.1	35.4	36.8	38.1	39.4
8	34.7	36.1	37.6	39.0	40.5	42.0	43.6	45.1
9	39.1	40.6	42.3	43.9	45.6	47.3	49.0	50.8
10	43.4	45.2	46.9	48.8	50.6	52.5	54.4	56.4
11	47.7	49.7	51.6	53.6	55.7	57.8	59.9	62.0
12	52.1	54.2	56.3	58.5	60.8	63.0	65.3	67.7
13	56.4	58.7	61.0	63.4	65.8	68.3	70.8	73.3
14	60.8	63.2	65.7	68.3	70.9	73.5	76.2	79.0
15	65.1	67.7	70.4	73.2	75.9	78.8	81.7	84.6
16	69.4	72.3	75.1	78.0	81.0	84.0	87.1	90.3
17	73.8	76.8	79.8	82.9	86.1	89.3	92.6	95.9
18	78.1	81.3	84.5	87.8	91.1	94.5	98.0	101.5
19	82.5	85.8	89.2	92.7	96.2	99.8	103.4	107.2
20	86.8	90.3	93.9	97.5	101.3	105.0	108.9	112.8
21	91.1	94.8	98.6	102.4	106.3	110.3	114.3	118.5
22	95.5	99.3	103.3	107.3	111.4	115.5	119.8	124.1
23	99.8	103.9	108.0	112.2	116.4	120.8	125.2	129.7
24	104.2	108.4	112.7	117.0	121.5	126.0	130.7	135.4
25	108.5	112.9	117.4	121.9	126.6	131.3	136.1	141.0
26	112.8	117.4	122.1	126.8	131.6	136.5	141.6	146.7
27	117.2	121.9	126.8	131.7	136.7	141.8	147.0	152.3
28	121.5	126.4	131.4	136.5	141.8	147.0	152.4	157.9
29	125.9	131.0	136.1	141.4	146.8	152.3	157.9	163.6
30	130.2	135.5	140.8	146.3	151.9	157.6	163.3	169.2
31	134.5	140.0	145.5	151.2	156.9	162.8	168.8	174.9
32	138.9	144.5	150.2	156.1	162.0	168.1	174.2	180.5
33	143.2	149.0	154.9	160.9	167.1	173.3	179.7	186.1
34	147.6	153.5	159.6	165.8	172.1	178.6	185.1	191.8
35	151.9	158.0	164.3	170.7	177.2	183.8	190.6	197.4
36	156.3	162.6	169.0	175.6	182.3	189.1	196.0	203.1
37	160.6	167.1	173.7	180.4	187.3	194.3	201.4	208.7
38	164.9	171.6	178.4	185.3	192.4	199.6	206.9	214.3
39	169.3	176.1	183.1	190.2	197.4	204.8	212.3	220.0
40	173.6	180.6	187.8	195.1	202.5	210.1	217.8	225.6

Len. in Feet	The Fourth part of the Girt in Inches.							
	29	29½	30	30½	31	31½	32	32½
1	5.8	6.0	6.3	6.5	6.7	6.9	7.1	7.3
2	11.7	12.1	12.5	12.9	13.3	13.8	14.2	14.7
3	17.5	18.1	18.8	19.4	20.0	20.7	21.3	22.0
4	23.4	24.2	25.0	25.8	26.7	27.6	28.4	29.3
5	29.2	30.2	31.3	32.3	33.4	34.5	35.6	36.7
6	35.0	36.3	37.5	38.8	40.0	41.3	42.7	44.0
7	40.9	42.3	43.8	45.2	46.7	48.2	49.8	51.3
8	46.7	48.3	50.0	51.7	53.4	55.1	56.9	58.7
9	52.6	54.4	56.3	58.1	60.1	62.0	64.0	66.0
10	58.4	60.4	62.5	64.6	66.7	68.9	71.1	73.4
11	64.2	66.5	68.8	71.1	73.4	75.8	78.2	80.7
12	70.1	72.5	75.0	77.5	80.1	82.7	85.3	88.0
13	75.9	78.6	81.3	84.0	86.8	89.6	92.4	95.4
14	81.8	84.6	87.5	90.4	93.4	96.5	99.6	102.7
15	87.6	90.7	93.8	96.9	100.1	103.4	106.7	110.0
16	93.4	96.7	100.0	103.4	106.8	110.3	113.8	117.4
17	99.3	102.7	106.3	109.8	113.5	117.1	120.9	124.7
18	105.1	108.8	112.5	116.3	120.1	124.0	128.0	132.0
19	111.0	114.8	118.8	122.7	125.8	130.9	135.1	139.4
20	116.8	120.9	125.0	129.2	133.5	137.8	142.2	146.7
21	122.6	126.9	131.3	135.7	140.1	144.7	149.3	154.0
22	128.5	133.0	137.5	142.2	146.8	151.6	156.4	161.4
23	134.3	139.0	143.8	148.6	153.5	158.5	163.6	168.7
24	140.2	145.0	150.0	155.0	160.2	165.4	170.7	176.0
25	146.0	151.1	156.3	161.5	166.8	172.3	177.8	183.4
26	151.8	157.1	162.5	168.0	173.5	179.2	184.9	190.7
27	157.7	163.2	168.8	174.4	180.2	186.0	192.0	198.0
28	163.5	169.2	175.0	180.9	186.9	192.9	199.1	205.4
29	169.4	175.3	181.3	187.3	193.5	199.8	206.2	212.7
30	175.2	181.3	187.5	193.8	200.2	206.7	213.3	220.1
31	181.0	187.3	193.8	200.3	206.9	213.6	220.4	227.4
32	186.9	193.4	200.0	206.7	213.6	220.5	227.6	234.7
33	192.7	199.4	206.3	213.2	220.2	227.4	234.7	242.1
34	198.6	205.5	212.5	219.6	226.9	234.3	241.8	249.4
35	204.4	211.5	218.8	226.1	233.6	241.2	248.9	256.7
36	210.3	217.6	225.0	232.6	240.3	248.1	256.0	264.1
37	216.1	223.6	231.3	239.0	246.9	255.0	263.1	271.4
38	221.9	229.6	237.5	245.5	253.6	261.8	270.2	278.7
39	227.8	235.7	243.8	251.0	260.3	268.7	277.3	286.1
40	233.6	241.7	250.0	258.4	266.9	275.6	284.4	293.4

Len. in Feet	The Fourth part of the Girt in Inches.							
	33	33½	34	34½	35	35½	36	36½
1	7.6	7.8	8.0	8.3	8.5	8.8	9.0	9.3
2	15.1	15.6	16.1	16.5	17.0	17.5	18.0	18.5
3	22.7	23.4	24.1	24.8	25.5	26.3	27.0	27.8
4	30.3	31.2	32.1	33.1	34.0	35.0	36.0	37.0
5	37.8	39.0	40.1	41.3	42.5	43.8	45.0	46.3
6	45.4	46.8	48.2	49.6	51.0	52.5	54.0	55.5
7	52.9	54.6	56.2	57.9	59.5	61.3	63.0	64.8
8	60.5	62.3	64.2	66.1	68.1	70.0	72.0	74.0
9	68.1	70.1	72.3	74.4	76.6	78.8	81.9	83.3
10	75.6	77.9	80.3	82.7	85.1	87.5	90.0	92.5
11	83.2	85.7	88.3	90.9	93.6	96.3	99.0	101.8
12	90.8	93.5	96.3	99.2	102.1	105.0	108.0	111.0
13	98.3	101.3	104.4	107.5	110.6	113.8	117.0	120.3
14	105.9	109.1	112.4	115.7	119.1	122.5	126.0	129.5
15	113.4	116.9	120.4	124.0	127.6	131.3	135.0	138.8
16	121.0	124.7	128.4	132.3	136.1	140.0	144.0	148.0
17	128.6	132.5	136.5	140.5	144.6	148.8	153.0	157.3
18	136.1	140.3	144.5	148.8	153.1	157.5	162.0	166.5
19	143.7	148.1	152.5	157.0	161.6	166.3	171.0	175.8
20	151.2	155.9	160.6	165.3	170.1	175.0	180.0	185.0
21	158.8	163.7	168.6	173.6	178.6	183.8	189.0	194.3
22	166.4	171.5	176.6	181.8	187.2	192.5	198.0	203.5
23	173.9	179.2	184.6	190.1	195.7	201.3	207.0	212.8
24	181.5	187.0	192.7	198.4	204.2	210.0	216.0	222.0
25	189.1	194.8	200.7	206.6	212.7	218.8	225.0	231.3
26	196.6	202.6	208.7	214.9	221.2	227.5	234.0	240.5
27	204.2	210.4	216.8	223.2	229.7	236.3	243.0	249.8
28	211.8	218.2	224.8	231.4	238.2	245.0	252.0	259.0
29	219.3	226.0	232.8	239.7	246.7	253.8	261.0	268.3
30	226.9	233.8	240.8	248.0	255.2	262.6	270.0	277.6
31	234.4	241.6	248.9	256.2	263.7	271.3	279.0	286.8
32	242.0	249.4	256.9	264.5	272.2	280.1	288.0	296.1
33	249.6	257.2	264.9	272.8	280.7	288.8	297.0	305.3
34	257.1	265.0	272.9	281.0	289.2	297.6	306.0	314.6
35	264.7	272.8	281.0	289.3	297.7	306.3	315.0	323.8
36	272.3	280.6	289.0	297.6	306.3	315.1	324.0	333.1
37	279.8	288.4	297.0	305.8	314.8	323.8	333.0	342.3
38	287.4	296.1	305.1	314.1	323.3	332.6	342.0	351.6
39	294.9	303.9	313.1	322.4	331.8	341.3	351.0	360.8
40	302.5	311.7	321.1	330.6	340.3	350.1	360.0	370.1

Len. in Feet	The Fourth part of the Girt in Inches.							
	37	37½	38	38½	39	39½	40	40½
1	9.5	9.8	10.0	10.3	10.6	10.8	11.1	11.4
2	19.0	19.5	20.1	20.6	21.1	21.7	22.2	22.8
3	28.5	29.3	30.1	30.9	31.7	32.5	33.3	34.2
4	38.0	39.1	40.1	41.2	42.3	43.3	44.4	45.6
5	47.5	48.8	50.1	51.5	52.8	54.2	55.6	57.0
6	57.0	58.6	60.2	61.8	63.4	65.0	66.7	68.3
7	66.5	68.4	70.2	72.1	73.9	75.8	77.8	79.7
8	76.1	78.1	80.2	82.3	84.5	86.7	88.9	91.1
9	85.6	87.9	90.3	92.6	95.1	97.5	100.0	102.5
10	95.1	97.7	100.3	102.9	105.6	108.4	111.1	113.9
11	104.6	107.4	110.3	113.2	116.2	119.2	122.2	125.3
12	114.1	117.2	120.3	123.5	126.8	130.0	133.3	136.7
13	123.6	127.0	130.4	133.8	137.3	140.9	144.4	148.1
14	133.1	136.7	140.4	144.1	147.9	151.7	155.6	159.5
15	142.6	146.5	150.4	154.4	158.4	162.5	166.7	170.9
16	152.1	156.3	160.4	164.7	169.0	173.4	177.8	182.3
17	161.6	166.0	170.5	175.0	179.6	184.2	188.9	193.6
18	171.1	175.8	180.5	185.3	190.1	195.0	200.0	205.0
19	180.6	185.5	190.5	195.6	200.7	205.9	211.1	216.4
20	190.1	195.3	200.6	205.9	211.3	216.7	222.2	227.8
21	199.6	205.1	210.6	216.2	221.8	227.5	233.3	239.2
22	209.2	214.8	220.6	226.5	232.4	238.4	244.4	250.6
23	218.7	224.6	230.6	236.7	242.9	249.2	255.6	262.0
24	228.2	234.4	240.7	247.0	253.5	260.0	266.7	273.4
25	237.7	244.1	250.7	257.3	264.1	270.9	277.8	284.8
26	247.2	253.9	260.7	267.6	274.6	281.7	288.9	296.2
27	256.7	263.7	270.8	277.9	285.2	292.5	300.0	307.5
28	266.2	273.4	280.8	288.2	295.8	303.4	311.1	318.9
29	275.7	283.2	290.8	298.5	306.3	314.2	322.2	330.3
30	285.2	293.0	300.8	308.8	316.9	325.1	333.3	341.7
31	294.7	302.7	310.9	319.1	327.4	335.9	344.4	353.1
32	304.2	312.5	320.9	329.4	338.0	346.7	355.6	364.5
33	313.7	322.3	330.9	339.7	348.6	357.6	366.7	375.9
34	323.2	332.0	340.9	350.0	359.1	368.4	377.8	387.3
35	332.7	341.8	351.0	360.3	369.7	379.2	388.9	398.7
36	342.3	351.6	361.0	370.6	380.3	390.1	400.0	410.1
37	351.8	361.3	371.0	380.9	390.8	400.9	411.1	421.5
38	361.3	371.1	381.1	391.1	401.4	411.7	422.2	432.8
39	370.8	380.9	391.1	401.4	411.9	422.6	433.3	444.2
40	380.3	390.6	401.1	411.7	422.5	433.4	444.4	455.6

Len. in Feet	The Fourth part of the Girt in Inches.							
	41	41½	42	42½	43	43½	44	44½
1	11.7	12.0	12.3	12.5	12.8	13.1	13.4	13.8
2	23.3	23.9	24.5	25.1	25.7	26.3	26.9	27.5
3	35.0	35.9	36.8	37.6	38.5	39.4	40.2	41.3
4	46.7	47.8	49.0	50.2	51.4	52.6	53.8	55.0
5	58.4	59.8	61.3	62.7	64.2	65.7	67.2	68.8
6	70.0	71.8	73.5	75.3	77.0	78.8	80.7	82.5
7	81.7	83.7	85.8	87.8	89.9	91.9	94.1	96.3
8	93.4	95.7	98.0	100.3	102.7	105.1	107.6	110.0
9	105.1	107.6	110.3	112.9	115.6	118.3	121.0	123.8
10	116.7	119.6	122.5	125.4	128.4	131.4	134.4	137.5
11	128.4	131.6	134.8	138.0	141.2	144.5	147.9	151.3
12	140.1	143.5	147.0	150.5	154.1	157.7	161.3	165.0
13	151.8	155.5	159.3	163.1	166.9	170.8	174.8	178.8
14	163.4	167.4	171.5	175.6	179.8	184.0	188.2	192.5
15	175.1	179.4	183.8	188.2	192.6	197.1	201.7	206.3
16	186.8	191.4	196.0	200.7	205.4	210.3	215.1	220.0
17	198.5	203.3	208.3	213.2	218.3	223.4	228.6	233.8
18	210.1	215.3	220.5	225.8	231.1	236.5	242.0	247.5
19	221.8	227.2	232.8	238.3	244.0	249.7	255.4	261.3
20	233.5	239.2	245.0	250.9	256.8	262.8	268.9	275.0
21	245.1	251.2	257.3	263.4	269.6	276.0	282.3	288.8
22	256.8	263.1	269.5	276.0	282.5	289.1	295.8	302.5
23	268.5	275.1	281.8	288.5	295.3	302.2	309.2	316.3
24	280.2	287.0	294.0	301.0	308.2	315.1	322.7	330.0
25	291.8	299.0	306.3	313.6	321.0	328.5	336.1	343.8
26	303.5	311.0	318.5	326.1	333.8	341.7	349.6	357.5
27	315.2	322.9	330.8	338.7	346.7	354.8	363.0	371.3
28	326.9	334.8	343.0	351.2	359.5	367.9	376.4	385.0
29	338.5	346.8	355.3	363.8	372.4	381.1	389.9	398.8
30	350.2	358.8	367.5	376.3	385.2	394.2	403.3	411.6
31	361.9	370.8	379.8	388.8	398.0	407.4	416.8	426.3
32	373.6	382.7	392.0	401.4	410.9	420.5	430.2	440.1
33	385.2	391.7	404.3	413.9	423.7	433.6	443.7	453.8
34	395.9	406.6	416.5	426.5	436.6	446.8	457.1	467.6
35	408.6	418.6	428.8	439.0	449.4	459.9	470.6	481.3
36	420.3	430.6	441.0	451.6	462.3	473.1	484.0	495.1
37	431.9	442.5	453.3	464.1	475.1	486.2	497.4	508.8
38	443.6	454.5	465.5	476.6	487.0	499.3	510.9	522.6
39	455.3	466.4	477.8	489.2	500.8	512.5	524.3	536.3
40	466.9	478.4	490.0	501.7	513.6	525.6	537.8	550.1

Len. in Feet.	The Fourth part of the Girt in Inches.							
	45	45½	46	46½	47	47½	48	48½
1	14.1	14.4	14.7	15.0	15.3	15.7	16.0	16.3
2	28.1	28.8	29.4	30.0	30.7	31.3	32.0	32.7
3	42.2	43.1	44.1	45.0	46.0	47.0	48.0	49.0
4	56.3	57.5	58.8	60.1	61.4	62.7	64.0	65.3
5	70.3	71.9	73.5	75.1	76.7	78.3	80.0	81.7
6	84.4	86.3	88.2	90.1	92.0	94.0	96.0	98.0
7	98.4	100.6	102.9	105.1	107.4	109.7	112.0	114.3
8	112.5	115.0	117.6	120.1	122.7	125.3	128.0	130.7
9	126.6	129.4	132.3	135.1	138.1	141.0	144.0	147.0
10	140.6	143.8	146.9	150.2	153.4	156.7	160.0	163.4
11	154.7	158.1	161.6	165.2	168.7	172.4	176.0	179.7
12	168.8	172.5	176.3	180.2	184.1	188.0	192.0	196.0
13	182.8	186.9	191.0	195.2	199.4	203.7	208.0	212.4
14	196.9	201.3	205.7	210.2	214.8	219.4	224.0	228.7
15	210.9	215.7	220.4	225.2	230.1	235.0	240.0	245.0
16	225.0	230.0	235.1	240.3	245.4	250.7	256.0	261.4
17	239.1	244.4	249.8	255.3	260.8	266.4	272.0	277.7
18	253.1	258.8	264.5	270.3	276.1	282.0	288.0	294.0
19	267.2	273.2	279.2	285.3	291.5	297.7	304.0	310.4
20	281.3	287.5	293.9	300.3	306.8	313.4	320.0	326.7
21	295.3	301.9	308.6	315.3	322.1	329.0	336.0	343.0
22	309.4	316.3	323.3	330.3	337.5	344.7	352.0	359.4
23	323.4	330.7	338.0	345.4	352.8	360.4	368.0	375.7
24	337.5	345.0	352.7	360.4	368.2	376.0	384.0	392.0
25	351.6	359.4	367.4	375.4	383.5	391.7	400.0	408.4
26	365.6	373.4	382.1	390.4	398.8	407.4	416.0	424.7
27	379.7	388.2	396.8	405.4	414.2	423.0	432.0	441.0
28	393.8	402.5	411.4	420.4	429.5	438.7	448.0	457.4
29	407.8	416.9	426.1	435.5	444.9	454.4	464.0	473.7
30	421.9	431.3	440.8	450.5	460.2	470.1	480.0	490.1
31	435.9	445.7	455.5	465.5	475.5	485.7	496.0	506.4
32	450.0	460.1	470.2	480.5	490.9	501.4	512.0	522.7
33	464.1	474.4	484.9	495.5	506.2	517.1	528.0	539.1
34	478.1	488.8	499.6	510.5	521.6	532.7	544.0	555.4
35	492.2	503.2	514.3	525.5	536.9	548.4	560.0	571.7
36	506.3	517.6	529.0	540.6	552.3	564.1	576.0	588.1
37	520.3	531.9	543.7	555.6	567.6	579.7	592.0	604.4
38	534.4	546.3	558.4	570.6	582.9	595.4	608.0	620.7
39	548.4	560.7	573.1	585.6	598.3	611.1	624.0	637.1
40	562.5	575.1	587.8	600.6	613.6	626.7	640.0	653.4

Len. in Feet.	The Fourth part of the Girt in Inches.							
	49	49½	50	50½	51	51½	52	52½
1	16.7	17.0	17.4	17.7	18.1	18.4	18.8	19.1
2	33.3	34.0	34.7	35.4	36.1	36.8	37.6	38.3
3	50.0	51.0	52.1	53.1	54.2	55.3	56.3	57.4
4	66.7	68.1	69.4	70.8	72.3	73.7	75.1	76.6
5	83.3	85.1	86.8	88.6	90.3	92.1	93.9	95.7
6	100.0	102.1	104.2	106.3	108.4	110.5	112.7	114.8
7	116.7	119.1	121.5	124.0	126.4	128.9	131.4	134.0
8	133.4	136.1	138.9	141.7	144.5	147.3	150.2	153.1
9	150.1	153.1	156.3	159.4	162.6	165.8	169.0	172.3
10	166.7	170.2	173.6	177.1	180.6	184.2	187.8	191.4
11	183.4	187.2	191.0	194.8	198.7	202.6	206.6	210.5
12	200.1	204.2	208.3	212.5	216.8	221.0	225.3	229.7
13	216.8	221.2	225.7	230.2	234.8	239.4	244.1	248.8
14	233.4	238.2	243.1	247.9	252.9	257.9	262.9	268.0
15	250.1	255.2	260.4	265.7	270.9	276.3	281.7	287.1
16	266.8	272.3	277.8	283.4	289.0	294.7	300.4	306.3
17	283.5	289.3	295.1	301.1	307.1	313.1	319.2	325.4
18	300.1	306.3	312.5	318.8	325.1	331.5	338.0	344.5
19	316.8	323.3	329.9	336.5	343.2	349.9	356.8	363.7
20	333.5	340.3	347.2	354.2	361.3	368.4	375.6	382.8
21	350.1	357.3	364.0	371.9	379.3	386.8	394.3	402.0
22	366.8	374.3	381.9	389.6	397.4	405.2	413.1	421.1
23	383.5	391.4	399.3	407.3	415.4	423.6	431.9	440.2
24	400.2	408.4	416.7	425.0	433.5	442.0	450.7	459.4
25	416.8	425.4	434.0	442.8	451.6	460.5	469.4	478.5
26	433.5	442.4	451.4	460.5	469.6	478.9	488.2	497.7
27	450.2	459.4	468.8	478.2	487.7	497.3	507.0	516.8
28	466.9	476.4	486.1	495.9	505.8	515.8	525.8	535.9
29	483.5	493.5	503.5	513.6	523.8	534.1	544.6	555.1
30	500.2	510.5	520.8	531.3	541.9	552.6	563.3	574.2
31	516.9	527.5	538.2	549.0	559.9	571.0	582.1	593.4
32	533.6	544.5	555.6	566.7	578.0	589.4	600.9	612.5
33	550.2	561.5	572.9	584.4	595.1	607.8	619.7	631.6
34	566.9	578.5	590.3	602.1	614.1	626.2	638.4	650.8
35	583.6	595.5	607.6	619.0	632.2	644.6	657.2	669.9
36	600.3	612.6	625.0	637.0	650.3	663.1	676.0	689.1
37	616.9	629.6	642.4	655.8	668.3	681.5	694.8	708.2
38	633.6	646.6	659.7	673.0	686.4	699.9	713.6	727.3
39	650.3	663.6	677.1	690.7	704.4	718.3	732.3	746.5
40	666.9	680.6	694.4	708.4	722.5	736.7	751.1	765.6

Len. in Feet	The Fourth part of the Girt in Inches.							
	53	53½	54	54½	55	55½	56	56½
1	19 .5	19 .9	20 .3	20 .6	21 .0	21 .4	21 .8	22 .2
2	39 .0	39 .8	40 .5	41 .3	42 .0	42 .8	43 .6	44 .3
3	58 .5	59 .6	60 .8	61 .9	63 .0	64 .2	65 .3	66 .5
4	78 .0	79 .5	81 .0	82 .5	84 .0	85 .6	87 .1	88 .7
5	97 .5	99 .4	101 .3	103 .1	105 .0	107 .0	108 .9	110 .8
6	117¾.0	119 .3	121 .5	123 .8	126 .0	128 .3	130 .7	133 .0
7	136 .5	139 .1	141 .8	144 .4	147 .0	149 .7	152 .4	155 .2
8	156 .1	159 .0	162 .0	165 .0	168 .0	171 .1	174 .2	177 .3
9	175 .6	178 .9	182 .3	185 .6	189 .1	192 .5	196 .0	199 .5
10	195 .1	198 .8	202 .5	206 .3	210 .1	213 .9	217 .8	221 .7
11	214 .6	218 .6	222 .8	226 .9	231 .1	235 .3	239 .6	243 .9
12	234 .1	238 .5	243 .0	247 .5	252 .1	256 .7	261 .3	266 .0
13	253 .6	258 .4	263 .3	268 .1	273 .1	278 .1	283 .1	288 .2
14	273 .1	278 .3	283 .5	288 .8	294 .1	299 .5	304 .9	310 .4
15	292 .6	298 .2	303 .8	309 .4	315 .1	320 .9	326 .7	332 .5
16	312 .1	318 .0	324 .0	330 .0	336 .1	342 .3	348 .4	354 .7
17	331 .6	337 .9	344 .3	350 .7	357 .1	363 .6	370 .2	376 .9
18	351 .1	357 .8	364 .5	371 .3	378 .1	385 .0	392 .0	399 .0
19	370 .6	377 .7	384 .8	391 .9	399 .1	406 .4	413 .8	421 .2
20	390 .1	397 .5	405 .0	412 .5	420 .1	427 .8	435 .6	443 .4
21	409 .6	417 .4	425 .3	433 .2	441 .1	449 .2	457 .3	465 .5
22	429 .1	437 .3	445 .5	453 .6	462 .2	470 .6	479 .1	487 .7
23	448 .7	457 .2	465 .8	474 .4	483 .2	492 .0	500 .9	509 .9
24	468 .2	477 .0	486 .0	495 .0	504 .2	513 .4	522 .7	532 .0
25	487 .7	496 .9	506 .3	515 .7	525 .2	534 .8	544 .4	554 .2
26	507 .2	516 .8	526 .5	536 .3	546 .2	556 .2	566 .2	576 .4
27	526 .7	536 .7	546 .8	556 .9	567 .2	577 .5	588 .0	598 .5
28	546 .2	556 .5	567 .0	577 .5	588 .2	598 .9	609 .8	620 .7
29	565 .7	576 .4	587 .3	598 .2	609 .2	620 .3	631 .6	642 .9
30	585 .2	596 .3	607 .5	618 .8	630 .2	641 .7	653 .3	665 .1
31	604 .7	616 .2	627 .8	639 .4	651 .2	663 .1	675 .1	687 .2
32	624 .2	636 .1	648 .0	660 .1	672 .2	684 .5	696 .9	709 .4
33	643 .7	655 .9	668 .3	680 .7	693 .2	705 .9	718 .7	731 .6
34	663 .2	675 .8	688 .5	701 .3	714 .2	727 .3	740 .4	753 .7
35	682 .7	695 .7	708 .8	721 .9	735 .2	748 .7	762 .2	775 .9
36	702 .3	715 .6	729 .0	742 .6	756 .3	770 .1	784 .0	798 .1
37	721 .8	735 .4	749 .3	763 .2	777 .3	791 .5	805 .8	820 .2
38	741 .3	755 .3	769 .5	783 .8	798 .3	812 .8	827 .6	842 .4
39	760 .8	775 .2	789 .8	804 .4	819 .3	834 .2	849 .3	864 .6
40	780 .3	795 .1	810 .0	825 .1	840 .3	855 .6	871 .1	886 .7

Len in Feet.	The Fourth part of the Girt in Inches.							
	57	57½	58	58½	59	59¼	60	60½
1	22.6	23.0	23.4	23.8	24.2	24.6	25.0	25.4
2	45.1	45.9	46.7	47.5	48.3	49.2	50.0	50.8
3	67.7	68.9	70.1	71.3	72.5	73.8	75.0	76.3
4	90.3	91.8	93.4	95.1	96.7	98.3	100.0	101.7
5	112.8	114.8	116.8	118.8	120.9	122.9	125.0	127.1
6	135.4	137.8	140.2	142.6	145.0	147.5	150.0	152.5
7	157.9	160.7	163.5	166.4	169.2	172.1	175.0	177.9
8	180.5	183.7	186.9	190.1	193.4	196.7	200.0	203.3
9	203.1	206.6	210.3	213.9	217.6	221.3	225.0	228.8
10	225.6	229.6	233.6	237.7	241.7	245.9	250.0	254.2
11	248.2	252.6	257.0	261.4	265.9	270.4	275.0	279.6
12	270.8	275.5	280.3	285.2	290.1	295.0	300.0	305.0
13	293.3	298.5	303.7	309.0	314.3	319.6	325.0	330.4
14	315.9	321.4	327.1	332.7	338.4	344.2	350.0	355.9
15	338.4	344.4	350.4	356.5	362.6	368.8	375.0	381.3
16	361.0	367.4	373.8	380.3	386.8	393.4	400.0	406.7
17	383.6	390.3	397.1	404.0	411.0	417.9	425.0	432.1
18	406.1	413.3	420.5	427.8	435.1	442.5	450.0	457.5
19	428.7	436.2	443.9	451.5	459.3	467.1	475.0	482.9
20	451.3	459.2	467.2	475.3	483.5	491.7	500.0	508.4
21	473.8	482.2	490.6	499.1	507.6	516.3	525.0	533.8
22	496.4	505.1	513.9	522.8	531.8	540.9	550.0	559.2
23	518.9	528.1	537.3	546.6	556.0	565.5	575.0	584.6
24	541.5	551.0	560.7	570.4	580.2	590.0	600.0	610.0
25	564.1	574.0	584.0	594.1	604.3	614.6	625.0	635.5
26	586.6	597.0	607.4	617.9	628.5	639.2	650.0	660.9
27	609.2	619.9	630.8	641.7	652.7	663.8	675.0	686.3
28	631.8	642.9	654.1	665.4	676.9	688.4	700.0	711.7
29	654.3	665.8	677.5	689.2	701.0	713.0	725.0	737.1
30	676.9	688.8	700.8	713.0	725.2	737.6	750.0	762.6
31	699.4	711.8	724.2	736.7	749.4	762.1	775.0	788.0
32	722.0	734.7	747.6	760.5	773.6	786.7	800.0	813.4
33	744.6	757.7	770.9	784.3	797.7	811.3	825.0	838.8
34	767.1	780.6	794.3	808.0	821.9	835.9	850.0	864.2
35	789.7	803.6	817.6	831.8	846.1	860.5	875.0	889.6
36	812.3	826.6	841.0	855.6	870.3	885.1	900.0	915.1
37	834.8	849.5	864.4	879.3	894.4	909.6	925.0	940.5
38	857.4	872.5	887.7	903.1	918.6	934.2	950.0	965.9
39	879.9	895.4	911.1	926.9	942.8	958.8	975.0	991.3
40	902.5	918.4	934.4	950.6	966.9	983.4	1000.0	1016.7

Len. in Feet	The Fourth part of the Girt in Inches.						
	61	61½	62	62½	63	63½	64
1	25.8	26.3	26.7	27.1	27.6	28.0	28.4
2	51.7	52.5	53.4	54.3	55.1	56.0	56.9
3	77.5	78.8	80.1	81.4	82.7	84.0	85.3
4	103.4	105.1	106.8	108.5	110.3	112.0	113.8
5	129.2	131.3	133.5	135.6	137.8	140.0	142.2
6	155.0	157.6	160.2	162.8	165.4	168.0	170.7
7	180.9	183.9	186.9	189.9	192.9	196.0	199.1
8	206.7	210.1	213.6	217.0	220.5	224.0	227.6
9	232.6	236.4	240.3	244.1	248.1	252.0	256.0
10	258.4	262.7	266.9	271.3	275.6	280.0	284.4
11	284.2	288.9	293.6	298.4	303.2	308.0	312.9
12	310.1	315.2	320.3	325.2	330.8	336.0	341.3
13	335.9	341.5	347.0	352.6	358.3	364.0	369.8
14	361.8	367.7	373.7	379.8	385.9	392.0	398.2
15	387.6	394.0	400.4	406.9	413.4	420.0	426.7
16	413.4	420.3	427.1	434.0	441.0	448.0	455.1
17	439.3	446.5	453.8	461.1	468.6	476.0	483.6
18	465.1	472.8	480.5	488.3	496.1	504.0	512.0
19	491.0	499.0	507.2	515.4	523.7	532.0	540.4
20	516.8	525.3	533.9	542.5	551.3	560.0	568.9
21	542.6	551.6	560.6	569.7	578.8	588.0	597.3
22	568.5	577.8	587.3	596.8	606.4	616.0	625.8
23	594.3	604.1	614.0	623.9	633.9	644.0	654.2
24	620.2	630.4	640.7	651.0	661.5	672.0	682.7
25	646.0	656.6	667.4	678.2	689.1	700.0	711.1
26	671.8	682.9	694.1	705.3	716.6	728.0	739.6
27	697.7	709.2	720.8	732.4	744.2	756.0	768.0
28	723.5	735.4	747.4	759.5	771.8	784.0	796.4
29	749.4	761.7	774.1	786.7	799.3	812.1	824.9
30	775.2	788.0	800.8	813.8	826.9	840.1	853.3
31	801.0	814.2	827.5	840.9	854.4	868.1	881.8
32	826.9	840.5	854.2	868.1	882.0	896.1	910.2
33	852.	866.8	880.9	895.2	909.6	924.1	938.7
34	878.6	893.0	907.6	922.3	937.1	952.1	967.1
35	904.4	919.3	934.3	949.4	964.7	980.1	995.6
36	930.3	945.6	961.0	976.6	992.3	1008.1	1024.0
37	956.1	971.8	987.7	1003.7	1019.8	1036.1	1052.4
38	981.9	998.1	1014.4	1030.8	1047.4	1064.1	1080.9
39	1007.8	1024.4	1041.1	1057.9	1074.9	1092.1	1109.3
40	1033.6	1050.6	1067.8	1085.1	1102.5	1120.1	1137.8

Len. in Feet.	The Fourth part of the Girt in Inches.						
	64½	65	65½	66	66½	67	67½
1	28.9	29.3	29.8	30.3	30.7	31.2	31.6
2	57.8	58.7	59.6	60.5	61.4	62.3	63.3
3	86.7	88.0	89.4	90.8	92.1	93.5	94.9
4	115.6	117.4	119.2	121.0	122.8	124.7	126.6
5	144.5	146.7	149.0	151.3	153.6	155.9	158.2
6	173.3	176.0	178.8	181.5	184.3	187.0	189.8
7	202.2	205.4	208.6	211.8	215.0	218.2	221.5
8	231.1	234.7	238.3	242.0	245.7	249.4	253.1
9	260.0	264.1	268.1	272.3	276.4	280.6	284.8
10	288.9	293.4	297.9	302.5	307.1	311.7	316.4
11	317.8	322.7	327.7	332.8	337.8	342.9	348.0
12	346.7	352.1	357.5	363.0	368.5	374.1	379.7
13	375.6	381.4	387.3	393.3	399.2	405.3	411.3
14	404.5	410.8	417.1	423.5	429.9	436.4	443.0
15	433.4	440.1	446.9	453.8	460.7	467.6	474.6
16	462.3	469.4	476.7	484.0	491.4	498.8	506.3
17	491.1	498.8	506.5	514.3	522.1	530.0	537.9
18	520.0	528.1	536.3	544.5	552.8	561.1	569.5
19	548.9	557.4	566.1	574.8	583.5	592.3	601.2
20	577.8	586.8	595.9	605.0	614.2	623.5	632.8
21	606.7	616.1	625.7	635.3	644.9	654.6	664.5
22	635.6	645.5	655.5	665.5	675.6	685.8	696.1
23	604.5	674.8	685.2	695.8	706.3	717.0	727.7
24	693.4	704.2	715.0	726.0	737.0	748.2	759.4
25	722.3	733.5	744.8	756.3	767.8	779.3	791.0
26	751.2	762.8	774.6	786.5	798.5	810.5	822.7
27	780.0	792.2	804.4	816.8	829.2	841.7	854.3
28	808.9	821.5	834.2	847.0	859.9	872.9	885.9
29	837.8	850.9	864.0	877.3	890.6	904.0	917.6
30	866.7	880.2	893.8	907.5	921.3	935.2	949.2
31	895.6	909.5	923.6	937.8	952.0	966.4	980.9
32	924.5	938.9	953.4	968.0	982.7	997.6	1012.5
33	953.4	968.2	983.2	998.3	1013.4	1028.7	1044.1
34	982.3	997.6	1013.0	1028.5	1044.1	1059.9	1075.8
35	1011.2	1026.9	1042.8	1058.8	1074.9	1091.1	1107.4
36	1040.1	1056.3	1072.6	1089.0	1105.6	1122.3	1139.1
37	1069.0	1085.6	1102.4	1119.3	1136.3	1153.4	1170.7
38	1097.8	1114.9	1132.1	1149.5	1167.0	1184.6	1202.3
39	1126.7	1144.3	1161.9	1179.8	1197.7	1215.8	1234.0
40	1155.6	1173.6	1191.7	1210.0	1228.4	1246.9	1265.6

Len. in Feet.	The Fourth part of the Girt in Inches.						
	68	68½	69	69½	70	70½	71
1	32.1	32.6	33.1	33.5	34.0	34.5	35.0
2	64.2	65.2	66.1	67.1	68.1	69.0	70.0
3	96.3	97.8	99.2	100.6	102.1	103.5	105.0
4	128.4	130.3	132.3	134.2	136.1	138.1	140.0
5	160.6	162.9	165.3	167.7	170.1	172.6	175.0
6	192.7	195.5	198.4	201.3	204.2	207.1	210.0
7	224.8	228.1	231.4	234.8	238.2	241.6	245.0
8	256.9	260.7	264.5	268.3	272.2	276.1	280.1
9	289.0	293.3	297.6	301.9	306.3	310.6	315.1
10	321.1	325.9	330.6	335.4	340.3	345.2	350.1
11	353.2	358.4	363.7	369.0	374.3	379.7	385.1
12	385.3	391.0	396.8	402.5	408.3	414.2	420.1
13	417.4	423.6	429.8	436.1	442.4	448.7	455.1
14	449.6	456.2	462.9	469.6	476.4	483.2	490.1
15	481.7	488.8	495.9	503.2	510.4	517.7	525.1
16	513.8	521.4	529.0	536.7	544.4	552.3	560.1
17	545.9	553.9	562.1	570.2	578.5	586.8	595.1
18	578.0	586.5	595.1	603.8	612.5	621.3	630.1
19	610.1	619.1	628.2	637.3	646.5	655.8	665.1
20	642.2	651.7	661.3	670.9	680.6	690.3	700.1
21	674.3	684.3	694.3	704.4	714.6	724.8	735.1
22	706.4	716.9	727.4	738.0	748.6	759.3	770.2
23	738.6	749.5	760.4	771.5	782.6	793.9	805.2
24	770.7	782.0	793.5	805.0	816.7	828.4	840.2
25	802.8	814.6	826.6	838.6	850.7	862.9	875.2
26	834.9	847.2	859.6	872.1	884.7	897.4	910.2
27	867.0	879.8	892.7	905.7	918.8	931.9	945.2
28	899.1	912.4	925.8	939.2	952.8	966.4	980.2
29	931.2	945.0	958.8	972.8	986.8	1001.0	1015.2
30	963.3	977.6	991.9	1006.3	1020.8	1035.5	1050.2
31	995.4	1010.1	1024.9	1039.3	1054.9	1070.0	1085.2
32	1027.6	1042.7	1058.0	1073.4	1088.9	1104.5	1120.2
33	1059.7	1075.3	1091.1	1106.9	1122.9	1139.0	1155.2
34	1091.8	1107.9	1124.1	1140.5	1156.9	1173.5	1190.2
35	1123.9	1140.5	1157.2	1174.0	1191.0	1208.0	1225.2
36	1156.0	1173.1	1190.3	1207.6	1225.0	1242.6	1260.3
37	1188.1	1205.6	1223.3	1241.1	1259.0	1277.1	1295.3
38	1220.2	1238.2	1256.4	1274.6	1293.1	1311.6	1330.3
39	1252.3	1270.8	1289.4	1308.2	1327.1	1346.1	1365.3
40	1284.4	1303.4	1322.5	1341.7	1361.1	1380.6	1400.3

R

Len. in Feet.	The Fourth part of the Girt in Inches.						
	71½	72	72½	73	73½	74	74½
1	35 .5	36 .0	36 .5	37 .0	37 .5	38 .0	38 .5
2	71 .0	72 .0	73 .0	74 .0	75 .0	76 .1	77 .1
3	106 .5	108 .0	109 .5	111 .0	112 .5	114 .1	115 .6
4	142 .0	144 .0	146 .0	148 .0	150 .1	152 .1	154 .2
5	177 .5	180 .0	182 .5	185 .0	187 .6	190 .1	192 .7
6	213 .0	216 .0	219 .0	222 .0	225 .1	228 .2	231 .3
7	248 .5	252 .0	255 .5	259 .0	262 .6	266 .2	269 .8
8	284 .0	288 .0	292 .0	296 .1	300 .1	304 .2	308 .3
9	319 .5	324 .0	328 .5	333 .1	337 .6	342 .3	346 .9
10	355 .0	360 .0	365 .0	370 .1	375 .2	380 .3	385 .4
11	390 .5	396 .0	401 .5	407 .1	412 .7	418 .3	424 .0
12	426 .0	432 .0	438 .0	444 .1	450 .2	456 .3	462 .5
13	461 .5	468 .0	474 .5	481 .1	487 .7	494 .4	501 .1
14	497 .0	504 .0	511 .0	518 .1	525 .2	532 .4	539 .6
15	532 .5	540 .0	547 .5	555 .1	562 .7	570 .4	578 .2
16	568 .0	576 .0	584 .0	592 .1	600 .3	608 .4	616 .7
17	603 .5	612 .0	620 .5	629 .1	637 .8	646 .5	655 .2
18	639 .0	648 .0	657 .0	666 .1	675 .3	684 .5	693 .8
19	674 .5	684 .0	693 .5	703 .1	712 .8	722 .5	732 .3
20	710 .0	720 .0	730 .0	740 .1	750 .3	760 .6	770 .9
21	745 .5	756 .0	766 .5	777 .1	787 .8	798 .6	809 .4
22	781 .0	792 .0	803 .0	814 .2	825 .3	836 .6	848 .0
23	816 .5	828 .0	839 .5	851 .2	862 .9	874 .6	886 .5
24	852 .0	864 .0	876 .0	888 .2	900 .4	912 .7	925 .0
25	887 .5	900 .0	912 .5	925 .2	937 .9	950 .7	963 .6
26	923 .0	936 .0	949 .0	962 .2	975 .4	988 .7	1002 .1
27	958 .5	972 .0	985 .5	999 .2	1012 .9	1026 .8	1040 .7
28	994 .0	1008 .0	1022 .0	1036 .2	1050 .4	1064 .8	1079 .2
29	1029 .6	1044 .0	1058 .6	1073 .2	1088 .0	1102 .8	1117 .8
30	1065 .1	1080 .0	1095 .1	1110 .2	1125 .5	1140 .8	1156 .3
31	1100 .6	1116 .0	1131 .6	1147 .2	1163 .0	1178 .9	1194 .8
32	1136 .1	1152 .0	1168 .1	1184 .2	1200 .5	1216 .9	1233 .4
33	1171 .6	1188 .0	1204 .6	1221 .2	1238 .0	1254 .9	1271 .9
34	1207 .1	1224 .0	1241 .1	1258 .2	1275 .5	1292 .9	1310 .5
35	1242 .6	1260 .0	1277 .6	1295 .2	1313 .0	1331 .0	1349 .0
36	1278 .1	1296 .0	1314 .1	1332 .3	1350 .6	1369 .0	1387 .6
37	1313 .6	1332 .0	1350 .6	1369 .3	1388 .1	1407 .0	1426 .1
38	1349 .1	1368 .0	1387 .1	1406 .3	1425 .6	1445 .1	1464 .6
39	1384 .6	1404 .0	1423 .6	1443 .3	1463 .1	1483 .1	1503 .2
40	1420 .1	1440 .0	1460 .1	1480 .3	1500 .6	1521 .1	1541 .7

AN APPENDIX,

SHEWING

The Way to PLENTY:

Propos'd to the FARMERS;

Wherein are laid down

General Rules and Directions for the *Management* and *Improvement* of a FARM.

I. 𝕎𝕚𝕝𝕕 𝕆𝕒𝕥𝕤 being one of the greatest Annoyances to the *Farmer*, no Care and Pains can be too much to destroy them. And altho' their Encrease be *chiefly* owing to a long continuance of *Plowing* and Tillage, yet the following Method pursued, (even in a regular Course of Husbandry) is found the best and most effectual way to destroy them, *viz.*

R 2　　　　　　AFTER

AFTER the *firſt* time of Summer-fallow-
ing the Land, (in *March* or *April* ſuppoſe)
in a month's time, and after a Shower, let
the Harrow be drawn over the Fallow, and
then you will quickly find the *wild Oats*
to ſpring and appear: Let them continue
to grow till the time of their *earing*, and
with a Scythe mow 'em down, and in a dry
Day, as ſoon after as may be, plow them
all in; which will be a means not only to
mellow and *enrich* the Ground, but to kill
and deſtroy that *pernicious Weed*, with the
help of the after-turnings of the Land. 'Tis
poſſible this firſt Experiment may not effectually and totally accompliſh the deſtruction
of this *Weed*, on the account of wet Seaſons,
or ſome other accidental Cauſes, but it is
known to be an *Excellent Remedy*, and
therefore a reſolute repetition of it will not
fail to compleat the Cure. The only Objection to this Method is, that the *Midſummer* Fallow is loſt, and the Land will not
have had ſufficient tillage for *Wheat* at *Michaelmas:* But the Anſwer is, that it will
do for *Barley* (which is not ſown till Spring)
by

by the help of an *Autumn* or *Winter*-fallowing ; and so the trial is to be made successively only on the Land intended for *Barley*.

II. **Instead** of *three* Fields for Tillage, (as the common practice is) *all* late Experience teacheth * **four** are better for the Farm and the Farmer ; *viz.* (1.) Wheat or Barley after the Fallows. (2.) Pease or Beans, or rather *both*. (3.) Oats ; and then (4.) the Summer Fallows. The reason of which is founded thus ; That a Crop of Beans and Pease do not (as most other Grain) take *from*, but give Riches *to* the Land, *mellowing* and disposing it for an After-crop : That the Straw of a mixt Crop of Beans and Pease is a great Relief to Cattle in the Winter, and excellently supplieth the want of Hay ; and, That a Crop of Beans is as good,

---

* In such places where the Soil is a rich Loame, this course of Husbandry has answer'd to a wonder : But in others, where the Soil is light, and not strong enough for Wheat and Beans, the common method of three Fields, or rather to take but one Crop, and then a Fallow, and so alternately, as is practis'd upon the light Lands in *Essex*, answers much the best.

and fometimes better than a Crop of *Wheat*.
Only becaufe it cannot be expected that the
Land fhould never be weary, and becaufe
'tis defirable to *improve* poor Land as much
as may be, therefore a fmall quantity of
fuch Dung as can be got fhould be laid upon the Bean-ftubbles, as well as the ufual
Proportion upon the Fallows.

I t fhould alfo be here remember'd, that
Beans and *Peafe* (let the Soil be never fo
ftrong) fhould be fown Under-furrow,
i. e. upon the Stubbles, and plow'd *in*; the
Furrow to be *thin*, and laid *flat* upon the
Beans: And this, if poffible, fhould be perform'd the latter end of *January*, or before the end of *February*, for no Froft will
hurt 'em after that: But as foon as they
begin to *peep*, in *March*, and after a Shower,
a Harrow fhould be drawn over 'em (*fear
not the tread of the Horfes*) to mellow and
loofen the Earth, and make it fit to receive
the fatning Dews. This Method beft fe-
cures the *Seed* from *Crows* and *Pigeons*,
and at the fame time gives a proper *depth
of Earth* as a Defence and Security againft
the

the Droughts at *Midsummer*, when they are in blossom, and when (for want of it) they are apt to shrink and *wither away*.

III. **When Land** is over-run with Shrubs, Underwood, Whins, Brakes, and by Age becomes *mossy*, and for want of trenching is poachy and full of Boggs, the first and only Remedy is, to clear the Ground of all the Trumpery, and then to *set in* the Plough for three years, sowing only *Oats* thereon successively, except it be good and proper enough to sow *Barley* the third year; still always remembring to keep a sufficient number of Trenches open to drain the Land; and with the third and last Crop to sow *Grafs-feeds* * suited to the nature of the Soil, such as *Clover, Trefoil, Rye-grafs*, &c. with a View to continue it in Pasture for three or four years, and then to *set in* the Plough again; and, if the Land is not of the best sort, to continue it so successively. But it should not be forgot, that before every third Crop is sown, a convenient quantity of

* See the Particulars at the end of this Appendix.

Coal-

Coal-afhes, if poffible, or fuch other Manure as the place will afford, fhould be laid
on, the better to make it fward over: ten
Wain-loads on an Acre will do pretty well.

IV. **Altho'** it be needlefs to fay, that all
Dungs are Improvers of Land, both Pafture
and Tillage, fuch as the Dung of Horfes,
Cows, Sheep, Hogs; as alfo *Fifh,* * *Sea-fand*
and *Shells, Rags, Leather, Tanners-Bark,
Kilp-afhes,* &c. yet becaufe it is not throughly underftood, and therefore too oft neglected, a ftrefs is to be laid upon the peculiar Excellency and Goodnefs of *Coal-
afhes,* (but efpecially the † Afhes of Sea-

* The great Neglect of the Tenants along the Northern Coafts, in not laying *Sea-Sand* upon their Tillage,
which chiefly confifts of a ftiff Clay, and would (of all
other Soils) be moft *Improv'd* by it.

† I was not a little *furpriz'd* when I firft went down
to furvey and let *His Grace the Duke of* BUCKINGHAM'S
Eftates in Yorkfhire, to find the Tenants had fuffer'd *Mil-
lions* of Loads of Sea-coal-afhes (made from the vaft
quantities of Coal ufed in the *Allom*-works at *Sandfend*)
to be wafh'd into the Sea for above 100 years laft paft,
without ever laying them upon their Pafture and Meadow Grounds. Had the Tenants known the Vertue of
thefe Coal-afhes from the beginning of the *Allom*-works,
the Eftate might have been confiderably *Improv'd*; but
fince, care has been taken to oblige all the Tenants to
follow the Example of the Tenants round *Sunderland*
and *Newcaftle,* who have made great *Improvements* very
lately, by virtue of this Noble Manure of Sea-coal-afhes.

Coal

Coal burnt) for all Pasture and Meadow Ground, provided they be well freed from the Cynders; the Nature and Vertue whereof is such, that it immediately disposeth the Land to produce wild *Trefoil,* and all the best and sweetest Grasses; and in such abundance also, that it will soon keep a double number of Stock, and produce double the Loads of Hay. As was said before, ten Loads on an Acre will do, but more is better, where it can easily be had.

V. **Experience** hath shewn, that even the worst Land may be so order'd that it shall in some measure *improve it self,* without any **Super-inductions** of Dung. *Turnips* for instance (which are too much neglected in the *North*) sown at *Midsummer,* and kept regularly * *houghed,* will not only *support,* but † *fatten* Sheep in the Winter in

---

* See the Method of houghing Turnips in the following pages, where 'tis fully describ'd.

† When Sheep are made fat with Turnips, 'tis adviseable to turn 'em into a Pasture for about a fortnight before they are kill'd, (especially if they are to be drove) by which means the nicest Palate cannot discover the Taste of Turnip-fed Mutton from the finest Grass Mutton.

great

great numbers, and confequently *enrich* the Soil by their *Dung* and *Urine*. And the very *Refuse* of the Turnips, after the Sheep have fcoop'd 'em, and are become rotten, do ftrangely mellow and fatten the Soil, richly difpofing it for a Crop of *Oats*, *Barley*, or *Spring-Wheat*, without any *Super-induction* of Dung. But in this procefs it is to be remember'd, that the Sheep are to be confined to *one Acre* at a time, by proper Hurdles, not fuffering them to *ramble* over the *whole* at once.

Again, Clover fown on indifferent Land, or Land *worn* out with plowing, if at *Midfummer* (when 'tis in its full bloffom and pride) it be plow'd in, will quickly fink and die away, and by its Salts give an uncommon fertility to the Soil, mellowing and *enriching* it for two or three Crops fucceffively, beginning with a Crop of *Wheat* in *Autumn*, after another Fallow. Much the fame (tho' not in fo good a degree) is to be faid with refpect to *Peafe*, *Vetches*, *Lentils*, and *Buck-wheat*. However, it fhould

not

not be *diſſembled* that the hazard of ſowing
Turnip ſon *very poor* Land is great, without
ſome additional help ; and therefore a ſprink-
ling of any rotten Dung, Hen or Pigeon-
dung, Malt-duſt, Coal or Kilp or Turf-
aſhes, may be proper to be thrown on before the Sowing at *Midſummer* or *Lammas*
after the Ground is made fine with the
Buſh-Harrow.

VI. 𝕮𝖑𝖔𝖛𝖊𝖗, 𝕿𝖗𝖊𝖋𝖔𝖎𝖑, 𝕾𝖆𝖎𝖓𝖙𝖋𝖔𝖎𝖓, 𝕽𝖞𝖊-
𝖌𝖗𝖆𝖘, &c. (of which ſee more in this Appendix) are vaſt Improvements to Lands,
eſpecially the worſt ſort, and thoſe that are
deſign'd to be laid down for Paſture, and
after a reaſonable time to be plow'd up a-
gain, by bringing them ſuddenly to Turf,
and by the richneſs of the Feed, cauſing
them to keep near three times the number
of Cattle which otherwiſe they could do.
But there is a Caution here to be obſerv'd,
eſpecially with reſpect to large Cattle, *viz.*
that for the *firſt Week* when they are turn'd
into it, you do not ſuffer them to continue in
it above an *Hour* at a time, (an *Hour* at each
Noon is ſufficient) for otherwiſe they will be
apt

apt to furfeit, to fwell and die. But the Improvement here fpoken of, manag'd with difcretion, is furprizing to them who have not feen it, and is one of the late means whereby Farmers have gain'd *great* Riches to themfelves. Thus the known Maxim here takes place, That *an Encreafe of the Stock is always a double Encreafe of the Profit*; return'd to the Farmer thefe two ways, both in the Profit of fat Cattle, and in the *Improvement* of his Land for another Year.

VII. Altho' the nature of Seed Corn, and the time of fowing it, is thought to be pretty well underftood, yet there are great Miftakes often committed by Farmers (of the *North* efpecially) in this Affair. All Winter-corn fhould be fown rather *before* than *after Michaelmas*, efpecially *Rye* on the lighteft Land; and therefore the *firft* fair and fettled Weather that offers after *September* fets in, fhould be chofen, and the *Fallows* fhou'd be difpos'd and prepar'd accordingly: Not but that, if the Seafon fuit not in *September*, or even *October*, he may

with

with a great deal of reaſon hope for Succeſs any time in *November,* and ſometimes
later; but yet, I repeat it again, if Choice
may be had, at or before *Michaelmas* is
beſt for moſt Land, eſpecially in the *North.*
In the management of his *Fallows,* the Farmer ſhould on no account go out with his
Team in a *wet* Day, ſuch practice conſtantly tending to *ſett* the Weeds, and to
make the Land lie *foul* at Seed-time.

𝕭𝖎𝖌 is a Grain known only in the *North,*
and deſerves to be *baniſh'd* thence; for the
Drink made of it is very diſagreeable to
Strangers, and affords not a proportionable
Strength equal to the ſame quantity of *Barley,* which yet always exceeds it in price
about two-pence in the Buſhel.   'Tis alſo
a Miſtake to think it will grow and thrive
where *Barley* will not; for it requires both
the *ſame Management* and the *ſame Soil:*
Neither will it afford a *greater Encreaſe*;
for tho' it hath a ſquare Ear, and *four Rows*
of Corn, yet that advantage is more than
counterbalanc'd by the *Leanneſs* of the Grain,
and the *Thickneſs* of the Skin.

𝕭𝖆𝖗𝖑𝖊𝖞

𝕭𝖆𝖗𝖑𝖊𝖞 is a hardier Grain than is commonly imagin'd, and therefore fhould be fown (if poffible) in *February*, the fucceeding Frofts never hurting it. The common and ufual way is, to harrow it in after plowing; which doth well enough with early fowing, or a wet Spring : But late Experience fhews, that except the Land be very ftrong indeed, fowing it 𝖀𝖓𝖉𝖊𝖗 𝕱𝖚𝖗𝖗𝖔𝖜 (like Beans) is the fureft way with all accidents to obtain a *great* Encreafe. Some take the middle way, fowing half *under*, and half *above* furrow, and have fucceeded very well. A very light Soil, that runs much to *Weeds*, is an Exception to an early fowing, but not to a late one 𝖀𝖓𝖉𝖊𝖗-𝖋𝖚𝖗𝖗𝖔𝖜. Great Care ought to be taken to weed both *Wheat* and *Barley* in *May* and *June*, for Experience fheweth that the higheft Expence in doing it is always repaid. *Carlock* is an harmlefs *Weed*, but no Grain fuffers fo much as *Wheat* and *Barley* by *Thiftles*, *Docks*, &c. If after weeding, the Crop appears thin, 'tis very advifeable to ftrow Pigeon or Hen-dung, or

Kilp-

Kilp-afhes, or Malt-duft over it, by which means it will ftrangely encreafe and *gather*; but this Work is moft proper to be done in rainy Weather.

VIII. 𝕭𝕖𝕔𝕒𝕦𝕗𝕖 𝕷𝕚𝕞𝕖 is found by all late Experience to be an excellent *Improver* of Tillage-Land, the Ufe of it is ftrongly re-commended, where-ever it can be had at any tolerable rate. It agrees with all forts of Soils, except the two Extreams, of a dufty *blowing Sand*, and the *ftrongeft Clays:* Where there is any good degree of the mix-ture of *both*, it never faileth to make *vaft Improvements*; for by its holding nature, when throughly dead and fallen, it adds *Tenacity* to light Soils, thereby hindring the Rains from falling too foon away ; and by its Salts, opens and relaxes the ftronger Soils, that they are not chill'd and ftarv'd by *ftagnating* Wets: For which reafon all *Heaths*, and *Moors*, and Grounds over-run with *Whins*, *Brakes*, *Broom,* or other brufhy Underwood, when turn'd up with the Plough, are furprizingly benefited by it; infomuch that many Lands, fuppos'd before

to

to be not worth above Two shillings an
Acre, are in the *North of* ENGLAND made
to be worth Twenty shillings an Acre, by
virtue of this noble Manure of **Lime,** Eighty or Ninety Bushels whereof being laid on
an *Acre* in Tillage, will last Four or Five
Years. But it should always be remember'd, that all loose, heathy, or moorish
light Soils, after sowing for three or four
years, or so long as the Soil continues hollow or spongy, should (as soon as the Spring-
Corn begins to appear) be *rolled* with a long
heavy wooden *Roll,* the better to fasten
the Ground, and to *close* the Corn to it;
which Practice is not yet understood in all
parts of the *North,* and therefore their
Crops often fail in a dry Summer for want
of it : Or they *weakly* content themselves
to lose the first year's Crop, and so are at
the charge of two or three *Fallows,* only
to obtain an End which is much better
obtain'd by ROLLING.

IX. **In laying down** the Land after
Tillage (always suppos'd to have been done
with sowing **Clover,** &c.) great care should
be

be taken that the Ridges be not laid *too high*, which always proves a damage to either Pasture or Meadow; for in *high* Ridges the good Soil is thrown up *deeper than necessary* at the *top*, and the Furrows laid bare to the *hungry bottom*, which bears nothing but coarse Grass or Rushes. But yet it should ever be remember'd, that proper Drains should be made from the *highest* to the *lowest* places, that the Water may not *stagnate* any where, but be carried into the Water-courses: For tho' a due quantity of Moisture be necessary for vegetation, yet Water (where-ever there is *too much*, so as to *stagnate*) always *impoverishes* the Land: And therefore, in this *necessary Work* of *draining*, let the Trench open'd be conveniently *wide* and *deep* enough: and what is taken out with the Spade should not be laid too near the side of the Drain, lest it be poach'd in again by the Feet of the Cattle.

X. **Great Improvements** are made in many parts of *Essex*, by laying on their Land the Earth and Mud which cometh

S   out

out of the Ditches when fcour'd and clean-
fed.   That which much contributes to the
richnefs of fuch Mud and Earth, is the
goodnefs of the Hedges, which are tall and
thick, and therefore fhed their Leaves plen-
tifully in *Autumn,* which mixing and rotting with the Earth, makes it fo *fat* and
ferviceable in Vegetation.   It is moreover a
good way to mix this *Ditch-Earth* with
fome Dung, which much improves and mol-
lifies it, efpecially after it hath lain fome
time in heaps. And yet if a fufficient quantity of this *Ditch-Earth* enrich'd with Leaves
cannot be got, 'tis a good way to mix *any*
fort of Earth with Dung, that it may be
fit for ufe and *rot* much the fooner, by
laying it on heaps to ferment.

XI. When Rye is cheap and plentiful,
(*i. e.* at Two Shillings a Bufhel, or under)
it has been found *richly* to anfwer the *Inte-*
reft of the Farmer, to fat his *Oxen* with it
after it is ground, tho' not too fmall. The
beft time for this practice is in Winter and
Spring, when *Beef* fells dear ; and the Ufe
of it is confirm'd with more reafon ftill, if
Hay

Hay happens to be fcarce. This, with many other Curiofities in Husbandry, I learnt
from Mr. *John Allen*, that ingenious and
faithful Steward to his Grace the Duke of
Kent, who hath practis'd it with good Succefs, and fent the Oxen to *London* for the
KING's Table, where the *Beef* was not a
little admir'd for its *delicious* Tafte.

To what has been faid before, it may be
very proper to add, that forafmuch as Ox-
Teams are found beft and moft profitable,
and that a conftant fucceffion of fat and lean
Cattle is abfolutely neceffary, every Farmer that keeps Ox-Teams (efpecially if he
buys *the long-Legg'd nimble fort* out of
Huntington-fhire) fhould rear two Oxen
and two Cow-Calves every year, to uphold
and preferve his Stock ; it being a known
Maxim in good Husbandry, That every
Farmer, who intends to *thrive*, fhould always be a *Seller* rather than a *Buyer*.

XII. 𝕲𝖔𝖔𝖉 𝕳𝖚𝖘𝖇𝖆𝖓𝖉𝖗𝖞 requires every
Farmer to keep his *Fallows* regular, and in
good order; not fuffering the Plough to

enter (efpecially the firft time) *too deep*;
and not to let the Land want the due number of *Tilths*, viz. four times for *Wheat*,
and five for *Barley* : But, above all, that he
take care to keep his *Fallows* as clean as
poffible from *Weeds*, which fpoil and eat
out the ftrength of his Land and Labour.
A great means of preventing this Damage
is, (as hath been before hinted) ever to ftir
the Land in *dry* Weather, and upon no
account to fuffer his Team to go out on that
Work in a *rainy* Day, it being a certain
Truth, that *it is better to do nothing, than
nothing to the purpofe.* The Cuftom practis'd in moft of the Southern Parts, of con-
fining and folding the *Sheep* by proper
Hurdles on the Fallows, fhould every where
be encourag'd, becaufe nothing is more proper and natural to all hard Corn than the
Dung and Urine of *Sheep* ; and the fooner
fuch Lands are plow'd after folding, the
better, that the Sun *exhale* not too much
of its *Vertue* and *Riches*.

XIII. **Moſt Farmers** are now convinc'd, that fteeping their Seed-corn (*Wheat*
efpecially)

especially) in a strong Brine or Sea-water,
and taking away the light Corn, that swims
at the top, is necessary to prevent the Smut:
but because this is often done so imperfect-
ly, either sometimes by only sprinkling it,
or only just putting it in, and taking it pre-
sently out again, I think it proper to advise the letting the Corn be steep'd therein
at the least 12 hours, not forgetting (after
the Corn is taken out) to sprinkle unflaked
Lime upon it, the better to separate the
Corn; for nothing less will entirely prevent
the Disease so fatal to some Grounds and
some Farmers. Neither should they forget
to change their *Seed*, and to chuse such as
grew on a Soil as different as possible from
that intended to be sown : However a
Change is necessary, it being a *Maxim* in
Husbandry, That all Grain *degenerates* by
being *sown* too long on the same Land, or
on the same sort of Land.

XIV. 𝕭𝖊𝖈𝖆𝖚𝖘𝖊 'tis greatly the Farmer's
Business and *Interest* to contrive all *honest*
ways of *improving* every Article, so as to
answer his Labour and Care, it may not

be amiſs to put the induſtrious in mind and
method of making the beſt of his Stock in
two particular *Articles,* much neglected in
the North Parts of *England,* and thoſe are
Veal and *Lamb. York, Durham,* and *New-
caſtle* are places *known* to be not only *rich,*
but exceeding populous ; to which alſo re-
ſort a vaſt concourſe of Nobility, Gentry,
and others, at all public times of Aſſizes,
Seſſions, Elections, Horſe-races, *&c.* And,
to make ſuch places more frequented by the
Gay Part of Mankind, they have (as in the
South) the Contrivances of Plays, Aſſemblies,
and Muſic-meetings : All which call for a
conſtant Demand of every thing eatable
which is good in its kind; and an *encouraging* price would be given by thoſe who love
to live *elegantly.* Accordingly tho' late
years have ſhewn a conſiderable *Improvement* in the two Articles above, yet an in-
ſtructive Method of managing theſe two
Particulars muſt needs be acceptable to the
Farmer. As to the firſt, it may be obſerv'd,

THAT the Myſtery of having good *Veal*
lieth in making it *fat, white,* and *well-
taſted.*

tafted. The laſt Quality is often wanted, even when the two former prevail; which is plainly owing to a too frequent and *over-bleeding.* To obtain therefore *all of them,* no better nor more certain Method can be had, than what I obtain'd from a near Relation, who, for the good of the Public, has given me leave to inſert it : Let the Calf be laid dry, on *clean Straw* every day laid upon the old, and coop'd up in a little room, but not too ſtifling where the Sun comes : His Bed ſhould be rais'd a Foot from the Ground, hollow'd with Hurdles, ſo that the Urine may quickly paſs away, at the ſame time taking care that the Calf may not come at the Wall or Ground, to lick it, as he greedily will if not prevented ; inſtead of which, a Chalk-ſtone ſhould be hung up in a String, to encourage his licking *that,* for it will add to the Beauty of the Veal. Thus far the Practice is pretty well *known* ; what follows is not ſo : For it is a great miſtake to let the Calf for the firſt fortnight *ſuck* as much as he will; juſt to keep him *alive* and *well,* is enough ; and after that, let him blood, and encreaſe his *quantum*

till

till he is three Weeks old, when you are to dose him with a 𝕻𝖎𝖑𝖑 Night and Morning, made up only of *Anifeed-water* and the powder of *Chalk*; the *Pill* fhould be about as big and as long as a Man's Thumb, made up to the confiftency of *Pafte,* at the fame time 'tis ufed, for otherwife 'twill be dry and hard. The reafon of the Prefcription is founded on this; That if the Calf is *laxative*, he never will thrive or be fat, and therefore all Art fhould be ufed to make him *coftive*; and this End is effectually obtain'd by this Compofition. And tho' it fomething abates his appetite to the Milk, yet he will notwithftanding grow very fat the laft fortnight, during the time of his *Pills*; for it is not profit to keep a Calf above five or fix Weeks at moft, altho' the practice about *London* extends further; yet neither is their Veal fo *delicate* or *well-tafted* as that which is thus manag'd, the Fat of which is obferv'd to be hard and firm, and the Flefh exquifitely white and fine by only *two* bleedings, once as before, and the fecond a Week before he dies.

THE

THE Method of having fat *Lamb* during the *Winter*, is more known, and lefs difficult: The chief of what I would fay upon this Head is, to *perfuade* the Farmers in the North to get more into the *Dorfetfhire* and *Wiltfhire* Breed of Sheep, and to provide *all* Conveniencies for houfing them, and keeping them clean and fweet; becaufe, as I have obferv'd before, there will be a *conftant Demand* for fuch Rarities, and an encouraging price will not be deny'd. Oats, Turnips, and Bran fhou'd be the chief Foods of the Ewes during the time of their giving Milk; of which if the Lambs have but enough, and are kept clean and warm, in *little Pens*, they will foon be very fat, and turn to great Profit; as may be guefs'd by the ordinary Price given; 15 *s.* for a fat Lamb at Five Weeks old, and 20 *s.* for a Calf of the fame age; but near *London* the Prices are greater.

XV. **Where Dungs**, Compofts, and moft of the feveral forts of Manures are fcarce or wanting, there is an **Art** to be learnt of
improving

improving poor Land, or rather of making poor Land *improve itself*, without **Super-inductions**: And this is an Art that should be highly regarded and minded by those who want *these Helps*, and would desire to grow *wiser* and *richer*. Of this, *several* Hints have been already given; but the whole Mystery, in short, lieth in sowing such *Seeds* upon *poor* or *worn-out Land*, that by *plowing* in the Crop at *Midsummer*, or by *eating* it with a number of *Sheep*, it will receive *Riches* sufficient to answer the Husbandman's Hopes in Tillage, without the *Charge* and *Trouble* of fetching Dung from distant places.

Clover, Vetches, Pease, Lintels, Buck-wheat, and **Turnips**, are all known to answer the purpose *here* spoken of; and therefore the sowing of them according to the *improv'd* Practice of the South Parts, should be more *encourag'd* and *practis'd*.

I am well aware that this Method of *improving* the poorer sort of Land, hath been the Occasion of the Complaints of some, and

and of lowering the price of the *richeſt*
and *beſt Land*, as it muſt in *reaſon* and of
conſequence be expected to do. But this
is no *juſt* or *real* Objection to the Practice,
as it relates either to the public or private ;
for if the whole Iſland was *all* made rich
by *Induſtry* and *Improvements*, the Nation
in *general* would be richer too by the quantity of its Products, and their Conſumption
in Trade : And as to *private Perſons*, 'tis
ſeldom known but that the *poorer Land*
has its ſhare in moſt *conſiderable Eſtates*,
and then the Advantages made will more
than over-balance the ſinking Rent of the
beſt Land.

To encourage therefore the great Improvements which are to be made by the ſeveral
ſorts of *artificial Graſs-ſeeds*, I have thought
fit to ſubjoin a *ſhort* (but *particular*) Account
of them, ſhewing the Quantity to be ſow'd
on an Acre ; the Soil they like ; the Time
of ſowing ; the uſual Produce, and the Price
of *Seed* in LONDON.

XVI.

XVI. 𝕮𝖑𝖔𝖛𝖊𝖗.

This is the *richeſt* and *beſt* of Graſſes, 11 pounds will ſow an Acre.

Delights in a Soil that is rather *dry* and *warm*, than moiſt and cold.

To be ſow'd * *alone* at *Michaelmas*, but moſt uſually with *Oats* or *Barley* in the Spring.

The Hay to be mow'd the middle of *May*, when it begins to knot.

The Produce of Seed from an Acre, two Buſhels.

The Price about 5 *d. per* pound in LONDON.

Will laſt about three years.

𝕽𝖞𝖊=𝖌𝖗𝖆𝖘𝖘.

Three Buſhels and an half ſow an Acre; but, if mixt with *Clover*, (which is gene-

---

* The moſt experienc'd Farmers of late years find, that ſowing theſe artificial Graſs-ſeeds *alone* at *Michaelmas*, anſwers *much* the beſt, becauſe the dropping of the Wet from *Oats, Barley*, &c. doth not a little leſſen the Crop of theſe artificial Graſſes when they are ſown together.

rally

rally thought beft) eight Pounds of *Clover* with one Bufhel of *Rye-grafs*.

It will grow on any cold, fowre, clayey, weeping Land.

It will laft about Seven Years.

The common Produce of *Seed* from an Acre is about 30 Bufhels.   And of Hay two or three Loads.

The middle Price of the *Seed* is 2 *s.* 6 *d.* a Bufhel.

Saint-foyn.

Four Bufhels fow an Acre.

Delights chiefly in a fhallow Ground, or Soil upon a *Lime-ftone*, *Rock*, or *Chalk*.

It will laft about twenty Years ; and if Soot is fpread upon the Land at the end of twenty Years, 'twill laft twenty Years more, or longer.

The greateft *Improver* of barren Land of all others.

To be fown alone about *Michaelmas.*

To be mow'd for * Hay about the middle

* This Grafs in particular fhould be mow'd the firft and fecond year, becaufe the treading of it with large Cattle, and their being provok'd by the fweetnefs of it
to

dle of *May* following, when it begins to flower.

The beft Hay for hard-working Horfes, and commonly produces about 3 or 4 Load from an Acre.

Its Produce of Seed, when fuffer'd to ftand till *Midfummer*, is 20 or 25 Bufhels from an Acre.

The Price about Three Shillings *per* Bufhel.

La Lucerne.

Fourteen pounds fows an Acre on warm Land, in the Spring.

To be mow'd twice a year, *viz.* the beginning of *May*, and again at *Midfummer*.

It is excellent Hay for Horfes, but will not make *any* Cattle fat in ten or twelve days, as *Mortimer* faith.

One Acre will keep three Horfes all the Year.

It will laft Twenty Years at leaft.

to bite too near the Ground, whilft the Roots are young and tender, is a great Injury to it, efpecially in wet weathei. *Note*, The Ground whereon this Grafs-feed is fown, fuffers the leaft of any by conftant mowing.

Vetches,

𝔙𝔢𝔱𝔠𝔥𝔢𝔰, 𝔏𝔢𝔫𝔱𝔦𝔩𝔰, 𝔗𝔞𝔯𝔢𝔰, *and* 𝔅𝔲𝔠𝔨=𝔴𝔥𝔢𝔞𝔱.

These are all profitable Grains, and great *Improvers* of Land, even after the Crop is reap'd; but much more so, if plow'd in when they are in *bloſſom*.

They require but an ordinary Ground, light Sand, or mellow.

Vetches are of two sorts; one will bear the Winter, and ſhould be sown in *November*, and the other in the Spring.

Lentils and *Tares* are vaſt Encreaſers, the Straw of which is one of the ſweeteſt Fodders, eſpecially for young Cattle, and the Seed peculiarly good for Pigeons.

One Buſhel of the 'foregoing Grains sows an Acre.

The Produce of which is ordinarily ſix Buſhels.

The middle Price about 4 *s.* a Buſhel.

Buck-wheat, one Buſhel sows an Acre; the Encreaſe is very great, yielding commonly

monly about 50 Bufhels upon an Acre:
'Tis an excellent Feed for *Hogs, Poultry,*
&c. and will grow upon any * dry barren
Land.

The time of fowing it is, the latter end
of *February*, or beginning of *May*.

The common Price is about 1 *s.* 6 *d. per*
Bufhel.

XVII. Turnips.

Becaufe the Turnip hath of late years
been found to be a very confiderable *Improver* of Land, and brings great *Profit* to
the Farmer, fown in large quantities, I rank
it among the *improving Grafs-feeds*, and
recommend the Ufe of it to all fuch as are
not *afham'd* to grow *wifer than their Fore-
fathers*, and will not be difcourag'd from
Experiments, the Succefs whereof have been
founded on *Reafon* and long *Experience*.
There are three forts of *Turnips*, the *round*,

* A Bufhel of *Buck-wheat* being fow'd upon an Acre
of dry barren Land, that has been *worn out* by *over-
plowing*, the Crop of which being plow'd in about *Midfummer*, when 'tis in its full *pride* and *bloffom*, will prove as
good a Manuring as Twenty Load of Dung upon an
Acre.

the

the *yellow*, and the *long*, which requires the deeper Soil: They may be sown from *Midsummer* to *Lammas*, or later; and the Land where they are sown shou'd be fallow'd twice, and made as *fine* as may be with the Harrow: And when the *Seed* is sown, it should be harrow'd in with Thorns on the back of the Harrow. After they appear with four Leaves, there will be a necessity of making use of the * Hough, which must not be neglected, though it be too often thought *unnecessary:* for without thinning and sorting them, they will never *bottom* well; and yet the *bottoms* are more profitable to Cattle than the *tops.*

IF the Land be *over-poor*, the *Turnips* are subject to be eaten by a *black Fly*; a sprinkling therefore of rotten Dung (or Soot rather, where it can be got conveniently) on the *top* before they are harrow'd, is very adviseable. Before or after a Shower,

---

* Turnips, when hough'd, ought to be 12 or 13 Inches asunder.

is

is the beſt time for Sowing; but if the firſt
or ſecond Sowing miſcarry, (*for miſcarry
they often will*) be not diſcourag'd, the
Seed is very cheap, and the *Labour* not
much, (being but 4 *d.* a pound, and two
pounds ſows an Acre.) The Practice of
giving the *Turnips* to Cattle in the Houſe,
ſhou'd not be encourag'd, for that is *robbing* the Land inſtead of *improving* it. The
moſt approv'd Method is, to reſerve them
for *Winter* Feed, and then the *Sheep* (for
they are the propereſt Cattle to eat them)
ſhou'd be confin'd by Hurdles to an Acre
at a time, till the *whole* be well eaten over;
and then 'twill be quickly obſerv'd that the
Dung and *Urine* of the *Sheep*, together
with the *rotted* Remains of the *Turnips*,
will have ſo mellōw'd and *enrich'd* the
Land, as to make it a fit Recipient for
Barley in the Spring, and for a Crop of
Beans or *Peaſe* the following Year, alſo
for a Crop of *Wheat* the third, after a Sum-
mer-fallow, without other *Helps*. Theſe
Crops are wonderfully uſeful to the per-
fecting the *Winter-Lamb*, by furniſhing
the *Ewes* with plenty of Milk.

It

I T may not be amifs here to inftruct the Farmer, that a dextrous Artift fhould provide a Hough fix or feven Inches wide, to determine nearly the diftance of the Plants after they have gotten four Leaves; for by fixing his Eye upon *One* only at a time, he procceds in a regular method, and clears his way. Four Men, at 12 *d.* a Day each, will in one Day finifh an Acre.

T H E fame Care that a Farmer takes to make his Land as *fine* as poffible for *Turnips*, fhould alfo be obferv'd with refpect to *artificial Grafs-feeds* abovemention'd; endeavouring to *free* the Land as much as poffible from all manner of *Trumpery*, fuch as Stones, Bryars, *&c.* The want of this Care, and a neglect in **Rolling** the Lands after fowing, have been the occafion of great Failures in the Crops, to the great Difcouragement of an *improvable Practice:* For 'tis to be confider'd, that thefe *Seeds* are fmall, and if the Mould is not bound *clofe* to them, they will fpend themfelves, without being ever able to

T 2 come

come forth out of the *Cavities* where they lie.

'TIS to be obferv'd, that the Farmers in fome parts of the *North* are not yet become fo dextrous in fowing thefe * *Tur-nip-feeds* and *Grafs-feeds*, as they are in the *South*, where conftant Practice makes it more familiar, they taking a little be-twixt their two Fingers and the Thumb. Till therefore this *Dexterity* can be obtain'd, 'tis advifable to mix the *Seeds* with a conve-nient quantity of fine *Sand* or *Duft*, the better to fill the *Hand*, in order to fow it with Exactnefs. But it fhou'd be remem-ber'd alfo, that it is not Wifdom to fow thefe *fmall Seeds*, except in a *ftill* Day.

* A pound of *Turnip-feed* fown (after Harveft) upon an Acre of light, fandy, or gravelly Land, that has been *worn out by over-plowing*, the Crop of which (*i. e.* the Leaves as well as Roots) being *plow'd in*, will (in about *two* Months after) die away and rot, and *ftrangely* enrich the Land, and prove as good a Manu-ring as 25 load of Dung upon an Acre. This Method of Husbandry has been practis'd with great Succefs by that ingenious Gentleman Mr. *Tho. Smith*, at *Eafhing* in the Parifh of *Godalmin* in *Surry*.

THE Farmers in the *North* have got a Notion that thefe *artificial Grafs-feeds* very much *impoverifh* the Land, and therefore are difcourag'd from fowing them in any great quantities: But this Difcouragement arifes from a *miftaken* Practice of conftant and *over-much* mowing the Crop, which is indeed the ready way to *beggar* the Land; as indeed the very fame Practice of *over-mowing* beggars the Meadows and Uplands where thefe *Seeds* are not fown: it being *now* a known *Maxim* among good Husbandmen, and founded on Experience, " That too often and too long *mowing*, is " as great a prejudice to them, as too of- " ten and too long *plowing* is to Til- " lage."

I would therefore *perfuade* every Farmer, for the fake of his own *Intereft*, to propagate thefe *Grafs-feeds* in a regular Method, by fometimes *Summer-eating*, as well as *mowing* the fame; not forgetting fometimes alfo to *plow* in a full Crop, when tis in its full *pride* and *bloffom*; and he

will

will quickly find the great Advantage thereof in the *richness* of the Land, nay, in feeing the Land Enrich itself. And this Method (as I have already obferv'd) is fingularly profitable and ufeful, where *Dung* and *Compofts* are not eafily obtain'd, or are to be fetch'd at a great diftance.

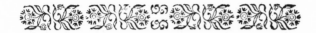

AN
ABSTRACT;

Or, a fhort Collection of the feveral Sorts of

Dungs *and* Compofts:

Together with

All *other Manures for the Improvement of the feveral forts of Land, as
practis'd in moft Counties in* England; *
being of ready Ufe to every Farmer, by
feeing in a little compafs their feveral
Natures and Properties.*

XVIII. **H**𝔬𝔯𝔰𝔢 and 𝕮𝕠𝔴-𝔇𝔲𝔫𝔤, &c.
being mixt with *Ditch-Earth*
where the Leaves of thick Hedges rot, or
being mixt with the Mud of Ponds, or
(for want of the faid rich *Ditch-earth*
or *Mud*) you may mix any fort of Earth
with the faid Dungs, and it will caufe it to
rot *much* fooner, and will prove an *admi-*
T 4 *rable*

rable Manure for moſt ſorts of Arable or
Paſture Land.   This Method is practis'd
very much in *Eſſex*, where they lay it in
great heaps, in a waſte place nigh where 'tis
intended to be ſpent.   The quantity of this
Compoſt for Clay-land is about 20 Loads
upon an Acre; but the red *Hazely* Brick-
earth, or light Sands, will not require above
10 or 15 Loads upon an Acre, becauſe it
muſt be renew'd oftner than the Clay-
lands.

Sheeps-Dung for cold-tillage Clay-
lands is the *beſt* of all Dungs; and becauſe
it cannot ſo conveniently be gather'd together as other Dungs, 'tis commonly convey'd upon the ſaid Lands by folding the
Sheep upon it, penn'd up together a-Nights
by proper Hurdles, by which means both
Dung and *Urine* are ſpent upon the Land.
I have ſeen good *Improvements* in *Eſſex*
by this Dung, where they fold the *Sheep*
in cover'd Folds, and mix their Dung with
Ditch-Earth, Mud, &c. as aforemention'd,
which cauſes the Dung to ſpread *much
further*.   Likewiſe in the *Weſtern* parts of
England

England (becaufe of the *Excellency* of this Dung *above all others*) they houfe their *Sheep* a-Nights, and litter them with clean Straw. This is found by *late Experience* the beft Manuring, and *well anfwers* the trouble.

𝕳𝖔𝖌𝖘-𝕯𝖚𝖓𝖌 (next to *Sheeps-Dung*) is the richeft and fatteft of any, both for *Tillage* and *Pafture*, efpecially the latter : One Load of this will go as far as two of others. It may likewife be mixt as above, to make it go the further.

𝕳𝖚𝖒𝖆𝖓𝖊 𝕺𝖉𝖔𝖚𝖗𝖊, for hot, dry, burning Lands, makes a *great Improvement*. To make it commodious for Carriage, 'tis often mixt with other Dungs or *Ditch-earth*, &c. as aforemention'd, and is us'd very much in *Kent*, &c. with good fuccefs, efpecially for Pafture Land.

𝕻𝖎𝖌𝖊𝖔𝖓𝖘-𝕯𝖚𝖓𝖌 being of a very *hot* nature, and *full* of Salts, agrees beft when laid on *cold* Lands, either *Tillage*, *Pafture*, or *Meadow*. When ufed for *Tillage*, it
fhou'd

fhou'd be fown by hand *after* the Grain is fow'd, and in the fame manner: About 30 Bufhels will fow an Acre. It anfwers for one Year only, but produces a great Crop, even on the moft *barren* Land, if the Year prove any thing dripping.

𝔥𝔢𝔫𝔰-𝔇𝔲𝔫𝔤, and the Dungs of other Poultry, are *all* very *good*, and full of *Ni-tre*, tho' none of them fo rich as *Pigeons-dung*. Becaufe of its hanging together, 'tis more difficult to fow than *Pigeons-dung*; therefore 'tis beft mixing it with other Dungs, or with *Afhes*, *Earth*, or *Sand*.

𝔖𝔢𝔞-𝔠𝔬𝔞𝔩-𝔄𝔣𝔥𝔢𝔰, for cold Meadow and Pafture Land, is an *admirable Improver*, caufing the Soil to run much to *wild Tre-foil* and *wild Clover*, (which of all others is the *fweeteft* and *richeft Feed* for Cattle) and in fuch *abundance* too, that it will keep a double number of Stock. 'Tis al-fo a very lafting Manure, efpecially if you have the opportunity to lay 20 or 25 Loads upon an Acre; tho' much lefs will anfwer

very

very well.   This Manure is not fo proper for *Tillage* as for *Pafture*.

Soap-Afhes (after the *Soap-boilers* have done with them) is an excellent Manure for both *Tillage* and *Pafture*; about 8 or 9 Loads will manure an Acre, and tends to the deftroying of *Furze*, *Broom*, and *Fern*, if apply'd after grubbing at Midfummer. This Manure will laft four or five Crops.

Pot-Afhes is a very good Manure for moft forts of *Pafture* Grounds; but becaufe the Wet is left in them by the *Potmen*, which has caufed the Lee to draw out good part of the Salts, therefore a *greater* quantity muft be laid on the Land than the aforefaid *Soap-afhes*.

Soot is an Extraordinary Manure for both Tillage and Pafture-Land, efpecially if it be Soot from *Sea-Coal*, becaufe 'tis much the ftrongeft, and fulleft of *Nitre*, and anfwers beft upon *cold Clays*, when about Forty Bufhels is laid upon an Acre; which

which will likewife be a means of deftroying *Weeds* and other *Trumpery.* If
once in four or five years you fow your
Land whereon *Saint-foyn* has been fown
with this Manure, 'twill very much encreafe the Crop, and make it laft feveral
Years longer.

𝕸𝖆𝖑𝖙=𝖉𝖚𝖘𝖙 is another confiderable *Improver* of Land, which muft be fow'd by
hand, as they do the *Seed*: It will give a
ftrange *Life* and *Encreafe* to a Crop of
Barley, efpecially after a Shower of Rain:
'Tis near as ftrong as *Pigeons-dung,* and
fhou'd be ufed in the fame manner, by
fowing about Forty Bufhels upon an Acre;
but you are not to expect more from it
than the Advantage of one Crop.

𝕽𝖆𝖌𝖘 of all forts, both *Linnen, Wool-
len,* and *Leather,* make a very great *Improvement* on chalky binding tillage Land,
vaft quantities of them being fetch'd from
London to *Dunftable* and other Parts
where chalky Hills are, only to lay on
their *Lands,* where they chop them very
fmall,

fmall, and ftrew them juft after the fowing of the Corn, allowing 24 Bufhels to
an Acre. Shreads of Leather, old Shoes,
Hats, or Stockings, as they are longer rotting and decaying, fo they *laft* the longer.

Wear, a Sea-weed growing chiefly on
fuch Rocks as are cover'd only at High-
water, is good to be laid on *Tillage* for
one Crop, the drying and burning of which
makes *Kilp*, ufed in making Glafs. This
Kilp alfo being *fteep'd* in Water, is ufed to
dilute the *Allom Liquor*. After the *Allom-
makers* have done with it, 'tis laid upon
the Land ; and altho' a great quantity of
the *Nitrous Particles* are drawn from it,
yet neverthelefs 'tis an *admirable Manure*
both for Tillage and Pafture Lands, and
has made *great Improvements* round *Sands-
end* in *Yorkfhire*, where the chief *Allom-
works* of His Grace the Duke of BUCKING-
HAM are. The common Allowance for either *Meadow* or *Pafture* is about fix Loads
upon an Acre. Thefe Afhes foon diffolve,
fo will not laft above four or five Crops of
Tillage ; but much longer, and are accounted

I   much

much better, for *Pasture* and *Meadow*, than *Tillage*.

Lime, of *all* other Manures, has (of late years) made the *greatest Improvement*, both of *Tillage* and *Pasture*, so that the *Industrious Farmer* thinks almost no Pains or Cost too much to procure it. It agrees with *all* sorts of Soils, except the two Extreams of a *dusty* Sand and the *strongest* Clays. It *improves* all light Soils, by adding *Tenacity* to them: Likewise all *heathy* and *moory* Grounds over-run with *Furze, Brakes, Broom,* &c. when turn'd up by the Plough, are *surprizingly* benefited by it, insomuch that many Lands, suppos'd not worth above Two shillings an Acre, are in the North of *England* made worth above Fifteen Shillings an Acre, by virtue of this Noble Manure of **Lime**; about Eighty or Ninety Bushels of which being laid upon an Acre in Tillage, will last five or six years.

Chalk, one Load of which should be mixt with two Loads of Dung or other

rich

rich Earth : According to this proportion, if you lay a good quantity in a heap to *ferment* and *incorporate*, 'tis an admirable Manure for all cold fowre, and also gravelly Land, and will produce incredible Crops of *Corn* for several years together, by laying about Twenty Loads upon an Acre. And when the time of Tillage is expir'd, in order to lay down the fame for Grafs, lay on Twenty Loads of *Chalk* alone upon an Acre, and it will perform wonders.

𝔐𝔞𝔯𝔩𝔢 is of several forts ; the *beft* is pure and unmixt, and will diffolve in *Water :* 'Tis an *excellent* Manure to fix light Sands, but it has been difputed whether it has any *fertilizing* Quality of itfelf, becaufe it doth not fend forth the *firft Year.* The common quantity in *Staffordfhire* is Three hundred Loads upon an Acre, which will laft without marling again above Twenty Years, if kept in Tillage and Pafture *interchangeably*, which is moft advifeable : And you ought to give the Land a fprinkling of Dung for every Crop of
Wheat

Wheat you reap; for this will keep the Land in a perfect *state of Health*, and help to loosen the binding Quality of the *Marle.*

It ſhould not be forgot, that the *Bottoms* and *Scourings of Ponds* (eſpecially ſuch as are ſurrounded with Hedges and Trees) are *excellent* for *all ſorts* of Soils, to be laid upon the Surface of *Meadows* and *Paſtures* in *Autumn, Winter,* or *Spring;* but the two firſt Seaſons are the beſt. The Leaves of Trees in proceſs of time do much *impregnate* the Mud with *Salts,* and therefore the *older* the *Ponds* are before they are ſcoured, the better. If the Meadow or Paſture be cover'd over pretty thick with it, as they ought, it will laſt many Years, and produce abundance of *Trefoil.*

SOME late Experience hath diſcover'd, that even the *black mooriſh* Soil taken off the *Fells,* which would not be perſuaded to bear or produce any thing but an unprofitable *Ling,* if 'tis laid together with *Lime,* and *Litter* or *long Dung* from the Stable,

Stable, in equal quantities, for a Year, 'twill make vaft Improvements on Meadow-ground laid on in the Spring: The *Lime* and *Dung* both tend to *ferment* and *rot* the Soil, and at the fame time give fuch *Tenacity* to it, that it foon becomes *mellow* and *rich*, and fit to anfwer the Expectations of a diligent Lover of *Improvements*.

𝕾𝖊𝖆-𝖘𝖆𝖓𝖉, to thofe who live within a mile or two of the Sea, and have any ftiff clayey Land to lay it on, is a moft *excellent* Manure, efpecially if it be taken *wet*, juft after the Tide has left it; and the more of it, the better. The reafon of its giving fuch *Fertility* to Land of a clayey nature is two-fold; *firft*, becaufe it tends to feparate the Parts of Clay, which otherwife would retain *ftagnating Water*, and thereby *Starve* and *Chill* all infant Plants: And, *fecondly*, becaufe being mixt with Salt, it gives much the fame *Riches* as are expected from Dung fill'd with *Nitre* and *Salt*. The fame is to be faid

U　　　　　with

with refpect to *Sea-fhells* and the *Bones and Refufe of Fifh, all* which are afforded in *great* quantities near the Fifhing-Towns on His Grace the Duke of *Buckingham's* Eftates in *Yorkfhire.*

A N

A N
ABSTRACT
Of the several Sorts of
Earths *and* Soils:

*On which the proper Dungs and
Manures are directed to be laid, agreeable to their several Natures.*

XIX. 𝔖𝔄𝔑𝔇, which of all others
wants generally moſt Help and
Improvement, and is in its nature looſe and
porous, quickly loſing the fattening Moi-
ſture that falls from the Heavens, is beſt
and moſt rationally mended by all ſuch
Dungs as give *Tenacity* and a holding Nature to it : And ſuch are the Dungs taken
from *Cows* and *Hogs*, which are cold and
binding.   There is indeed much difference
in the Nature of *Sands*; ſome are *cold,*

U 2   and

and others *hot* ; fome are *rich*, and others
poor : but all of them want fomething to
hold their Parts together, which is beft done,
as is before faid, by the Dung of *Cows*,
Oxen, or *Hogs*.

MUCH the fame is to be faid of *Gravel*,
efpecially when it is not mixt with *Clay*,
Chalk, or *Loam* ; there all holding and
binding Dungs are moft proper, *Humane
Ordure* not excepted, and *Rags* included.

THERE are alfo other light Soils, that
are not properly either Sand or Gravel,
which muft be mended with the aforefaid
Dungs, and thefe are light *chifelly Soils*,
lying on the top of fcaley Rocks of *Free*
or *Lime-Stone,* and are of confequence
mixt with many fmall Stones, which turn
up with the Plow. Befides the aforefaid
holding Dungs, thefe Soils are alfo properly mended with *Chalk*, *Clay*, *Marle*, or
the *Bottoms of Ponds :* But if thefe Soils (as
commonly they do) prove fhallow upon the
Rock, the beft way to improve and enrich
them, is, to lay them down with *Saint-foyn.*

Clay,

Clay, when 'tis pretty much unmixt, is the other Extream to what went before, and r ift have different Manures for its Tillage, as *Horſe-dung, Sea-coal Aſhes, Sea-ſand, Drift-ſand, Pigeon* and *Hen-dung*, and the *Bottoms of Wood-yards*, and all little enough to mellow and looſen the Parts of ſome untractable *Clays*.

Chalk has moſt of the Properties of *Clay*, eſpecially that of holding the Water, and wanting ſomething to looſen its Parts, tho' it is generally of a warmer nature : Accordingly all the Dungs named under the laſt Article (as alſo *Rags*) improve and mend it. And when ſo mended, 'tis obſerv'd to bear the *beſt* and the *fineſt Wheat*.

Loam, properly ſo call'd, is that Soil which partakes of a due mixture of both *Clay* and *Sand*, having all the *good* Properties of *both*, and none of the *bad* ones ; and is generally of ſuch a ſufficient depth, that it bears all ſorts of *Vegetables* to perfection, both Trees, Plants, and Grain. Accordingly 'tis to be remark'd, that juſt ſo far as the

Clay

Clay on the one hand, or the *Sand* on the other, are obferv'd to prevail and to exceed their Proportion in thefe forts of mixt *Earths,* fo far they are proportionably *worfe,* and lefs ufeful for Vegetation, in their own Nature : And therefore of confequence the proper and difcreet *Application* of Dungs muft be made accordingly, as directed above. But yet fuch happy Soils and mixt Earths, as we call *Loam,* are frequently to be met with ; which therefore muft rationally be fuppos'd to be mended, enrich'd, and improv'd (when *worn out*) by a mixture of all forts of Manures and Dungs both of a *holding* and *loofening* nature.

The Conclusion.

XX. **WIthout** entring upon (or at-tempting) a general Syſtem, but to make this Treatiſe as uſeful as may be, I think it not improper to let the FAR-MER know *how* ſome general Annoyances to a FARM may be remov'd without any great Charge.

Whins or **Furze** may eaſily be de-ſtroy'd when they return or come up again, as ſoon as the Land is laid down for Graſs after Tillage ; for 'tis obſerv'd, that they are by Hand eaſily pluck'd up by the Roots after a Froſt, when the Ground is looſe and tender : This in the *Weſt of England* is cal-led *Weeding* the Land. Conſtant mowing them down while young, will do the ſame thing

Broom

𝔅𝔯𝔬𝔬𝔪 is easily destroy'd by *cutting*, *chopping*, and afterwards *mowing* it down at 𝔐𝔦𝔡𝔰𝔲𝔪𝔪𝔢𝔯, within two or three Inches of the Ground : After which if it should have a *resurrection*, yet the *second* Tryal will *effectually* compleat the *Cure*.

𝔎𝔲𝔰𝔥𝔢𝔰 are also easily destroy'd by *mowing* them down near the Ground at *Spring* and *Midsummer*, not forgetting to lay a good sprinkling of *Lime*, or a good quantity of *Horse*, *Pigeon*, or *Hen-dung* at the Roots, and you'll see no more of them.

𝔉𝔢𝔯𝔫 is more difficult to destroy than any of the 'foremention'd, because they strike such a *deep* root into the Earth ; but nevertheless constant mowing in *Spring*, and at *Midsummer*, and afterwards laying *Dung* or *Lime* at the Roots, will answer the End in destroying them in a great measure.

F I N I S.

HISTORY OF MANAGEMENT THOUGHT

An Arno Press Collection

Arnold, Horace Lucian. **The Complete Cost-Keeper.** 1901

Austin, Bertram and W. Francis Lloyd. **The Secret of High Wages.** 1926

Berriman, A. E., et al. **Industrial Administration.** 1920

Cadbury, Edward. **Experiments In Industrial Organization.** 1912

Carlson, Sune. **Executive Behaviour.** 1951

Carney, Edward M. et al. **The American Business Manual.** 1914

Casson, Herbert N. **Factory Efficiency.** 1917

Chandler, Alfred D., editor. **The Application of Modern Systematic Management.** 1979

Chandler, Alfred D., editor. **Management Thought in Great Britain.** 1979

Chandler, Alfred D., editor. **Managerial Innovation at General Motors.** 1979

Chandler, Alfred D., editor. **Pioneers in Modern Factory Management.** 1979

Chandler, Alfred D., editor. **Precursors of Modern Management.** 1979

Chandler, Alfred D., editor. **The Railroads.** 1979

Church, A. Hamilton. **The Proper Distribution Of Expense Burden.** 1908

Davis, Ralph Currier. **The Fundamentals Of Top Management.** 1951

Devinat, Paul. **Scientific Management In Europe.** 1927

Diemer, Hugo. **Factory Organization and Administration.** 1910 and 1935

Elbourne, Edward T. **Factory Administration and Accounts.** 1919

Elbourne, Edward T. **Fundamentals of Industrial Administration.** 1934

Emerson, Harrington. **Efficiency as a Basis for Operation and Wages.** 1909

Kirkman, Marshall M[onroe]. **Railway Revenue.** 1879

Kirkman, Marshall M[onroe]. **Railway Expenditures.** 1880

Laurence, Edward. **The Duty and Office of a Land Steward.** 1731

Lee, John. **Management.** 1921

Lee, John, editor. **Pitman's Dictionary of Industrial Administration.** 1928

McKinsey, James O. **Managerial Accounting.** 1924

Rowntree, B. Seebohm. **The Human Factor in Business.** 1921

Schell, Erwin Haskell. **The Technique of Executive Control.** 1924

Sheldon, Oliver. **The Philosophy of Management.** 1923

Tead, Ordway and Henry C. Metcalfe. **Personnel Administration.** 1926

Urwick, L[yndall]. **The Golden Book of Management.** 1956

Urwick, L[yndall]. **Management of Tomorrow.** 1933